CROSSING
GALILEE

CROSSING GALILEE

Architectures of Contact
in the Occupied
Land of Jesus

Marianne Sawicki

TRINITY PRESS INTERNATIONAL
Harrisburg, Pennsylvania

Copyright © 2000 Marianne Sawicki

Trinity Press International
P.O. Box 1321, Harrisburg, PA 17105
Trinity Press International is a division of The Morehouse Group.

Cover art: Drawing of the basilica building at Sepphoris by James F. Strange.

Cover design: Annika Baumgardner

LIBRARY OF CONGRESS CATALOGING-IN-PUBLICATION DATA

Crossing Galilee : architecture of contact in the occupied land of Jesus / Marianne Sawicki.
        p.   cm.
   Includes bibliographical references and index.
   ISBN 1-56338-307-1 (pbk. : alk. paper)
   1. Sociology, Christian—History—Early church, ca. 30-600.
2. Women in Christianity—History—Early church, 30-600.
3. Mediterranean Region—Social conditions. 4. Palestine—Social conditions. 5. Sociology, Biblical. 6. Bible—Antiquities. I. Title.
BR166 .S29 2000
225.9'5—dc21   99-053038

Printed in the United States of America

00 01 02 03 04 05   10 9 8 7 6 5 4 3 2 1

Contents

Illustrations

Acknowledgments

THIS VOLUME REPORTS the findings of field research in Israel during the summers of 1993 and 1996, made possible by grants from the Committee on Research and Publications of the Society of Biblical Literature (SBL). I am deeply grateful to my colleagues in the SBL for this support. The plan of the book was created during my fellowship year at the Erasmus Institute at the University of Notre Dame, 1998–99, and the final editing was done at Ghost Ranch, New Mexico, a Christian education center of the Presbyterian Church USA (PCUSA). Heartfelt thanks go to Erasmus Institute and to the PCUSA for their hospitality.

Conversations with archaeologists and historians have helped me frame my theoretical approach to the Galilee of Jesus. In particular, I must thank Professor James F. Strange, director of the University of South Florida Excavations at Sepphoris; and Professor Douglas R. Edwards of the University of Puget Sound, project director of the excavations at Cana of the Galilee. In historical Jesus studies, I profited from conversations with Professor Seán Freyne of Trinity College, Dublin; Professor Joshua Schwartz of Bar-Ilan University, Ramat-Gan, Israel; Emeritus Professor John Dominic Crossan of DePaul University, Chicago; Robert Funk of Westar Institute, Santa Rosa, California; and Professor Robert J. Miller of Midway College, Kentucky, who is my husband. I thank each of these men for their generosity and patience. Each will see his influence in these pages, although none would endorse everything here.

This work builds upon my earlier electronic and print publications in the archaeology of gender. Portions of chapters three, four, five, six, and nine are revisions of essays whose drafts were made available electronically, starting in 1992, on the IOUDAIOS server and then through the DIOTIMA web pages at the Department of Classics of the University of Kentucky. Chapter four draws material from my paper "Making the Best of Jesus" for the 1992 meeting of the Society of Biblical Literature; from chapter six of my book *Body, Text, and Science* (Dordrecht: Kluwer, 1997), with kind permission from Kluwer Academic Publishers; and from my 1995 article "Caste and Contact in the Galilee of Jesus: Research Beyond Positivism and Constructionism," contributed for a volume that was never published.

Chapter five updates portions of my articles "Caste and Contact" and "Spatial Management of Gender and Labor in Greco-Roman Galilee," *Archaeology and the World of Galilee: Texts and Contexts in the Roman and Byzantine Periods,* edited by Douglas R. Edwards and Thomas McCollough (Atlanta: Scholars Press, 1997). Portions of chapter six are revisions of material from "Spatial Management." Chapter seven is expanded from a paper presented at the 1997 meeting of the Society of Biblical Literature, which was also the basis for my essay "Magdalenes and Tiberiennes: City Women in the Entourage of Jesus," to appear in *Transformative Encounters: Jesus and Women Re-Viewed,* edited by Ingrid Rosa Kitzberger (Leiden: Brill, forthcoming). Chapter eight is a revision and update of my essay "Salt and Leaven: Resistances to Empire in the Street-Smart Paleochurch," adapted from *The Church as Counterculture,* edited by Michael I. Budde and Robert Brimlow (New York: SUNY Press, forthcoming) by permission of the State University of New York Press, all rights reserved. Chapter nine incorporates additional portions of "Caste and Contact."

Ancient Christian texts have been cited in translation from the Scholars Version: *The Complete Gospels: Annotated Scholars Version,* revised and expanded, edited by Robert J. Miller (Sonoma, CA: Polebridge Press, 1994).

1 A Reorientation of Jesus Studies

THE OBJECT IS JESUS. Jesus of Nazareth was and is also much more than an object, certainly. But in this book Jesus must be regarded as an object of study.

In saying that Jesus is an object, I mean to affirm that some information about Jesus can be known "objectively," by any careful inquirer, regardless of the kind of personal relationship that inquirer may or may not have with Jesus. I mean to suggest as well that those who claim to have a relationship with Jesus must be prepared to say how they know that the one with whom they are relating is really Jesus, and not some fantasy or human contrivance. Objective information about Jesus can be acquired through critical academic investigation. Study of this kind is a means to increase information, but the activity of study does not generate the information arbitrarily. In other words, "objectivity" is not a euphemism for "hegemony" or the opinion of the powerful majority, whatever that might happen to be. The reality of Jesus is available for study by methods whose validity is open to impartial assessment.

Investigators approach Jesus from various angles. The commitments required for doing so are the same allegiances and responsibilities generally embraced by any researcher who undertakes historical study. Those academic commitments are complicated and problematic, to be sure; they may even be faith-like, in their own secular way. Whatever the angle of approach may be, the objectivity of historical study of Jesus consists in the intention to work "in the sunshine." Sunshine means visibility. Thus when results are offered to the reading public, the methods and intentions that were operative in their acquisition will be visible as well. Because the results remain visibly supported by the methods that reached them, they can always be corrected. Findings of historical study are not dogmatic, and do not

1

take the place of religious dogma. So the metaphor of sunshine fits the historical study of Jesus in at least two ways: this study illuminates its object, Jesus, from some definite direction; and the discipline's illumination opens it up to anyone's gaze.

This book, then, is about a discipline. It is about the "studies" part of the academic field of Jesus Studies. This field features both landmarks and shadows, and I mean to examine it in a new light. This intention brings out a third metaphoric sense of "illumination." The angle of illumination can shift. If you will, the "sunshine" of this examination will shift the shadows across the field. In my view the early morning of Jesus Studies is past; the afternoon sun lights up another side of things and casts previous certainties into shade. In that morning, we used to go "questing" for Jesus. Now it is time to turn to the task of considering the pathways that allow critical inquirers to come unto him.

New angles of illumination enhance what has already been learned about Jesus through previous historical study. If they erode current consensus on some points, that by no means signals a surrender to the so-called radical perspectivalism of knowledge, much less a total collapse into epistemological relativism, as some may fear. Real things have sides. Otherwise they would not be real material objects at all. Analogously, with objectively knowable objects such as Jesus, we may reasonably expect to augment our understanding when we shift the angle of illumination by altering the kinds of questions asked.

Jesus—which is to say, that which we can objectively know about Jesus—is surrounded by and embedded in various other objects of our knowledge: his historical era, his home country, his language, the common motifs and stories of Israelite religious traditions in the first century, and the economic and ideological conflicts of that time and place. Those are the sorts of objects that are studied in historical-Jesus Studies. Those objects are going to appear different after the shift in conceptual illumination that this book describes and helps to carry out. This disciplinary phenomenon characterizes Jesus Studies now at the turn of the century, as the shift of illumination is occurring along several arcs of emphasis:

> from land to water;
> from situating to crossing;
> from homogenized "cross-cultural" models to indigenous modeling;
> from social causality to idiomatic expression;
> from gender to kinship;
> from Europe to Africa and Babylon;

from Pauline letters to Synoptic Gospels;
from texts to material culture;
from "making Jesus" to "crossing with Jesus."

These are changes in the orientations from which research questions are brought to bear upon the evidence. That is to say, they are changes in the constitution of the evidence. To describe and promote these reorientations will be the work of this entire book. But these shifts can be briefly introduced here.

(1) FROM LAND TO WATER. Readers of the Christian Scripture know that Palestine is a strip of territory between the Mediterranean Sea and the Jordan River. It is a "holy land," a "promised land," the principal arena for Israel's experience of divine justice and faithfulness. Until recently, studies of Jesus have paid surprisingly little attention to the land, regarding it merely as a kind of stage or neutral platform supporting the events told in the Gospels. Since the 1990s, ever increasing attention has been paid to the ownership and the agricultural wealth of the land in Greco-Roman times.

But the land itself, as land, is also a living system. Its soil yields crops, and its rock formations retain water from the seasonal rains. It undergoes temporal cycles, not only with the agricultural and weather cycles of the seasons, but also with the inheritance cycles that develop through marriages, births, and deaths; with the sabbatical and jubilee cycles of the Mosaic law; and with the tithing and taxing cycles imposed by authorities. The land *as lived*, that is, the cultural and cultivated landscape, was more than a platform that supported people in place and fed them. It had meaning for the indigenous people, as symbol and vehicle of their relationship with their God.

Ancient Palestine was a fluid land for its native inhabitants, a land in motion. To their minds, everything on the land had its own proper tendency or valence. For example, and this example is the paradigm case, water came down from the heavens, into the village cisterns and wells, and along the river channels and aqueducts. The water ran its natural course through the land. Culturally and religiously, people and commodities had their own proper valences as well. The land was a landscape of pathways for fluids: both the real material waterways, and the built or culturally secured patterns of circulation for people, their labor, and their goods. To understand the land and life upon it, we must follow the water and what happened to the water in the first century. Consider the Sea of Galilee. Hellenistic interests—probably Hasmonean-Judean, but possibly Ptolemaic or Seleucid—had organized and expanded the fish-packing facilities on its western shore. Then when Jesus was a young man, Herod Antipas changed the character of the Lake again by building himself a new capital on the cliff-side at Tiberias. After that, as we shall see, the fishing was never the same again. Moreover, alterations analogous to those of the water were wrought in Galilee's cultural and economic fluids as well: its labor, its wheat and wine, and the streams of its kinship and inheritance patterns. We must look at displacements of these flows: where they go after the Herods redesign the channels.

(2) FROM SITUATING TO CROSSING. Writers go to and over Palestine as well. Where Jesus lived has often been mapped. To map is mental work. It is an analytic exercise of selection, description, and connection that is meant to render the land available for human uses of various kinds. Maps are texts. They differ from the real territory in the means of access that they offer. Access to a map is visual: your glance easily jumps from one place-name to another in whatever direction you please, quicker than you can even say the name. Gospel narratives, being texts, traverse Galilee in this random-access mapping mode.

But crossing the real landscape is more complicated. To find a route from here to there, people living in the land have to reckon with hills, swamps, hostile villages, alien cities, police patrols, heat, storms, and the provision of food, water, and shelter. Moreover, Galilee's landscape was progressively re-made by various colonial interests: Ptolemies, Seleucids, Hasmonean-Judeans, and then Herodian-Romans. Each of those powers annexed Galilee to another territory. Each of them "opened up" the circulation patterns of Galilean people, labor, and commodities, draining Galilee for the benefit of a distant capital. When Jesus was a young man, Antipas re-mapped and re-landscaped Galilee. Tiberias, his new capital, diverted the Babylonian tourist traffic across the Lake and into Galilee. Antipas effectively re-designed the Sea of Galilee into a little Aegean Sea. His father, Herod the Great, had architecturally Romanized Jerusalem and its Temple; now Herod Antipas turned the Jordan into a little Tiber, leading tourists from Tiberias—Herodian port of entry into the promised land—on up to Jerusalem. Downstream, John the Baptist positioned himself astride the river, turning its water back into a vehicle of divine governance of the land, and turning the tourists away from Antipas. The ideological struggle for Galilee was waged in terms of the real traffic patterns and trade routes that crossed the land. It had to be resisted on the same terms.

The key to understanding this is to recognize that physical spaces can be simultaneously used by different individuals with different class identities and agendas. Housing is one index of social status, but knowledge of housing design does not directly translate into demographic data. Families are more than the places that they build to define and contain themselves. It would be incorrect to assign rich people exclusively to lavish urban villas and poor peasants exclusively to little village houses. Working men and women were to be found in the villas and in urban service facilities at all hours of the day and night. They might be found at home in the villages during planting and rainy seasons, but at other times traveling for trade or to find waged work. A man, a woman, or a child might sleep in one edifice, work in another, and eat in a third; and those arrangements might vary from summer to winter. The question of situation, then, becomes less significant than the question of what adaptive uses were made of the various available built environments.

(3) FROM HOMOGENIZED "CROSS-CULTURAL" MODELS TO INDIGENOUS MODELING. In the 1980s and 1990s, Jesus Studies as an academic field was enriched through applications of social-scientific methods, with analytic tools borrowed from the sociologies and the anthropologies of the 1960s and 1970s. This time lag is understandable in interdisciplinary work. However, social science has not stood still in the meantime. Within social theory, new critiques have developed around some of the very aspects of the "modeling" of social systems that have been most widely appropriated into recent social-scientific biblical scholarship. In particular, the notions of an "honor and shame" society, a discrete "Mediterranean" cultural identity, and the economic constructions of the "Lenski-Kautsky model" now must be re-evaluated. Post-colonial studies of the 1990s have precipitated revisions of all those constructs in sociology and anthropology.

Moreover, through refinement of archaeological techniques in Israel, we are becoming less dependent upon imported models and more able to describe relations proper to first-century Galilee itself. Rather than extrapolate data from the composite account of "a commercializing agrarian empire," we can examine material evidence of economic activity that is recoverable from the remains of the built environment of Greco-Roman Palestine itself. Rather than import general kinship categories from an anthropology textbook, we must listen to the Mishnah's rulings on caste status and we must also trace the pathways for the circulation of brides, commodities, land ownership, social obligation, and legitimacies of various kinds—all of which were constructed materially in architecture and can still be read there, at least fragmentarily.

Social scientists today recognize that earlier "cross-cultural" models covertly generalized Western categories and Western concerns, and were therefore blind to much that was unique and distinctive about particular peoples. While comparative analysis is still done in social and cultural anthropology today, it is usually attempted between individual case studies. Peoples and their ways of life are no longer interpreted as if they were mere instantiations of a general cultural rule, a rule whose formulation was somehow exempt from cultural determination itself. Jesus Studies needs to catch up with these developments in general social theory.

(4) FROM SOCIAL CAUSALITY TO IDIOMATIC EXPRESSION. The trouble with models of human social behavior from the 1960s and 1970s is that they were built like models of physical systems. The components of a modeled system are environmental influences and "states." These are linked by arrows of causality. In a well-built model, any given state is supposed to be completely predictable and explainable in terms of all the states that preceded it in its causal sequence; and once you have explained that state, you can predict the states that will follow it. There is no room for discretion or surprise. The state of affairs at "time one" devolves inexorably into the state of affairs at "time two" in social-science models of the New Testament world.

But this strategy of explanation turns out not to fit human affairs too well. Under the influence of systems theory, prevalent in mid-twentieth-century physical sciences, those social-scientific models interpreted human cultural activities as if they too were the effects of environmental factors. A certain configuration of resources and social structures, it was assumed, just automatically evoked certain predictable cultural adaptations. On the average, such expectations might be confirmed more often than not. Unfortunately, the model shed no light upon the anomalies, the unpredicted responses. These were the most interesting cases: the instances where unique or clever innovations circumvented the "system" and even altered it.

Systems theory cannot adequately interpret individual or collective creative agency. The only "general rules" operating causally to determine human behavior are those of biology: genetics, nutrition, disease processes, or the chemistry of metabolism and mood, for example. This is a rather restricted sector of human experience. In hindsight, the social models of the 1960s are now seen to have overestimated the range of behaviors in which relations of cause and effect are operative. Humans are innovators. We "play" on systems as if they were game boards.

The colonial powers intervening in Galilee were tampering with the land's indigenous economic and cultural system. Nothing "caused" them to do so; they were rationally motivated by greed or lust for power, or perhaps even by a worthy political vision of their own. But nothing "caused" Galilean resistance either. In a process more linguistic than mechanical, Galileans responded to incursions by making clever and novel uses of their land's material resources and of their cultural resources as well. We should regard those resources as a common idiom in which material compliance could at the same time offer expressive resistance. I will argue that circulation patterns (of brides, foodstuffs, water, and so forth) across thresholds (of homes, markets, territorial borders, and so forth) will show us the indigenous logic of Galileans, the logic in which the gospel first was articulated. This logic governed more than words. It guided the design of the Galilean built environment as well, and it still may be read off of urban, village, and lakeside ruins, in doorsteps, highways, fortifications, and floor plans.

(5) FROM GENDER TO KINSHIP. Anyone who wants to know about Jesus must seek him on his native turf, in his own land and landscape. Precisely *there*, a crucially important role was played by gender, or more precisely, by behaviors and expectations that we would call gender. There is indeed a causal component within gender, which anthropologists call sex. It accounts for procreation, is influenced by physical causality, and is common to our whole species regardless of culture. Gender, however, is what we make of sex culturally. But this aspect of the world of Jesus was ignored in academic study until relatively recently.

There are now two contrasting approaches to the study of gender in ancient Palestine. One uses techniques borrowed from feminist literary analysis. This approach gives a gendered reading of texts, but cannot easily be adapted to interpret artifacts, architecture, and other elements of the material culture. The other approach is more empirical, but has yielded meager results and has shifted its target of inquiry several times. An archaeology of women was at first oriented toward finding things that women had possessed and used; for example, their clothing, ornaments, or grooming utensils, or the tools of women's technologies such as needles and loom accessories. But the association of such things with women often was quite weak, having been inferred from some textual reference or from sheer nostalgic imagination. Archaeologists then switched their quest to places that may have belonged in some special way to women: the kitchen, the "women's quarters" of the urban villa, the women's section of a synagogue, the village well, or the *miqveh*. But again, the inference from structure to function was weak. The gendering was not supported by the materials themselves, but had to be assigned on the basis of textual mentions or contemporary anthropological parallels.

The question of women's places resolved itself into a question whether there were any places where women could not go. Was an exclusively male gendering imposed upon any space? Rabbinic texts suggest that women were barred from study houses. Otherwise, this question receives a negative answer, which serves to underscore the mobility of women with respect to the built environment and the natural landscape. Women went almost anywhere that men went, including into the newly introduced venues of the Hellenistic cities and the villas and estates surrounding them. But there was one move that women alone made: their move as brides from the father's house to the husband's. This suggests that questions about gender in Greco-Roman Palestine can be meaningfully framed and addressed in terms of motion across various thresholds, but that this can be done only in the larger conceptual context of kinship. Gender as we know it, as a bipolar assignment of identity and relationship potential, carried by individuals, does not seem to be a meaningful descriptive category for ancient Galileans.

In first-century Galilee, as in other Israelite cultures and in many other societies, gender was assigned and modified through kinship and so cannot be understood adequately apart from that context. The cultural idiom of the Galilee of Jesus owes its structuration to kinship management strategies, including but not limited to practices that we regard as constructing gender. The capacity of those strategies for flexible resistance enabled people to respond adaptively under conditions of imperial contact; that is, during cultural, economic, and agrarian expansion by Hasmonean Judeans into Galilee, and then during Roman co-optation of Judean hegemony as well. Maleness and femaleness were defined and experienced within a social logic of caste whose function was to preserve Israelite identity and land ownership intergenerationally. Thus, caste and kinship provide the indigenous context in which to pose meaningful questions about gender, its possibilities, and its limitations, for Jesus and for his early followers. Israelite caste practices assigned access to goods and prestige unequally among individuals, but the logic of that assignment was not a simple "gender oppression" as understood in 1980s feminist political theory.

(6) FROM EUROPE TO AFRICA AND BABYLON. Most practitioners of intellectual disciplines in the West, including scholars whose ancestors

were African or Asian or Amerindian, have been trained to frame analytic questions in terms of social practices indigenous to Europe. We
take the Greeks as definers and originators of the quest for wisdom and
reliable knowledge—"philosophy" so-called. Like the Romans, we
practice both material and conceptual colonization, and we overlay
other cultures with our categories of understanding. This intellectual
heritage cannot be undone, but it can be made self-conscious and can
be modified when appropriate.

For example, we can recognize the work of abstraction and sup-
pression that went into constructing "the Mediterranean" as a homogeneous cultural unit in the anthropology of the 1960s. In Antiquity, the
Mediterranean was a navigable body of water that brought diverse cultures into contact. Palestine was no more and no less "Mediterranean"
than it was "African" and "Babylonian" and "Asian." It had cultural contacts of long standing in all directions. Successive administrators—the
Ptolemies, the Seleucids, the Hasmoneans, the Herodians; and their
predecessors and followers—promoted economic and cultural contact
with lands to the east, west, south, and north of Palestine. There is no
way to recover a baseline "indigenous" or pure culture beneath those
influences. But we can talk about the persistence of kinship practices
and strategies, insofar as these were an intentional effort to constitute
Israelite identity in the midst of those incursions.

In some respects, Israel-defining kinship practices are comparable
to the practices that anthropologists have studied in nineteenth- and
twentieth-century societies in the lands around the Mediterranean
Sea. But in other respects, they are more like the kinship practices for
managing labor and land use in traditional African societies. The
anthropology of kinship in East Africa and in West Africa can illumi-
nate some important aspects of kinship and caste in Palestine that
Mediterranean-area anthropology leaves altogether in shadow. This is
not to presume any causal link between African and Israelite cultural
practices, although contact between Palestine and the civilizations of
the Nile is certainly older than history itself. It is merely to observe that
the more recent and better-understood African societies show us just
how resourceful and adaptable a repertoire of traditional kinship practices can be, and therefore an understanding of traditional African societies can suggest avenues of analysis for the ancient evidence.

Moreover, to draw cases for comparative study from geographically
diverse areas helps to counteract a tendency recognized within cultural
anthropology. Investigators are always prone to emphasize whatever
aspects of Israelite culture may happen to resemble their own culture,
taking those particular aspects to be emblematic of the culture as a

whole. This sort of bias is widely recognized in the salience of certain gender practices for Euro-American male anthropologists. Similarly, practices projecting "honor and shame" in ancient societies will be most salient to those of us who come from cultures in which these categories happen to be especially meaningful, such as Polish-American immigrant culture. Alternately, the opposition between peasant village and imperial city will take center stage for investigators whose own social experience featured such conflict, such as writers whose families came from rural Ireland. Comparison of ancient Israelite social practices with European ones is valid, but surely needs to be enhanced and brought into focus by comparative study of other peoples. Rabbinics, Africanist anthropology, and Americanist archaeology of gender are some under-exploited sources of illumination for Jesus Studies.

(7) FROM PAUL TO THE SYNOPTIC GOSPELS. Paul's letters to churches in the cities of the Roman Empire are the oldest texts of the Jesus movement, but they do not depict the practices of Jesus and his neighbors and cousins. More information about Jesus and about early Christian practices is to be had in the Gospels of Mark, Matthew, and Luke. Those documents can be read as layered compositions, as collages of earlier expressions. They yield new information when questioned from the cumulative reorientations suggested above. In the Gospels, what *moves*, and what is *held back*? How does the indigenous grammar lend sense to the expressions of Jesus? How is the power of caste status subverted by a claim of divine sonship? How would Jesus' messages have been heard and understood? Before there was a church and a new religion, what did Jesus mean? This is not to say that distortions were introduced by the ecclesial and religious modifications of the "original" meaning of Jesus. Rather, it is to suggest that we do not really understand the church and its religion until we take the trouble to inquire into what they might be modifications *of*.

(8) FROM TEXTS TO MATERIAL CULTURE. Texts give us only a portion of the available evidence. In recent decades, Jesus Studies has expanded its database beyond the canonical texts of the New Testament to embrace many other ancient texts, such as the Gospel of Thomas, the targums, early rabbinic materials, Dead Sea Scrolls, Philo, Josephus, and various inscriptions and non-literary papyri. Some tentative correlations have been attempted between those texts and material remains of the first century, such as household artifacts or the ruins of cities and towns. But we have hardly begun to read the landscape. "Material culture" includes more than pots and walls. The design of

housing, the placement and use of trade routes, the provision of water and food for villages or urban centers, the fortification of selected settlements, the emergence of new kinds of edifices and industries—all of these must be "read" in coordination with the texts. Animal and vegetable remains from the first century tell a story about diet, and the analysis of human bone yields a record of the quality of life. In Israel, the practices of archaeology are currently being revised to incorporate innovations developed in excavations in the Americas and elsewhere. Archaeologists are also guided by on-going conversations in Jesus Studies. There is need for a reading strategy that mediates between textual evidence and the evidence of material culture, without reducing either one to the other.

(9) FROM "MAKING JESUS" TO "CROSSING WITH JESUS." In earlier work I investigated the "making" of Jesus. Starting from the event of Calvary, when his friends confronted the unavailability of the living body of Jesus, I asked what they made of that situation. The work of early Christian redesign of Jesus was a poietic work by women, at its start, and it led into the various textual, educational, and intellectual practices that I explored in my 1994 book *Seeing the Lord*. I concluded that the Gospels prescribe two preconditions for "seeing the Lord," that is, for recognizing the christic identity and living ecclesial availability of Jesus after Calvary. One condition is pneumatic: the dynamic presence in the community of an empowering spirit, the "one who stands among you whom you do not know" (John 1:26). The other condition is mnemonic: the memory of definite details about the personality and message of Jesus as he lived and taught before Calvary. To recognize the Risen Lord is to make the connection between that presence and that memory. The recognition of the Lord is the insight of the identity between who Jesus was then and what he is doing now.

Recovery of that second ingredient, the memory of the pre-Calvary historical details, is not at all a theological task. It is a historical task, which continues in this book. The task here is to bring Jesus up to Calvary, not down from there, as I did in my earlier book. The focus in the present book is still upon cultural creativity, but not the creativity in what the women made of Jesus after Calvary. Here we will examine the common cultural idiom that was available to Jesus himself, the idiom in which he framed the confrontative messages that took him to Calvary. Before the cross, there were crossings. Galilee was multiply and perversely crossed by imperial incursions before Jesus was crucified. His offense was to cross those crossings, as it were. Like John the Baptist, who diverted the waterworks of Antipas and died for it, Jesus used the culturally meaningful discourse of caste in order to mock the imperially compromised legitimacy of Judean authority. Whatever timeless significance the words and deeds of Jesus may have achieved, their meaning first took flesh in and still depends upon the cultural idiom of the time and place in which they were framed. We do not now have, nor will we ever have, a complete understanding of that idiom. But even a partial understanding is surely worth securing.

■　■　■

Reorientation of inquiry into the meanings of Jesus is the concern of this book. In the next chapter, we begin to sketch the material expressions of an indigenous Israelite logic of circulation and containment. Subsequent chapters show how that logic also gave structure to indigenous social practices for the management of caste, of labor, and of commodities. As we will see, this idiom of containment and diversion is the grammar of Israelite religious ideology as well. In the first century it became a powerful resource for cultural and even physical survival, as it enabled people to accommodate to the incursions of empire while offering real and symbolic resistance.

My case is built upon the work of many other investigators. For the sake of coherence and readability, I have chosen not to interrupt my argument with authoritative references. Instead, a bibliographic essay at the end of the work offers a focused discussion of my sources. Readers will find there an account of where I agree with, borrow from, or object to the initiatives of recent scholarship. More importantly, you will find a doorway into that scholarship to assist your own further inquiry into matters described in this book.

My proposal that one idiom frames both the material and the textual expressions of first-century Galilee is designed to be equally provocative to archaeologists and to biblical scholars. It will please neither side. It is a first attempt to provide a common platform for the analysis of textual artifacts alongside of architecture and landscape, and to forge a common hermeneutical practice for understanding the congruent technologies through which they were produced.

2 Containment Designs in the Kinneret Region

THE ARCHAEOLOGY OF MIND is a project of interrogating material cultural remains for information about people's ways of thinking and understanding. What is "material culture"? People build things at various scales and of various materials: tiny jewelry and coins, jars and cooking pots, benches and tables, rooms, villages, roads and aqueducts, granaries and warehouses, theaters and fortresses, harbors, cities, caravan routes, empires. Each of these fits into human living in some functional way. Each has its associated technology and practical routines. As people use those places, tools, implements and ornaments, they are providing for their biological needs, but they are also reminding themselves of who they are. That is, they are reinforcing their culture and establishing their personal identities in the terms which that culture offers. They are constructing the distinctive reality of their shared social world; they are maintaining it and passing it on to the rising generations. All this can be regarded as a work of cultivation, in which the values and meanings of the people are realized and preserved in the materials around them. This cultural work piggybacks upon whatever functional work is overtly accomplished in the use of artifacts.

People make things, but the things reciprocally "make" the people as well. In using an artifact, people repeat the motions that dance their world into being. The choreography of filling a jar, docking a boat, closing a door, walking a road, casting a net, or stringing a loom provides a somatic experience of the distinctive and apparently obligatory way in which this particular world coheres, and of one's own placement within it. These gestures often are wordless, never are they meaningless. Their meaning is their "fit" into a larger pattern. This relational pattern is read, affirmed, strengthened, and perhaps modified through the on-going engagement of people with their stuff and their built environment. The equipment of the world is said to work "recursively" upon those who use it or inhabit it, in that it molds the hands and feet of its users. Literally, bone shapes itself to the habitual tasks and technologies of everyday life. Poietically, the contours of the built environment both conform and conform to the springs of the mind in the routines of human habitation.

Any engineered environment, together with the artifacts that furnish it, expresses the terms in which its residents value their world and negotiate their identity. The landscape is also a mindscape. It is difficult to begin to understand the landscape of a foreign culture such as that of Roman-era Galilee. The first difficulty is to convince ourselves that the residents of that land were not exactly like us. To be sure, the basic material needs of human beings are similar no matter where or when they live. So the houses and cisterns of Galilee are analogous to houses and water mains in the United States inasmuch as they provide for physical needs. Some of the differences in their design undoubtedly are owing to differences in climate and available materials. However, the social and symbolic meanings of those structures may be quite different, in ways that environmental factors cannot entirely explain.

Therefore, at some point in the interpretive process, we must make a switch in analogies. Instead of pursuing the analogy between contemporary America and ancient Galilee, comparing house with house in terms of their similar sheltering functions, we must try to discern the analogies at different scales within Galilee itself. For example, perhaps a Galilean house is similar to a Galilean cooking pot, because both are containers, both hold their contents securely until it's time to let them out, and both are open to the sky only sometimes. (No such analogy seems to hold between an American dwelling and, say, a microwave oven.) This tentative search for analogous structures will not get very far, obviously, unless we set aside the presumption that the meaning of a thing is equivalent to its function in fulfilling human biological needs. This search, if it is to progress at all, has to proceed by hunches. Slowly we move from one artifact to another, and gradually a network of congruent meanings begins to take shape. Each time a similar pattern is glimpsed in another structure, we become more confident that something meaningful has been detected, and that the congruences are not mere coincidence. If the pattern shows up in social practices as well as in material forms, then it may truly be a component of the indigenous cultural idiom.

This chapter examines a selection of architectural designs from Galilee and Judea. It presents something of a guided tour, with detailed commentary aided by some pictures of the designs. Words upon a printed page are not the best medium for conveying the somatic sense of the places and spaces of the ancient built environment. It is hoped that some readers have already visited the sites mentioned here, or will do so in the future. Meanwhile, imagination will assist in depicting these structures as containers that selectively admit, retain, and release what enters them. The forms that will be considered here are: the house, the study house, tanks and pipelines, synagogues, wharves, the city of Tiberias, the rebuilt Temple, and the book. In subsequent chapters we will go on to examine how these forms adaptively stabilize labor, kinship, ideology, and gender in the Land of Israel in the midst of imperial incursions in the first century BCE and the first two centuries CE.

THE HOUSE. Houses have been excavated at various locations in Israel. Some are small and simple, others are quite grand. What was their function? How did they work? What did they mean? We begin to interpret Galilean houses by analogy with houses in our own experience. You as a human being already know about houses. You know that there are certain basic sheltering functions that a house must perform if human life is to flourish within it. The house should have a roof and walls to shelter its occupants from the blazing sun and the heat in summer, the driving rain and the chill in winter. Houses in Galilee did this with rock walls thick enough to provide passive solar heating in the winter. By the same principle, they stayed cool during summer days. The native rock is either black basalt or white limestone. Both are plentiful, are easily worked, and are re-usable. Most houses were constructed of boulders and field stones; only the grandest villas used dressed stone. While alternative building materials are possible, they are not likely. Wood in Galilee was a cash crop; it was too rare and valuable to use for constructing the walls of houses, and lacked the climate-control capabilities of rock. Mud brick would melt in the yearly rains; and why bother to make bricks when rocks lay so conveniently all around?

The roofs of village houses probably were thatched over undressed beams, although this organic material does not survive. Some roofs, or portions of roofs, may have been tiled and guttered. Portions of the residential space were left open to the sky as courtyards or stockyards. Rooftops also were used for sleeping and other domestic activities in the summer. The simplest houses were not heated, and they had no chimneys or vents. Their ovens and cookfires were placed in unroofed areas, and may not have been lit every day since fuel was scarce. The houses had two kinds of floors. In the roofed rooms, floors usually were of packed earth, while the surfaces of courtyards were paved. The pavement could help to collect rainwater and channel it down into limestone cisterns carved into the bedrock below the courtyard. Runoff from the roof would also help to fill the cistern, in case the roof was tiled. If the house was not located over bedrock, then water had to be drawn up from a well or carried from a nearby spring or stream.

Common houses, then, controlled and facilitated "vertical access" to the resources of the sky. The roofs kept out sun and rain, but also functioned as platforms where sleepers or diners could catch a refreshing breeze in summer. The unroofed courtyards admitted the light and air needed for tasks like cooking, spinning, weaving, and pot manufacture. Their pavements kept rainwater from making mudpuddles, and let it run off instead into cisterns below the ground for later use. This controlled vertical access, engineered into the design of the common house, suggests that openness to the sky was perceived as a necessary functional capability. Did it have any additional cultural meaning? So it would seem. Since time immemorial in Palestine, the sky was associated with deity, and the high God was worshiped in high places like mountains and hilltop shrines. In historical times, the poetic language of prophecy and psalm often depicted divine favor as something that dropped from heaven like rain or dew. Moreover, customs for the harvest festival of Sukkoth included the erection of a temporary "booth," a holiday house open to the sky; and during that special time, activities normally done under cover of the house's roof, such as sleeping and dining, were done in the walled but uncovered space of the booth—in closer proximity to the heavens, so to speak. Thus, we begin to formulate a hunch: the opening and closing of access to the sky seems to have carried meanings beyond its bare functional usefulness. Architectural access to the sky and to sky intrusions—light, heat, water, fresh air— expressed human access to the divine as well as divine providence toward the human.

But what about "horizontal access"? What controls did the house provide for comings and goings? The house had doors, but it probably lacked windows. (It is difficult to be certain about the windows, since our information comes from ruins where the walls are no longer preserved to any great height.) In fact, much care was taken with the design of the doorjambs. In a house whose walls were of dry-laid fieldstone, the threshold might be the only dressed stone used in the construction. Thus, more effort and care went into the carving and placement of the doorjambs and threshold than into the walls for the rest of the house. In fact, it may have taken a special artisan to set the door stones and hang the doors right, someone analogous to a subcontractor.

(Jesus and his family apparently did this sort of work.) Wall masonry, by contrast, could be laid competently by a gang of one's uncles and brothers-in law.

There are several thresholds to be seen in the archaeological park at Qatzrin in the Golan. Although their dates are uncertain and they may have been carved in the late Roman era, there is no reason to suppose that they are not representative of a persistent indigenous design commonly in use in villages from long before Jesus' day. These thresholds are distinctively carved to receive the posts for a set of double doors and to permit those doors to open inward or to be shut and locked.

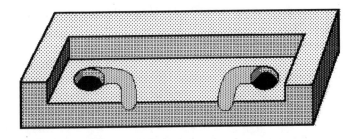

FIGURE 1: *Threshold design for village doors at Qatzrin. The stone is approximately 80 centimeters wide.*

The design of the stone threshold allows us to infer something of the design and operation of the wooden doors, which as organic material have not survived.

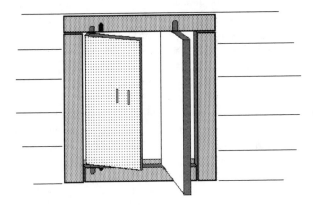

FIGURE 2: *Reconstruction of wooden doors to fit the carved threshold, as seen from within the house.*

We can see that the stone was meant to hold a pair of wooden doors that must have worked as illustrated. The stone threshold permitted the doors to swing inward on their posts. They could be opened only from the inside. Moreover, they would open in two stages. First, they swing inward just an inch or so, so that one side can clear the inner edge of the other. But the outer edges of the doors soon strike the sill, preventing the doors from swinging any further until they are lifted. If a door is lifted and pulled sideways, its post can slide along the curved channel toward the occupant of the house, and the doors will open wide. This design allows the occupant to take a look at whoever is outside before granting admission. An unwelcome intruder would have to stoop and reach inward to grasp the bottom of the door to raise it, and could be hit over the head or kicked while attempting to do so. In closed position, the doors could be further secured by sliding a latch through the handles. The whole door could slide entirely off the track when it was necessary to replace worn wooden posts.

The ingenuity of this design, and the care and expense of carving it, attest to the perceived significance of controlling horizontal access to the house. Importantly, the doors like the roofs must open at the appropriate times and for the appropriate reasons. Like the roofs, they are built of a relatively costly and perishable organic material, wood. Beyond its functional utility, does this door design carry a cultural significance as well? If so, then the everyday use of the doors would also cultivate a sense of the naturalness and necessity of the analogous cultural structures. For example, it takes two doors properly joined to secure the house, but it takes only one defective or derailed door to permit leakage in or out. The daily choreography of coming and going across that threshold, of opening and closing those doors, would make real the definitions of "belonging" to the house. Culturally, the very broad semantic range of the term "house" in Aramaic and Hebrew suggests that ownership and kinship structures might work analogously with the physical operation of that threshold and those doors.

What lay beyond the doors, within the house? There were two kinds of spaces: covered rooms, and open courtyards or stockyards. In villages like Capernaum and towns like Bethsaida, the walls of a house enclosed several clusters of two or three rooms each, positioned around one or more courtyards. This design is called an *insula*. In the countryside, the rooms were clustered at the corner of a larger walled yard or pen. This design has been termed a farmhouse.

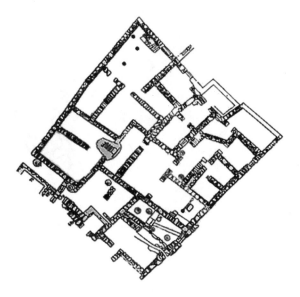

FIGURE 3: *Insula II at Capernaum, first century* CE, *after Corbo. This block of houses is about 26 meters square.*

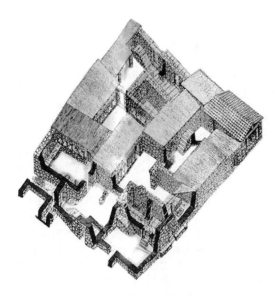

FIGURE 4: *Reconstruction of Insula II at Capernaum, suggesting walls, roofs, and open yards. After Corbo. Courtyards are 6 to 7 meters long by 3 to 4 meters wide. Roofed rooms are roughly half that size.*

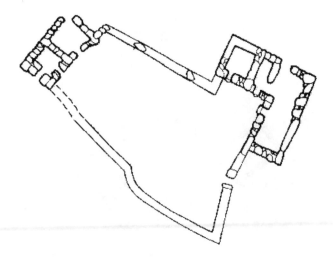

FIGURE 5: *Plan of "farmhouse" in northern Samaria near the town of Umm Rihan, after Guijarro. The yard is about 16 meters long.*

From these arrangements we can infer that people lived near their domestic animals, and that working, sleeping, and eating all occurred within the same enclosure. What we cannot infer is that people lived or worked with their own kin exclusively. In other words, the cultural rules for defining kinship may not have coincided with the various floor plans of the houses. The size, number, and layout of the rooms reflected the ingenuity of those who remodeled and occupied them and the kind of work they did there. There is no evidence that the configuration of rooms within houses is an unambiguous indicator of "family type." For one thing, the floor plan could not change as rapidly as the family did. Being stone, the house materially persisted while individuals were born, grew up, married out or married in, and died. This flux of occupation indeed requires a certain flexibility of the enclosure as a whole, with the rooms serving various needs at various times. At most, the layout might generally accommodate adjustments as the kin group expanded or shrank. The house clearly is not analogous to some specific and static shape of "family." Rather, in its persistence and elasticity, the house is analogous to a kinship lineage. Living in such a house reinforces the perceived reality of the lineage as a stable enclosure that is selectively permeable for births, marriages, and deaths. The closeness of the quarters may also encourage non-kin workers in the house to join its lineage through marriage, where possible. (We will return to the complex questions of kinship in a later chapter.)

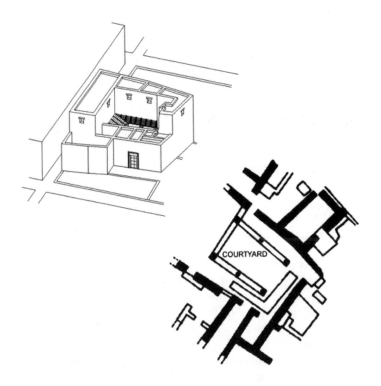

FIGURE 6: *The Hasmonean-era villa at Sepphoris. Top: Reconstruction suggested by James F. Strange. Bottom: plan of the ruin. Built in the first century BCE, this villa may have been part of Hasmonean settlement on the northern and western slopes of the acropolis. The courtyard is about 9 by 11 meters, including a shaded area defined by columns and an inner court of about 4 by 7 meters open to the sky.*

The insula and the farmhouse were the commonest house designs. Besides those, in Hellenistic times grand mansions began to appear in Galilee like those in Judea and in other lands around the Mediterranean. These houses were much larger, finely decorated and furnished, and designed to require maintenance by a staff of workers. For example, a distinctive feature was the large "triclinium" dining room. It accommodated couches for reclining at leisurely meals— meals that therefore had to be served by someone other than the reclining diners.

To be a Roman-era triclinium, a room must be large enough to hold couches arranged on three sides of a rectangle, surrounded by serving pathways. The term would eventually come to designate any domestic space presumed to have been dedicated to formal dining, and some reconstructions of ancient houses mistakenly label a smaller space as a triclinium. The people who were domiciled or fed or employed in a Hellenistic mansion were not all of one kinship group. Managers of mansions who needed to recruit a household staff would have had to extract some of the people and activities from the indigenous houses, at least for some of the time. These grand villas offered or imposed an alternative choreography to that of the village house, thereby challenging indigenous relationships and destabilizing their perceived inevitability. As we shall see, the crossing and clashing of cultures in the Galilee of Jesus was sited in and around Hellenistic mansion houses.

THE STUDY HOUSE. The term "house" also applies to one specially adapted kind of architecture that is of interest to us mostly because it had not yet appeared at the time of Jesus, but would soon afterwards. The little that is known about the design of the rabbinic *bet midrash* or "house of study" comes from ancient texts. No known example has yet been excavated, although there is an inscribed lintel on display in Qatzrin that may have come from a study house.

The surprising thing about the *bet midrash* is this: that religious studies began to require a designated and dedicated urban space about the year 300 CE. Textual sources indicate that this space had a door and a doorkeeper who charged admission; it belonged to a particular rabbi, who taught there. Importantly, the erection of the first study house was not the beginning of the institution of rabbinic teaching, much less the beginning of any organized religious instruction in Galilee. It was only the authoritative cloistering of such instruction. This architectural development is congruent with a trend to protect and stabilize instruction, using the same material technology by which lineage itself was stabilized: the lockable house. The suggestion of a perceived cultural congruence between legitimate instruction and legitimate kinship will be explored further in subsequent chapters.

FIGURE 7: *Lintel from "the house of study of Rabbi Eliezer Ha-Kappar" at Dabbura in the Golan, identified by Dan Urman.*

THE PLUMBING: CISTERNS, AQUEDUCTS, AND *MIQVA'OT*. It is often said that the land itself is the primary material correlate of Israelite social identity. But the land means nothing without its water. The key to the significance of the non-moveable real estate of Galilee is the moving water: where it comes from, where it goes, how it gets there, and what it does along the way. The water architecture of Galilee works like the house, in some respects. In the midst of natural patterns of flow, it catches, contains, covers, and then releases the water at the proper times, somewhat as the house takes in people selectively and sends them forth again in their daily and generational cycles.

An ideal site for a Galilean settlement is halfway up a hillside on a bedrock formation of limestone karst. Limestone is soft rock. It is honeycombed with natural caverns, and these can easily be enlarged, modified with steps for access and a protective cover, and even plastered to control seepage. These caverns fill up during the torrential winter rains, and this water supply can be shielded from evaporation so that it lasts through the dry summer months. The source of cistern water is rain, which drops from heaven in the natural weather cycle. But once fallen, the water has to be lifted out of the cistern by human hands, in a bucket or jug.

Cistern water was deemed to be unsuitable for many of the ritual purifications prescribed in Jewish law. They require "living water," which means running water, or more exactly, water whose natural downward valence from the heavens has not been interrupted by human hands. The water of a river or creek or even a sea will suffice. But cistern water cannot be used, because it has been lifted and thus is perceived to have acquired a contrary valence. Ingeniously, however, city dwellers in Hellenistic times invented an architectural design for ritual bathing in those situations where rivers and seas were too far distant for convenient access. The *miqveh* (plural *miqva'ot*) with its special supply tank, the *otzar*, catches rainwater passively. In fact, this installation uses a small amount of living water to "revive" the original dropped-from-heaven valence of a quantity of other, more convenient water (such as aqueduct water). This produces a volume sufficient for the bath. Obviously, there is no chemical difference between "living" and "drawn" water. The perceived character of the water is a meaning that derives from knowledge of the way in which the water has moved. Thus the architecture of the *miqveh* installation can provide for a change in the character of water and in its potency by, in effect, correcting the perceived direction of its movement.

Water, then, is significant to people of Israelite heritage not only in its capacity to satisfy physical needs, but also in its capacity both to carry a valence and to correct the valence or trajectory of other fluids, including other volumes of water as well as people, utensils, and commodities in motion across the landscape. The way water moves is important, not only to the physical well-being of people, livestock, and crops, but also for the management of cultural meanings. Or, to put it another way: to the indigenous imagination, what is important about water is the way it is moving.

So when Herodian engineers built the massive aqueduct systems to support cities like Caesarea or Sepphoris, they accomplished something more than civic improvements. They secularized the water. It no longer came from heaven; it came from Rome. "From Rome" means that Roman engineering brought it into homes and courtyards from far-off mountain springs, conveniently, automatically, without regard to the natural vicissitudes of the weather or the seasons, and without any apparent assistance from divine providence. In this regard, we can see that the *miqveh* installation in a Greco-Roman city functions to re-orient the flow of this secularized public water so that it becomes suitable for religious ritual. Aqueducts as such were by no means a Roman innovation in Jerusalem or Galilee. The Temple city had ancient water tunnels, and the waterworks at Sepphoris probably were founded by the Hasmoneans. But unlike those earlier installations, the Herodian- and Roman-era aqueducts were monumentally built and called attention to themselves by their size and design. They matched the massive civic architecture of theaters, colonnaded avenues, temples, and so forth that constituted the "urban overlay" of the Greco-Roman cities in Galilee. *Miqva'ot* in and around Jerusalem first are found at Hasmonean-era sites, in both domestic and industrial contexts. In Galilee, where they also appear at Hasmonean sites such as Yodefat and Gamla, this architectural form seems to have been imported from Judea about the first century BCE.

The *miqveh* pool itself is a stone tank that retains enough water for complete immersion of that which requires ritual purification: for example, jars, other utensils, or the human body. Later rabbinic texts tell us that it should have seven steps leading down into the water, it should be fed by gravity from an *otzar* where "living water" collects, and it should have no drain. The *miqva'ot* excavated in association with agricultural production facilities in Judea are large and may have separate steps for entry and exit. Those found within houses are smaller and simpler. The identification of any particular stepped pool as a *miqveh* is always doubtful, since ritual use cannot be inferred from design. But hundreds of similar tanks have been excavated in homes and on farms. In either context, these tanks would be irrationally redundant if their function were merely to wash and cleanse someone or something. They are built for meaning.

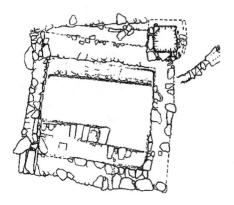

FIGURE 8: *Plan of the excavated* miqveh *at Gamla, first century* BCE, *after a drawing on Donald D. Binder's synagogue website. The exterior walls are 4.5 by 4 meters. Inside the tank, the walls are about 3.1 meters high. Water apparently rose halfway up the walls to the level of a ledge, from which the steps descend.*

We can formulate the hunch that, in a house or farm enclosure, the stepped pool does something that the lockable doors cannot do, or perhaps can no longer do. The doors can selectively admit and release. The *miqveh-otzar* installation, as we have seen, not only admits and retains fluids, but also changes the character of fluids by changing their direction of flow, their "valence." Analogous to the house, the ritual tank admits, retains, and releases items. In addition, this special tank corrects the social momentum of that which bathes in it. The persons and utensils that have been bathed in the *miqveh* emerge with a new spin, that is, with the directionality of their circulation corrected and restored to what it was when they left the hand of the Creator. They now reassume their places and activities within the flow of daily life. These would be perceived cultural meanings, of course. The architectural design of the stepped pool seems to manifest what we may tentatively term a grammar or idiom of the flow of relationships.

THE SYNAGOGUE HALL. The earliest identifiable synagogue structures in Galilee are built like large stepped pools. However they were never meant to hold water, because they lack waterproof plaster. Instead, they seem to be tanks of light. The structures designated as synagogues by the excavators of Gamla and Magdala are rectangular, with ranks of stone steps on all sides for seating. Instead of water from heaven, these tanks bathe people in sky light. Instead of an *otzar*, these tanks have high clerestory windows to collect heavenly illumination and channel it downward onto the central pavement across which the seated people are facing one another. This is the space in which "items" of community concern are discussed and settled. People's affairs can have their "spin" corrected here and the correct momentum of relationships can be maintained. If the synagogues at this period also functioned as prayer halls and venues for the reading of the scripture, that use is also congruent with the ritual use of the *miqveh*.

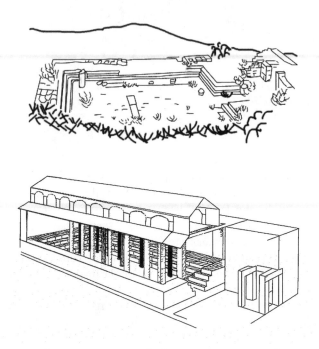

FIGURE 9: *The synagogue at Gamla, first century BCE. Top: drawing of the ruin, looking south from the hillside across the brow of the gorge. Bottom: reconstructed cutaway view, after a drawing by James F. Strange. This side of the synagogue, the north, was set into the hillside. The clerestory would collect sunlight from the exposed south side. The structure was 25.5 by 17 meters. The interior floor is 13.4 by 9.3 meters, surrounded by ranks of stone benches on all four sides.*

It is worth noting what those early Galilean synagogues were not. They were not enclosed behind locked doors. They were not houses, in either sense: neither homes nor "houses of study." They were not distinctively "Galilean," in comparison with synagogue design in Judea or the cities of the Diaspora. They were, rather, "homes away from home." That is, the architectural form of the synagogue seems to have come to Galilee with Judean settlers and developers in the wake of the Hasmonean expansion. We formulate the hunch, then, that in the towns of Galilee the perceived need for an architecture of community affairs—that is, an architecture to regulate and adjust the momentum of community affairs—coincided with social changes wrought by Hellenistic expansion into Galilee in general, and by Hasmonean administrative innovations in particular.

WHARVES AROUND THE KINNERET. The impact of colonial administration upon Galilee affected the regional landscape, not just the architectural designs of individual buildings. The Ptolemies of Egypt (ruling in Palestine after 312 BCE), the Seleucids (after 198 BCE), and the Hasmoneans (after 160 BCE) all appreciated the inherent fecundity and exploitable resources of the Galilee: the agricultural potential of the land to produce wheat, wine, olives and olive oil, wool, flax, and textiles; and the potential of the Sea of Galilee to produce fish and processed fish sauces. Politically, during the lifetime of Jesus the Kinneret, or Sea of Galilee, was the eastern border of the territory governed by Antipas. Socially, economically, and culturally, however, it was by no means a marginal area. The Lake was a center of industry, the hub of commerce, the point of embarkation for shipping produce northward and eastward, and the gateway to Israel for business travelers and pilgrims arriving from Syria and Babylon.

The Kinneret is not physically connected with the Mediterranean. It is a nice big sea nevertheless. So it could be built up in ways that *felt* Mediterranean, which is to say, felt exotically Alexandrian or Aegean. There is no way to establish a baseline or a "before" state for the built environment of the Sea of Galilee as it was prior to the time when the Hasmoneans annexed the territory. All around the shoreline, the remains of ancient harbor facilities have been found during those rare seasons when the water line is low enough to expose the bottom of the Lake. These indicate that ship-borne activities, namely fishing and transport, were well organized in ancient times. If there were docks, then we are talking about vessels bigger than boats of the size that could be hauled out onto the beach. We can infer industrial activity: ship-building and repair, sail-making, net-making, fish markets, fish-processing, fish-packing, the import of lumber, salt and vinegar, and trans-shipping from distant cities. The archaeological record does not yet allow secure

dating of the ruins of the ancient docks, much less an account of when
the industries flourished or declined. Famously, one boat from the first
century has been found and restored at Kibbutz Gennesar, on the western shore just north of the ancient harbor of Magdala.

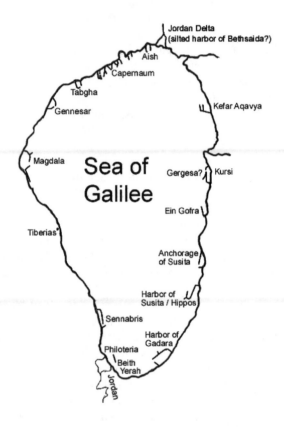

FIGURE 10: *Ancient harbors, jetties, and docks around Lake Kinneret, the
"Sea of Galilee," after Rousseau and Arav. The Lake is 13 miles long and 8
miles wide.*

The Judeans extended their administrative control to encompass the
Kinneret completely during the rule of Alexander Jannaeus, by about 80
BCE. Hellenistic buildings at Magdala, including the synagogue, date
from this period at the earliest. Owing to the breadth of territory that
they controlled, the Hasmoneans created a business climate favorable to
what we might term vertical monopoly within the fishing industry, which
would make large-scale fishpacking more economical and lucrative.

Besides fish from the Lake, they could supply salt, vinegar, jars, lumber and sails for the fishing fleet, as well as safe and passable roads for transporting those materials to the drydocks and packing plants at Magdala. It is possible that the Seleucids and the Ptolemies also did this earlier. In any event, by the time of Mary and Joseph, the Kinneret was certainly developed as region participating in international trade. The Lake was ringed by harbors. Moreover, it offered relief to people who were finding it increasingly difficult to make a living by farming, as wealthy landowners enlarged their estates through creative mortgage and foreclosure tactics. The Lake itself held fish for the catching, and paid jobs were available at the harbors. In other words, the lakeshore as a built environment attracted people into alternative patterns of circulation at a time when the lockable doors of the traditional house were assailed by economic and political developments.

Yet under the Hasmoneans, life on the Lake was not yet so very different from life on the land. The water retained its character of "living water" whose perceived momentum was flowing from the divine hand. The wind in the sails and the fish in the nets were analogous to light, rainfall, and summer breezes. Temporal rhythms of day and night, winter and summer, controlled the fishing no less than they regulated planting and harvest. Perhaps the major cultural incongruity was that the products that left the Lake went far away and did not return.

TIBERIAS. Something did return from where the Lake's produce was sent. What returned were people: pilgrims, foreign businessmen, tourists. But this stream of foreigners had no reason to cross the Lake into Galilee until Antipas built the city of Tiberias to attract them, about the year 19 CE. In Hasmonean times and during the reign of Herod the Great, all of the Lake region lay within the same administrative district. But after 4 BCE, the Kinneret became the eastern border of Antipas' territory. At first Sepphoris was his capital. But it lay inland and was not near to the major international routes to Jerusalem. Traffic from the east approached the Temple city along a route that ran down the eastern shore of the Lake and never crossed into the jurisdiction of Antipas.

Antipas chose the spot for his new capital, Tiberias, on the western shore within sight of travelers arriving at Gamla and the harbor towns of the eastern shore. He built a palace on the hillside. Presumably he built docks below, where today the tourist beach clubs and hotels line the shore at modern Tiberias. This new city was designed to divert the international overland Jerusalem traffic into Antipas' region, by boat. Travel by boat was fashionable, besides offering a pleasant change after the trek across the Syrian desert from Damascus. The imperial cities of

Rome, Alexandria, and even Caesarea were all approached by water. In the case of Rome, Ostia was the port and the Tiber river led up to the great capital itself. In effect, when Antipas built Tiberias as a port of welcome to the land of Israel, he "italianized" the Lake and the lower Jordan. The need to transport elite international travelers over the Kinneret, and to entertain them while they rested at Tiberias, invited the establishment of a new kind of industry: imperial tourism. This may well have brought material disruptions of the fishing businesses; it certainly changed the perceived character of the water.

FIGURE 11: *Herod Antipas governed the territories of Galilee and Perea. Drawing by Corey Kent, after Rousseau and Arav. The old pilgrimage route from Damascus brought eastern visitors to Gamla and to cities of the Decapolis like Hippos, Gadara, and Scythopolis before turning south along the Jordan toward Jericho and Jerusalem. It did not cross Galilee. Tiberias was sited to attract elite travelers into a pleasant detour west across the Lake into Antipas' northern territory.*

THE TEMPLE AND JERUSALEM. The Herods knew how to circulate people, money, power, and commodities. Herod the Great, father of Antipas, had promoted Jerusalem as a destination for international travel in various ways. Not only had he built the Mediterranean port of Caesarea, he had redesigned the Temple itself. Although the Temple Mount has not been excavated, literary sources indicate that people and livestock circulated through Herod's Temple in greater numbers and with greater speed and efficiency than in any previous design. They moved in a different pattern as well. For the first time, gendered space was introduced into Jewish worship by Herod's Temple. Its design can be read as a template for the construction of Israelite identity, as we shall see.

THE BOOK. The series of forms that we have been considering has progressed from smaller to larger and from the local to the regional and national scale. Why does the book, as a form, come last in this series? Why is it placed into this series at all? Like the other architectures, the book materializes structures of identity management that are taken for granted by those who use it. The book accepts, contains, and releases ideology. It does this important cultural work by admitting the reader, conducting him or her along certain pathways, and then sending that reader forth on a readjusted life-trajectory. Both as scrolls and as codices, books are built to do just this. When used, and quite apart from whatever their "content" may happen to be, books act recursively upon their users to replicate the template of "containing," following, and releasing in the readers' subsequent behavior. Book, as an architecture, was not indigenous to the Land of Israel. However it naturalized itself there and became part of the repertoire for securing identity and intergenerational continuity. As gospel, testament, mishnah, and talmud, the book materially defined and secured legitimacy.

The book, then, is the biggest and most extensive of the architectural forms. It has covered the whole earth. Herod's Temple was a sucking mechanism. It drew people, wealth, animals, and imaginations toward Jerusalem from all across the empire and from the Babylonian East as well. Building upon ancient customs, Herod secured Jerusalem as the focal point of international Jewish identity by enlarging and refurbishing the Temple, and by supplying an infrastructure of pleasant ports and safe roads that promoted international travel to and from the Temple city. This worked all too well, for in 70 CE the Temple drew down the wrath of Rome. The whole city was destroyed. By comparison, the book did not attract; instead, it replicated and disseminated itself. With the book, there is no one physical place to be defended, won, or lost.

Wherever the book goes becomes the center. The book carries the pattern for legitimation and identification, and the book can be carried everywhere. It is an architecture of diffusion, not concentration.

Books represented an advanced technology, supported at considerable cost. The physical format of books in Antiquity was the papyrus or parchment scroll, carefully hand-lettered by a skilled scribe, protected in a case of wood or leather. Some ancient scrolls have been found hidden in ceramic jars. Alternately, notebooks or codices also were used in the first century. Each individual copy was quite fragile, since it was made of perishable organic material, and since variances could so easily creep into the text in the copying. But the resilience of this architectural form consists in its copy-ability. Making a copy of an ancient book was difficult, but not nearly so difficult as building a temple, an aqueduct, or even a house. Making many, many copies tended to insure that the book would continue to work, somewhere, even after temples, aqueducts, and houses were razed. The book attained its most resilient and persistent form when it became a book of books, that is a canon. Canons identify and unify the members of communities. They constitute a new kinship, and they connect community members even after the people leave their houses or cities or native lands, even when the people of the book are separated by great spans of space and time. The book is the ultimate imperial architecture.

▪ ▪ ▪

This chapter has briefly sketched several design features that developed in, and thereby developed, the Land of Israel. They ranged in scale from small and large edifices to a city, a cluster of harbors, a regional route, and trans-national structures of assembly and dispersion. Each architectural form facilitates circulation in a different way. But a certain congruence has been suggested, as each seems to invoke and materialize an indigenous logic of containment and selective opening. The next chapter will elaborate on the meanings of those patterns of circulation, drawing them into a synthetic account.

3 | What Moved Across Galilee

COGNITIVE ARCHAEOLOGY ATTEMPTS TO RECOVER the indigenous principles of organization that were enacted in the everyday tasks of an ancient people, although never explicitly formulated by them. Both in the building of their environment and in their use of it, Galileans and Judeans established the meanings that made sense of their lives.

Designs for containment were introduced in the last chapter as distinctive material features of the Palestinian landscape. The exemplar in our exposition was the Israelite house, built to accommodate the selective admission and release of people, possessions, sun, and rain. On a grander scale, Galilee itself was a container newly breached by the cities of Herod the Great and Antipas, after centuries of negotiating partial material and cultural closures amid incursions by various Hellenistic colonial powers. We saw that the landscape of Galilee within the Land of Israel was also a mindscape, that is, a dynamic field of meaning potential.

The nested containers comprising this material and cultural terrain are "containers" in regard to something movable. What were those "fluid" elements? What kinds of entities were in motion between containers, having their trajectories adjusted and modulated by means of temporary containment and periodic release? I suggested in the last chapter that water was the simplest case of a managed fluid in Palestine. Water was perceived to have both physical and cultural properties. Physically, it moved through the built environment propelled by gravity or by the lifting power of humans and draft animals. Culturally, its character was determined by the perceived momentum of that flow. Accordingly, "living" water had ritual uses for which drawn water was not suitable. A distinctive plumbing installation, the architecture of the *miqveh* with its *otzar*, was invented for the restoration and management of living water in the midst of situations where aqueducts were delivering most of the available water and where Greco-Roman public baths were organizing civic life.

There is a certain logic built into the plumbing of the *miqveh* and, in turn, built up and reinforced by the use of this plumbing. Its design works recursively, to make the meanings of the circulation patterns seem natural and inevitable to those who routinely use the architectural fixtures. In addition, there are other elements of the landscape, such as the house with its lockable doors and its partial roofing, that also channel certain moving entities along patterns analogous to those that water follows on its way through the ritual plumbing. The house in its own way seems to be able to stabilize what it houses, modulating and correcting the perceived momentum of the persons and things that pass through it.

Moments of circulation, stabilization, and re-direction, then, appear to be the basic idiom in which the various architectural designs express their meanings and impart their spin to what moves across the Land of Israel. Israelite kinship, too, is constructed on this template. The idiom of directed circulation provides for the expression of ethical and ritual meanings as well. The distinction between justice and injustice, and the distinction between ritual cleanness and uncleanness, while not equivalent distinctions, both are constructed in the same basic idiom. Law and lawfulness materialize in and through the architectures that supply the grounding points in that circuit.

This construction strategy emphasizes fluidity. In this, it contrasts sharply with the modern Western bias toward stabilization. For our part, we typically seek to secure justice by investing static individuals with static possessions, properties, rights, and duties. But the logic of correct circulation that we encounter in Hasmonean and Roman Palestine is incommensurate with our own familiar logic of honoring rights and duties. Holiness, for example, is perceived to obtain in the land of Israel when everything moving across the land is maintaining its own proper momentum. The holy land itself is regarded as the most stable element, and so it is understood to be a stabilizer, magnet, and modulator of that which crosses it. Places are not holy in any static sense, by virtue of being separated from other spaces as integral, self-contained units. The notion of holiness as separation was an analytic model constructed within the academic discipline of the history of religions, and it can be applied only with difficulty in the interpretation of Israel's experience. In Israel, a place is holy when things move rightly within it and moreover, when it can rectify the trajectory of what crosses it. Thus, what profanes is whatever moves the wrong way. The profane is not imagined to be the outside or the boundary that localizes the holy sphere. That interpretive model—holiness as separation—may work for other societies, but it does not fit Israel too well.

Destination, not location, appears to be the significant social issue negotiated in spatial designs in Israel. This motif repeats itself in various cultural spheres. If we wish to discern the indigenous meaning complex, then we must take care not to allow our own customary vocabulary to overwrite the indigenous material and verbal expressions. As we shall see in this chapter, then, a woman who marries and goes to reside in the house of her husband's family would thereby stabilize the lineage of her children and secure for them and herself an accessible accumulation of the fruits of her labor. She would regard herself as an active tributary in a network of moving and grounding elements, and not as a repository of "rights." Only in terms of non-indigenous Western social categories could she be an exploited possession, a chattel. She herself would not be capable of describing her situation in those terms, for she would not experience herself in a "situation" at all. She might indeed experience injustice; but if so, she would experience that injustice as a misdirection, a diversion of what ought to be coming her way, a detour of her own productivity away from the circuits of traditional kin-based redistribution patterns. The distinction between the two descriptions is subtle, but without it we risk missing the sense that Galilee made to ancient Galileans.

Caste in Israel, then, may be regarded as a status and a determinant of personal identity only from the modern Western angle of vision. To the ancient people caste was descent: the proper flow pattern of one's parentage, the momentum toward legitimate marriage and offspring for one's children. Gender, then, was an integral component of caste and it cannot be understood apart from caste. Gender in contemporary Western societies is conceived as a system for the assignment of status and personal identity. But in the Kinneret region at roughly the time of Jesus and the Tannaim, gender was neither static nor personal. More precisely, the social functions that contemporary social science correlates with personal gender status were instead accomplished through the larger reciprocal social architecture of kinship.

Kinship and gender relations can be illuminated in various ways. They can be interpreted through a model derived from the architectural structures introduced in the last chapter, which are the structures that the people themselves used for managing at least the material comings and goings of their own lives. Such a model would formalize the terms of grounding structure, circulating fluid, and redirective spin, and would apply those categories to interpret indigenous behaviors and practices. But would such a model truly be an indigenous model? On one hand, to "model" anything by imposing abstract categories, as an exercise in social analysis, would certainly not be a practice familiar to ancient Galileans. It is a contemporary scientific practice, and is indigenous to our own culture. On the other hand, the terms of this modeling would be culturally much closer to the indigenous idiom of the ancient people than are the terms currently used in other common modeling schemes.

There are three major alternative models in use among scholars today that are challenged by my attempt to formalize the indigenous Israelite idiom of circulation and grounding. (These alternatives are mentioned in passing here, and receive a fuller consideration in chapter four. Further technical discussion is reserved for chapter ten.)

(1) *an economic conflict model*, in which the peasant majority is said to be oppressed by the urban imperial minority, with occasional eruptions of violence punctuating longer periods of collaboration when benefits accrue to both sides. Those who use this model differ on the relative weight given to the oppression versus the benefits. Important works by Seán Freyne, John Dominic Crossan, Richard Horsley, and Douglas Edwards have recourse to this basic interpretation of social reality in Greco-Roman Galilee.

(2) *a gender-ideological conflict model*, in which females and non-elite males are said to be disparaged by the elite male minority, with occasional outbreaks of counter-hegemonic assertion. Important works by Elisabeth Schüssler Fiorenza and her followers invoke this model. It places emphasis on verbal expression, including rhetoric in texts, but it neglects material practices involving texts as artifacts whose indigenous meaning would be defined by their use in the ancient context and in concert with other items of material culture. Kathleen Corley, Cynthia Baker, and Miriam Peskowitz are among the scholars who rely upon this interpretive strategy.

(3) *an "honor-shame" model*, in which social standing is said to be continually wagered and enhanced or decreased in game-like transactions supervening upon all social exchanges. This interpretation derives from anthropological studies of twentieth-century traditional societies that were carried out in the 1960s. Also called the "social science" approach, this program of interpretation was pioneered by Bruce Malina and is elaborated by Jerome Neyrey, John Pilch, and participants in The Context Group.

Each of those models has advanced the critical study of first-century Palestine beyond the level of a mere retelling of the traditional accounts, or a nostalgic retrojection of contemporary relations into the past. But each carries the risk of importing its own interests into the ancient materials and mixing them with the data. Of course, data never appear in a pure state. A pure induction of categories from the ancient materials is impossible. For one thing, the very intent of "inducing categories" of analysis is an intent that belongs to us as alien investigators. Yet without it, the only understanding available is that which would arise from living in the midst of the ancient structures as the ancient people did. But we no longer can do that; we live here, while the ancient architecture lies in ruins. Yet the effort to induce our analytic categories out of their material artifacts has the advantage of illuminating a crucial issue. Every name we give to something of theirs is given analogously. Recognizing this fact, we can assess in each case how close or distant the analogy may be. For example, our term "circulation" seems quite a close approximation of what water has always done in pipes and tanks. "Gender" is a less than perfect analog for the ancient assignment of productive and reproductive social roles through sex and marriage. "Honor" is rather different from most of the terms actually used in Galilean society, which was a nexus of troubled contact among several cultures and languages. Only Greek offered an equivalent for our term "honor." The intention to construct an indigenous model of Galilee includes an intention to find close analogs between ancient experience and our own. The closest will be the somatic ones: those that express how human bodies like ours managed their physical environment by building architectures, implements, and roadways that are still there in ruins.

Both in the ruins and in texts, there are ample resources for building such an indigenous model, that is, for an archaeology of Galilean mind. A mirror of the ancient mindscape already exists in the Mishnah, a text compiled about 200 CE. The chronicles of Josephus, architectural details, and the topography of Eretz Israel itself also help reconstruct what Galileans "had in mind" in the first century. An archaeology of mind for Galilee must be deployed heuristically, and must not be allowed to manufacture data. Our premise is that, as indicated by both their kinship practices and their indigenous architecture, Galileans conceived status in terms of circulation. Which is to say: what we call a "place" in the physical or social sense was understood by them as directionality or even gravitation. The holiness of the Land of Israel depended on having things travel across it in the right direction: produce, labor, brides, cattle, words, and so forth. Let us take a look at the evidence that supports this claim.

Kinship in the Mishnah

In contemporary anthropology, "kinship" is one of the basic analytical categories applied to any human society. All people have ways of receiving each new baby into a perceived pattern of relationships, and of providing for the replication of that pattern intergenerationally. The patterns vary widely across cultures, and the terms for the relationships are notoriously difficult to translate. There are no scientifically collected anthropological data from ancient Galilee. However, Paul Flesher has presented a meticulous account of the logic of the kinship system reflected in the Mishnah, and his discussion is the basis for the following account.

The Mishnah is by no means an ethnographic report. But as a collection of detailed legal decisions and cases, it gives us a window on how people managed their obligations and their entitlements. Compiled about 200 CE from older sources, the Mishnah is relatively close in time to the Galilee of Jesus. It offers a historical witness to how people of a certain class were reasoning about economic and social relations. It is less reliable as evidence of how everybody actually behaved. Yet for the question at hand—intergenerational kinship reckoning—the very nature of the problem enhances the historical reliability of this early-third-century text. It stands to reason that, if elite families in the year 200 were maintaining marriage records and recalling betrothal customs that reached back beyond the fourth generation, obviously they meant to convey information that they took to be information about the first century.

The term "caste" is an anthropological shorthand for the transgenerational assignment of a ranked social identity. Like the term "family," it is not indigenous to Galilean society but belongs to our own descriptive vocabulary. The mishnaic terms are priest, levite, pure Israelite, and those with defective caste status: proselytes, freed slaves, slaves, various kinds of bastards, and the "people of the land" who did not bother to offer rhetorical defenses of their parentage at all. It is we who recognize this as resembling the "caste" assignments that are known in numerous other cultures, both today and in the recent past. The framers of the Mishnah were preserving and interpreting laws for life as a Jew. In the thinking of the people whom the Mishnah describes, the logic of caste was complex and asymmetrical. Caste was more than a category of personal identity and cultic prerogative. It was a system for distributing property and food. Caste placed things and people into categories, it provided procedures for alternating among those categories, and it assigned power to moderate or control the powers of others.

The Mishnah regards the householder as the central or basic kind of human being. Women, minors, and bond workers are defined by their lack of something that the householder has. Obviously, this scheme is a social construct. It may or may not have served as a means of (what *we* might see as) economic oppression or gender disparagement. That cannot be determined *a priori*, from the structure itself. One must first attempt to understand Israelite caste on its own terms as a social ideal, even a legal fiction. Whether and how this ideal actually functioned to distribute food and property is a question requiring empirical investigation, especially archaeological examination of the physical remains of habitation sites.

The basic category of "householders" is defined in relation to an architectural form that we examined in the last chapter: the house. The physical function of the house, that is, its selective containment of people and things, may very well correlate with some of the details of the prerogatives of this group, householders. In the mishnaic reckoning, each of the groups defined as non-householders participates in the privileges of the caste of the householder to whom he or she belongs: the priestly, the levitical, the "pure Israelite" (anachronistically so called), or one of the non-castes whose nationality is dubious (i.e., converts to Judaism, freed slaves, and people whose parents were ineligible to marry one another). An important caste privilege for priests (and, theoretically, for levites as well) is that portions of the harvest and meat from sacrifices are allotted to their households. This food can be eaten only by members of those households. This description probably does not correspond to actual distribution practices in the third century, since the Temple had been destroyed in 70 CE. It reflects how things are "supposed to" work. It preserves this ideal for some imagined future time when a restored Temple will need personnel with proper lineages. And it reflects memories of lineage-based distribution as practiced before 70 CE.

Across the generations, then, marriages are arranged in order to maintain caste and the resultant household eligibility to consume those rations and exercise other important social prerogatives. This is "how it is supposed to be," notwithstanding actual practices in the third century, or even in the first century. "Pure Israelite" households are defined as those whose daughters may marry priests or levites, eat their rations, and produce children who may also eat such rations. These daughters are precisely those for whom an effective rhetorical case can be made that every marriage in their lineage for four generations back (or for very elite caste, ten) was legally contracted between spouses of unimpeachable Israelite caste or better. It is the lineages of the daughters that require defense. The sons are secured by the fact of their residence within the paternal household since birth. The marriage rules are quite complex. Violations of them produce the outcastes, who can marry only one another or those who in effect have no ancestry: proselytes and freed slaves.

The Mishnah's account does not cover the marriage strategies of all of the people who resided in the Galilee in the first century. Men of foreign nationality who had married local women probably did not care about claiming that their children were Israelite. People whose parents and grandparents had not registered their marriages, for whatever reason, would not care. People who had lost their houses and farms through military or economic conquest had more pressing concerns than whose daughters their sons might marry and whose houses they might marry their daughters into. Those issues were rendered moot when the house itself was gone and the sons and daughters were sleeping on their employers' floors.

But these caste-maintaining regulations were still economically significant in the first century. Tithes cannot be collected unless caste logic is obvious to everyone, and unless lineages are documentable or otherwise rhetorically defensible. The fact that tithes are mentioned both in the Mishnah and in first-century texts indicates that people recognized what it meant to be a priest in general and, in terms of that understanding, also recognized the lineage of the man who proposed to collect the tithe. Even people who did not bother about caste when arranging their own marriages had a working knowledge of this structure, for it defined claims upon their labor and productivity that could be brought to bear by priests and levites. This indigenous logic is universally accessible to people who profess descent from Abraham and subscribe to the laws of Moses.

Maintaining a proper and defensible lineage was a matter of great importance for the most elite priestly families, who resided in Jerusalem and managed the Temple economy. Their share of tithes and sacrifices could support large workforces, for all of the slaves and freedmen engaged in agricultural or industrial production in one's house and lands could be fed on the meat and grain coming in as one's priestly ration. That ration, while it could not be sold, could be converted into labor and thereby into commodities for the market. The nutritional privileges of caste could constitute a considerable business advantage. Thus, the motives for maintaining caste through proper marriage were not entirely religious. Besides nutritional privilege, caste imparted eligibility to hold civic and religious administrative positions (and receive any associated stipends). Theoretically, only "pure

Israelites" could be judges, clerks, notaries, or managers of charities, and only levites or priests could hold the various liturgical and other offices in the Temple administration. The Mishnah's mentioning of offices that ceased to function in 70 CE, when the Temple was destroyed, suggests that this way of reckoning caste was already in place for at least several centuries before the Mishnah was committed to writing.

In all cases, only free adult males of the right caste are to hold those offices. However, a man's caste could not be secured through his patrilineal descent alone. Caste depended on certification that brides marrying into his family were properly pedigreed as well. The lineage of a prospective bride had to be traced back for several generations, and marriage documents were archived for that purpose. Patrilineal caste, then, was not static. It was imagined as something in need of renewal and stabilization in each generation by a bride carrying the right caste credentials through the lines of both her patrilineal and matrilineal descent. Otherwise, the children of the family could no longer claim their fathers' caste and privileges. Obviously, the mindscape of caste mattered most to those who had most to gain or lose in terms of their caste privileges. The exception that proves the rule is the Herodian dynasty, whose Roman connections enabled them to hold power (but not the affections of the populace) despite their irregular marriages. John the Baptist was able to do political damage to Herod Antipas with rhetoric citing Herodian violations of caste practices, which included both wrong marriages and tampering with the prerogatives of the priesthood. These events indicate that the logic of caste was intelligible to and accepted by the populace. Even those who could claim no caste privilege of their own still recognized and accepted caste itself as the basis for legitimate claims to receive tithes and exercise certain governmental roles. People could tell the difference between a marriage that maintained caste and one that destroyed it. The power of caste was rhetorical, it was the ability to get one's claims to power and resources accepted, and it was constructed in the architecture of meaning. Antipas had to resort to violence because he lacked the power of caste.

Proper marriage is the only way to maintain caste over time within a household. Entitlement to tithes is a special case of the entitlements conferred by kinship in general. Proper marriage maintains entitlements to inheritance as well as the whole mutual webwork of obligations toward one's kin. A household is a node in a web of patrilineal households linked by the exchange of brides. Brides, then, are construed as mobile in comparison with men, who are grounded in their fathers' houses and castes. Yet this is not a simple opposition. Women's mobility is necessary to the intergenerational maintenance of that groundedness, yet also permanently threatens it. Women are "grounded" by marriage, but the wife is not statically enclosed by the house. She comes and goes through the doors. She belongs to the house as someone whose productivity and children accrue to it.

Women's potential and kinetic energy

Mishnaic discussions of women's work clearly invoke this rationale. The goods that women produce and the wages they earn are supposed to travel back to the household, where they are controlled by a male relative designated through a complicated system of kinship assignment. Miriam Peskowitz has reviewed the mishnaic case law pertaining to textile production in Roman-era Palestine, coordinating the mishnaic texts with archaeological evidence and considering carefully the intricate technological and ergonomic details of spinning and weaving. In her view, the Mishnah discloses information about the ideological construction of femininity by the sages of the early third century who compiled it. She calls attention to the rhetorical techniques by which they masked the real economic value of women's work; that is, by which they "decommodified" that work. The economic pressures of empire were acutely felt in Galilee, and kinship strategies adapted to cope with them.

Thus, it appears that women's labor was both a real component of the material economy and an ideal feature in a cultural mindscape. The latter was skillfully wielded to manage the former. As an *economic reality*, women's labor produced food (grain, bread, fruits, vegetables, olives, oil, wine, milk, cheese, meat), textiles (wool, flax, thread, raw cloth, dyed cloth, clothing, military cloaks, embroidery), equipment (pottery, jewelry, tools, baskets, bags), and services (fuel gathering, laundry, hygiene, maintenance of public buildings like the baths, cooking and cleaning in private homes, hairdressing, wet-nursing, property management, negotiation of betrothals). But as a *cultural symbol*, women's labor was construed to be a kind of current that circulated through city and countryside but ultimately was supposed to pour back into the household to which the worker was attached. This symbolization permitted the woman to "stay" in the household to which the kinship system assigned her, even while she physically traveled to various locations outside it, whether a few yards or a few miles away. Her labor, or more precisely its fruit, was imagined as something continually pouring back into the house where she belonged.

At any given time, a woman's labor—"the work of her hands," in the rabbinic phrase adopted by Peskowitz—also means her potential for productivity in the future. The sages of the Mishnah reason concretely about potentials as if they were tokens passing from one person to another. Thus, a girl's labor first belongs to her father, and if he should die before she marries, it passes to her brothers. The bride's future productivity is a bargaining chip in negotiating the marriage contract. Because its value would be lost if the woman were injured or killed, it therefore creates an interest enabling a husband to bring suit in such an event. The wife's productive potential is the basis for what we might term the husband's power of attorney over her affairs. This token (ideally) transfers in exactly the same way as caste. That is, the woman's productivity always belongs to the household that defines her caste. Marriage means that her labor and its fruits will henceforth flow into the husband's household, just as her children will belong to his caste (rather than that of her father). This legal construct, "the work of her hands," is the symbolic token that marks the economic reality of women in the Mishnah.

Did everyday practices in Galilee conform to this symbolic structure? As Peskowitz shows, the sages applied its principles inconsistently and ignored them when expedient. There is no reliable information about what percentage of the first-century Galilean population considered themselves "Jewish" (an identity that was contested and variously defined at that time, in Eretz Israel as well as in the Diaspora), much less the percentages of (those perceived as) freedmen, bondmen, proselytes, offspring of irregular unions, priests, or levites. It seems safe to make two generalizations. First, Hasmonean expansion into the Galilee and the Golan in the first century BCE heightened the salience of those categories. Second, subsequent Herodian urbanization precipitated cultural and commercial contacts that disrupted the caste classifications in various ways. For whom were these developments most salient? For two groups: for those with the greatest stake in maintaining caste—levites, priests, and their bride-givers, the "pure Israelites"—and for people who paid tithes if, and only if, the caste of the recipient was recognizable and rhetorically defensible.

The right kind of brides had to cross the right kind of thresholds in order to insure the proper flow of commodities into tithes and into other apportionments to kin—as well as a fresh supply of the right kind of brides for the next generation. Materially, that is the only kind of caste there is. Nothing like a DNA test for parentage existed. A challenge to one's caste would have to be overcome either through brute force or through argumentation based on shared principles. Nevertheless, there is no necessary association between caste and wealth. A well-to-do family without "pure Israelite" caste might be less successful in bride-giving than a poor family with Israelite caste. Yet the situation might change in times of severe economic distress, when the out-caste status of a prospective bride might become less significant than the material resources she could bring into a household. Kinship, then, is not a system that functions automatically, by inexorable social causality. It is a cultural strategy for managing material resources, and it enables people to adapt to changing historical conditions. The idiom of kinship is a cultural resource for creative expression. It is adaptable because it is a repertoire of dynamic flow patterns.

Immersion and instruction

In caste we can discern the paradigm for a whole array of cultural analogs. Brides, commodities, labor, caste, kinship, and the prerogatives of caste and kinship all seem to move like water through the built environment of Galilee according to patterns built into Galilean mind. Correctness and legitimacy are established as a proper momentum and grounding. We can now observe an analogous treatment for yet another fluid: instruction. In a careful study of sectarian viewpoints on ritual purity, Carol Selkin has identified a conceptual linkage between the management of water and the disciplining of interpretive instruction. Her findings are congruent with our circulation model, and they allow us to refine it further.

A new architectural form, the ritual immersion pool or *miqveh*, begins to appear in the first centuries BCE and CE, precisely at the temporal and spatial horizons between Hasmonean and Herodian-Roman occupation: at Gamla, Magdala, Yodefat, Jericho, Sepphoris, and Jerusalem, to name some of the sites where *miqva'ot* have been excavated so far. It is essential to distinguish between the architecture and the practice that it housed. Ritual bathing predates the special architecture that was designed to accommodate it. Conversely, not every stepped pool excavated is a ritual bath. Some of these pools are just utilitarian reservoirs, covered to retard evaporation, and provided with steps for access to the receding water level during the dry season. But after Roman cultural and political hegemony is achieved, ritual bathing and the tanks in which it is done become the focus of sectarian disputes. As Selkin explains, the practical religious issues arise from the twofold halakhic role of water. Under some circumstances water transmits certain kinds of ritual impurity, while under other circumstances it removes them. Water is perceived as making objects susceptible to impurity, not carrying impurity in the sense that we might think of water as carrying bacteria or chemical pollutants.

Generally speaking, water that was anchored into the ground by an immobile container could purify any smaller portable vessel that had become impure through contamination of its contents by a source of impurity. But opinions differed over just how grounded a container had to be in order to be considered a pool rather than a vessel. There was also disagreement about the varieties of drawn water and living water, and about how either could be turned into the other. Sectarian positions on such issues helped to define the social boundaries of the various factions within Judaism in the Greco-Roman period, Selkin suggests. Moreover it is plausible, on philological grounds, that the notion of attaining ritual purity by immersing oneself in a grounded pool supported the analogous notion of attaining exegetical purity by "immersing" oneself in interpretations of the Torah that were "grounded" in authoritative teachers or, increasingly, in a canon of written texts. This metaphor was active and productive of meaning in the indigenous imagination. Teaching of Torah seemed to be something like water. It could purify or be polluted, depending on the "grounding" of its human "container" and the direction of its "flow." Teachings were credible to the extent that they were perceived to be collected and contained under the name of a reliable rabbi, and to the extent that he transmitted the teachings stemming from a line of reliable teachers.

The interdependent categories of "the grounded" and "transmission," brought to light by Selkin in relation to "containers" such as pools, pots, texts, and human beings, seem now to offer an interpretive key for the kinship strategies explored by Flesher and the gender management described by Peskowitz for a somewhat later period in Roman-era Palestine. One detects a certain congruence in their structure. This is why we can speak of an indigenous logic of social organization operative in Hasmonean-Herodian Galilee. This logic came under stress and yielded new adaptive meanings in that conflictive context.

Circulation routes

Ancient scientific accounts of material elements held that each substance has a natural tendency to move in a certain direction. Earthly materials, for example, want to go downward, fire wants to rise, grass wants to grow into grain and be harvested, clouds want to blow in and drop rain. Today we describe the same physical phenomena in terms of gravity. We imagine that earth sucks; ancient people imagined that falling objects and rising smoke were merely trying to move in their proper directions. We imagine social relations as a struggle to rise to the top against an inexorable gravitational drag by breaking through a crust of competitors. To its ancient inhabitants, Eretz Israel did not have such a top and a bottom. The forms in which we spontaneously apprehend social structuration—stratified pyramids and binary oppositions—are quite alien to the imaginations of first-century Judeans and Galileans. They organize their society in patterns of circulation and grounding. For every element in Israel's everyday world, there is a direction in which it should go respective to other elements, the land, and the people, rather than a place to which it "belongs." An indigenous principle of grounding and circulation provided the symbolic idiom in which people of Israelite heritage managed their affairs and made sense of their lives in Judea and also in Galilee. In other words, this way of perceiving the world would have been fundamental to the common cultural heritage shared by indigenous Galilean villagers and the Hasmoneans who took over the administration of the Galilee in the first century BCE. This common understanding would have contrasted with Greek and Roman perceptions. But the Hasmoneans, for their part, understood Mediterranean cultural logic as well. They were Hellenists as well as Israelites. Indeed, the biculturalism of the Judeans and of Jews from the Western Diaspora should be understood as a competence to alternate and translate between the two idioms: the indigenous-Israelite idiom of grounding circulation, and its Aegean counterpart.

The logic of circulation in Eretz Israel is quite subtle and nuanced. What "circulates" are fluids and the containers that carry them, both literally and figuratively. Their mobility can go right or go wrong, but it is always going. These elements are on the move in relation to stationary things, which are capable of "grounding" them. Grounding means regulating the direction of their circulation and correcting it when it goes wrong. But there are complications, for the "movers" and the "fixers" are mutually affecting. Each kind of object needs the other one continually to define, maintain, and enhance its character. Stasis is never achieved.

The "grounded" things include such constructions as the household, the patrilineal line of descent, the *miqveh*, and the Torah. None is grounded invulnerably, as is evident in the kinship strategies. Their grounding needs to be secured by "mobile" things, yet mobile things are capable of moving in ways that can destabilize or uproot. For example, women as procreators and cooks are needed to maintain the "grounding" power of the household and the lineage; but women can also spoil it through their flawed ancestry or their culinary or reproductive malpractice.

Besides grounded containers and mobile containers, the other element of this logical system is comprised by the fluids that the containers carry. Water, caste, agricultural produce, Torah teaching, women's fertility and "the work of women's hands" are all construed to be fluids. They are "living" and are intimately involved with the propagation and sustenance of human life. When they circulate in the prescribed ways, they ensure the "groundedness" of Israel in the Land of the Promise. But when they backwash or go wrong, they erode that "groundedness" and also lose their own life power. For example, oral Torah is like water because when pure it can give life, but when tainted with wrong interpretations it can kill.

Things regarded as "fluids" have ambiguous value: each one has a right way and one or more wrong ways to go. These fluid or mobile elements can be in motion either materially or figuratively. Material fluids include water, liquid food (oil, wine, honey, sauce), solid food (grain, meat, tithes, sacrifices), bodily secretions (saliva, menses, semen, urine), and corpses. Each of these has a prescribed way in which it must be moved and handled, relative to the other elements in the system. Figurative fluids behave analogously; they include labor (productivity, "the work of women's hands," the fruit of women's wombs), caste, and Torah instruction.

Things regarded as "containers" for those fluids may hold them either literally or figuratively. Containers may be relatively mobile and therefore liable to "go wrong," or they may be relatively stable and thus able to ground and orient the circulation of other mobile things. On a scale from most mobile to most stable, "containers" include: open pots and baskets; covered pots and baskets; unmarried women of Israelite, levite, or priestly caste; slaves of either sex; freedmen and freedwomen; households; men of Israelite, levite, or priestly caste; lineages; tombs; cisterns and wells; stone jars; *miqva'ot*; rivers and lakes. Generally speaking, the more stable entities can ground the less stable, but the more mobile can also make the stable things go wrong. The most stable and stabilizing thing of all is the land itself. The natural environment (as we might call it), supporting all human and nonhuman life, is set in proper motion by the hand of the Creator. The Temple and the (written) Torah, then, are versions or symbolizations of this, crafted by human hands.

But the hegemony of the Jerusalem Temple in Jesus' day was relatively recently established and had been achieved by the shutting down of numerous other cultic sites. The dominance of written Torah was still being secured through the technologies of writing and the shutting up or shutting down of variant oral traditions. The impulse toward architecture and literacy in Eretz Israel, therefore, is the desire to provide grounded and grounding containers to facilitate proper circulation. As the patrilineal caste needs a house, the Torah needs a written text and the produce of the land needs the Temple. These physical points of reference orient the circulation of fluids and their mobile carriers around the land.

Moreover, when circulation goes awry it requires correction. Regrounding and re-turning are accomplished by means of specialized architectural forms. These function like fulcrums or pivots to modulate the movement of fluids, altering their direction as necessary. Such adjustment maintains the perceived orderliness of creation because it orchestrates human affairs in sync with the divinely ordained rhythms of rainfall and agricultural productivity and procreation, in a grand choreography across the land. For example, grain is deemed inedible until the tithe is separated and sent on its way to the Temple or the local priest. Immersion in a *miqveh* cleanses pots and people from ritual impurity—that is, rectifies their "circulation"—because the tank is embraced by the earth and retains a large volume of water gathered directly from natural rain runoff without the intervention of any mobile container. On the other hand, the caste of a child whose parents were ineligible to marry one another can never be repaired. (But Flesher finds a loophole in the system that could in effect repair the "birth defect" of outcaste status. In the Mishnah, he reasons, slavery cancels ancestry. Theoretically, if an illegitimate son were sold as a slave and then freed, he would acquire the status of a freedman. He could then find a bride, because freedmen were eligible to marry members of any caste except for priests. The trouble with this suggestion is that the illegitimate son unfortunately would have no one with the paternal competence to sell him! But this hypothetical case illustrates the logic of adjusting the momentum of one's perceived circulation.)

We have reviewed the textual evidence of the Mishnah concerning caste and kinship reckoning, management of women's labor, and immersion practices. That evidence has strengthened the hunch that circulation and grounding were an indigenous idiom of cultural expression. Now we are ready to advance this "archaeology of Galilean mind" by reviewing the architectural forms introduced in the last chapter.

Buildings for circulation

Beyond question, the Jerusalem Temple was the destination of international pilgrimage for many centuries. From within Judea and Galilee it attracted people, livestock, and produce every day, but particularly for annual festivals. Why? The commonplace modern answer, "through religious piety," begs the question. Religion is never entirely self-referential.

Religious practices, stories, and edifices may convey their meanings by referring to one another. But they also refer to the material components of human life. The Temple in Jerusalem was a slaughterhouse. Animals walked in; meat came out. This is the material fact. Whatever cultural and religious meanings may be enacted through animal slaughter depend upon its physical accomplishment. As an edifice, the Temple had to accommodate complex movements of animals as well as people. This fact is brought to light by our circulation model. It is overlooked in the most insightful discussion of the Temple space available, that of Jonathan Z. Smith, which presents the data and interpretation that will be reviewed in what follows.

The architectural design of the Temple should be interpreted in terms of concrete material and social factors, as an expression in the indigenous idiom of circulation and grounding. There have been at least three Temples in Jerusalem, with different designs. Their floor plans are not currently recoverable in the archaeological record, and no blueprints survive. But we do have several sets of descriptive texts to go on. An idealized account of the Temple's layout comes from the period after the destruction of the First Temple ("Solomon's Temple," in 587 BCE) and probably also after the building of the Second Temple (dedicated in 515 BCE). This text is Ezekiel 40–48, which Smith has characterized as a postexilic priestly ideology of place. The text recounts a visionary experience, which Smith has translated into floor plans of the Temple that the author envisioned.

This ideal Temple, as the author of Ezekiel 40–48 understood it, would provide nested spheres for various categories of people. Foreigners were outside, surrounding a sphere of the people, which in turn surrounded a central axis with adjacent areas for the levites, the Zadokite priests, and the deity. Smith maps these spheres into several diagrams and interprets them as expressing a hierarchy of status.

The following map probably does not correspond to the physical layout of either the First or the Second Temple. But the Ezekiel floor plans are appropriate evidence for our archaeology of mind —whether or not they correspond to what actually was built. Smith has marked the diagrams with the paths along which people would move through the Temple compound. He suggests that these ritual movements reconciled the hierarchy of cultic status, expressed in the floor plan, with the contrasting hierarchy of royal political power, expressed in the person of the king, who traveled and stood in a more prestigious place than other lay people did. Though Smith considers motion, his interpretation tries to translate the idiom of movements into the idiom of status and hierarchy. He also overlooks the movement of the animals.

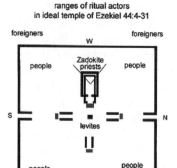

ranges of ritual actors
in ideal temple of Ezekiel 44:4-31

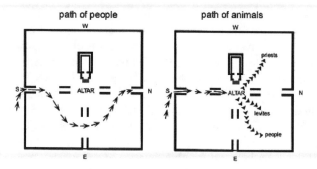

FIGURE 12: *Reconstruction of the plan of the Temple projected in Ezekiel 40–48, after Smith, who does not consider the paths of the animals. The slaughter, butchering, and distribution of meat to priests, levites, and people also defined their respective roles.*

Leaving aside the imported terminology of status and hierarchy, let us review the progress of people and animals through this design. According to the Ezekiel vision, people entering the Temple through the south gate exited through the north gate, after their paths took a swerve to the right (east) in order to avoid walking through the center of the compound where the animals were being sacrificed. All along the way they would be passing the people who entered by the north gate and exited by the south, swerving left (east) to avoid the center.

The Temple is there for people to walk through it. What both Ezekiel and Smith seem to ignore, however, is the fact that the Temple is also a slaughterhouse. People are supposed to enter with animals, and the animals do not swerve. That is, the cattle go straight ahead and are handed off to levites and priests. They are slaughtered, butchered, skinned, and roasted. Then the hides and part of the meat are diverted to priests and levites as their share, and part of the meat is handed back to the people as they complete their swerve and head on out the gate opposite the one through which they entered. The Temple circulates and redistributes meat.

In contrast with Ezekiel's idealized vision, the Mishnah and Josephus preserve eye-witness descriptions of the rituals, the furniture, and the edifice of the Temple—presumably the so-called Third Temple produced by extensive renovations of the Second Temple begun by Herod in 20–19 BCE. This Temple's floor plan also facilitated the circulation of people and the slaughtering of livestock, but in a rather different pattern.

The Temple compound that Josephus and the sages remember admitted people through a gate on the south side. They went up a tunnel with ramps and steps, emerging into a large open paved area surrounded by colonnades to the left, right, and behind. This was "the Court of Gentiles," which anyone might visit. It completely surrounded the central enclosure, which tourists and pilgrims walked around counterclockwise before exiting down a tunnel-ramp on the south side, near the one through which they had entered. In Herod's Temple, all the human traffic flowed in one direction, circling the center instead of merely swerving to pass it. People could also linger under the colonnaded portico, or if Israelite, they could enter the central area.

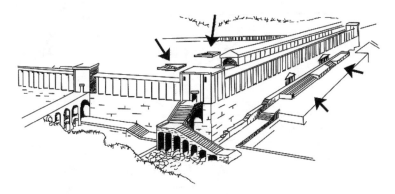

FIGURE 13: *Reconstruction of the southern part of the Temple Mount as renovated by Herod the Great. The Western Wall is in the left foreground. The arrows indicate the Hulda Gates, which admitted people to ramp tunnels that ran under Herod's Royal Stoa and opened into the Court of Gentiles.*

The central enclosure within the Court of Gentiles marked off areas of restricted access, with gates on the west, south, and east. These admitted Jewish men and women into the open-air "Court of the Women," in whose north side the Nicanor Gate opened onto the area for slaughter and sacrifice. Only men could pass through that gate into the "Court of the Israelites," a pavement forming the southern margin of the "Court of the Priests." That is where males of the priestly and levitical castes performed their cultic duties at the huge altar and slaughtering facilities. Apparently, in the Herodian period people no longer brought their own animals with them to be sacrificed. A man purchased one on the spot from the Temple staff, patted the beast to assert ownership, and received his prescribed portion of meat. The profit from the sale of animals for sacrifice was controlled by priestly families, in addition to the income they received directly from tithes. Plausibly, Jesus' frustration with this practice led to the "Temple-cleansing" incident recounted in the Gospels.

FIGURE 14: *The Court of Gentiles surrounds the Temple enclosure, on the right. The openings for the ramps down to the Hulda Gates are arranged so that throngs of people could come up through one, walk around the enclosure, and exit down the other. Beyond the ramp openings is the Royal Stoa of Herod. The Stoa ran the entire width of the southern edge of the Temple Mount, about 300 meters. It was as tall as a 10-story building and about 35 meters wide, according to dimensions given by Josephus. Commercial activities could be accommodated there, and may have spilled out into the Court of the Gentiles in the area near the entrance and exit ramps. The colonnaded southern exposure of Herod's stoa collected sunlight in winter, provided cool shade in summer, and cast its shadow toward the Temple enclosure.*

The Herodian design was much more efficient, streamlined, and convenient than that of the earlier layout. Livestock came and went unseen, except for the moment of high drama in which they were dispatched in the various prescribed directions. This design also introduces gendered space into Jewish cult. Women are barred from proximity to the act of sacrifice. Yet interestingly, the area where all and only Jews may go is called "Court of Women." Thus the place with the gender-restrictive name is in fact accessible to both genders, while the place with the inclusive name, "Court of Israelites," is for men only.

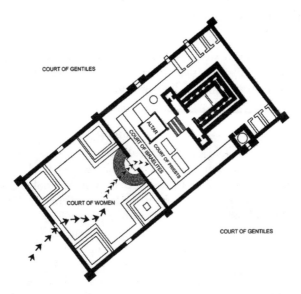

FIGURE 15: *Reconstructed plan of the Temple enclosure, after Rousseau and Arav. The enclosure was about 62 by 135 meters. As the arrows indicate, Israelite men and men of the priestly and levite castes are those whose path of approach to the altar of sacrifice passes through women of pure descent who have completed rituals of purification. The semicircular stairway leading to the Nicanor Gate is the place where a wife accused of adultery undergoes trial by ordeal in order to remove (or, confirm) any doubt about the lineage of her children. Gentiles are those who may not approach or pass among the women of Israel.*

Thus, men must go through the Court of Women in order to emerge as "Israelites." The Nicanor Gate, which admits men to the Court of Israelites, is the place where women who are accused of having endangered caste through adultery must appear for the rite of *sotah* (Num 5:11–31). It is also where women are purified after childbirth, and where the recovery of lepers is certified. Jews are those who pass through the Gentiles to emerge into the sacred enclosure. This makes good sense without having to be translated into the categories of "status" and "hierarchy." In the indigenous idiom of circulation, one is a Jew—an Israelite, a levite, a priest—by virtue of the way one moves through this design. Being a Jew means stepping away from Gentiles, through mothers, with the produce of one's land, toward observance of Covenant obligations, and then receiving back a proper portion of the produce and carrying it home. The Temple accommodates and defines this motion.

Selective admission and release

The Temple is not a secret place. It is an emphatically public statement in stone. All are welcome to admire this enclosure from without. Indeed, the Temple was remembered as an architectural marvel that people came from all over the world to see. Gates and enclosures were culturally significant features, as the archaeological record attests. They served to define gender and nationality at once. In common village housing as well, as we saw in the last chapter, passages between the household and the outside signaled personal status and economic function. Stones for the doorjambs, thresholds, sills, and lintels were cut with greatest care; often they are the only features of a house that remain. For example, in the talmudic-era ruin of Qatzrin, windowsills and thresholds are cut with an ingenious double curved channel (discussed in chapter two, figures 1 and 2.) This feature allowed doors or shutters to open by rising up and swiveling inward, but also let them lock securely as they swung closed and dropped their posts into the sockets. Aside from utilitarian use, these designs attest to the cultural significance of being able to gather one's people and cattle and labor into a defined and defining place. The finely-worked stone closure apparatuses are physical analogues of the lineage and therefore of the nation. They close securely when both sides are properly supported and engaged. A defect on either side defeats the lock and allows leakages. But the doors must also open selectively for the life of the house to continue.

Thus, village doorways had significance beyond their simple material functions of climate control and regulation of people's entries into and exits from the household. Analogously, the city gate at an earlier period was symbolically and functionally the "heart" of the city, the location where its self-defining and self-regulating institutions were housed. As Lee Levine remarks, the city gate was the main communal setting in the life of every community in pre-Hellenistic times. Thus, gates were not mere holes in the walls. Rather, they were built with several large chambers to accommodate court proceedings, markets, meetings, religious ceremonies, and all kinds of public and private business. These uses ceased, Levine argues, only when Greek advances in military technology, such as siege engines and catapults, made it necessary to redesign the city gate as a primarily defensive edifice. At that point, throughout the Hellenistic world there emerged both a new, simpler gate design, and new forms of civic architecture. Social institutions that previously had been accommodated in the grand spaces of the city gates now moved into edifices specially designed to house them.

Levine suggests that the origin of synagogue architecture lies in this development. The synagogue as an edifice was meant to house the various functions that the community (*synagogē*, gathering of the people) needed to pursue in order to conduct its communal life and provide for the common welfare. These functions were secular as well as religious. Among them Levine lists "political meetings, social gatherings, courts, schools, hostels, charity activities, slave manumission, meals (sacred or otherwise), and, of course, religious-liturgical functions" (1996: 432).

Levine's suggestion lends support to my hypothesis that maintaining correct grounding and circulation constituted the basic idiom of Judean and Galilean social organization and its architectural expressions. There need be no question of whether and when the synagogue "took the place of" the Temple after the latter was destroyed in 70 CE. The two edifices are simply to be read as different expressions in the same common idiom. The synagogue is like a gate, in the old sense of the community's heart. Through the functions listed by Levine, this heart "beats" and regulates the passage of persons, ideas, property, commodities, throughout the social organism. The synagogue edifice houses the functions that keep community affairs running on track. It is also a place where wrongs can be righted and things can get back on track when they have gone awry. This is not primarily a matter of inclusion and exclusion (as alleged in John 9:22 and 16:2). Rather, it is what I have termed "grounding": rectification of the pathways along which people and things travel.

Levine's proposal helps to account for why people decided that these vital community institutions needed a special building to house them. It does not yet say anything about the distinctive design of such a building. James Strange takes up this question in a discussion of four sites with ruins identified as first-century synagogues: Gamla, Magdala, Masada, and Herodium. These would be the oldest synagogues of Eretz Israel, if authentic. All four identifications are still contested, so we add them to our first-century database with caution.

The structures thought to be synagogues are all rectangular spaces provided with three to five tiers of masonry steps for seating along the walls. (For drawings of the synagogue at Gamla, see Figure 9 in chapter two.) Columns stand in a line in front of the seats on two or three of the walls. Those columns, rising quite close to the knees of people seated on the lowest tier and obscuring their view of the central area, support the roof. More precisely, they support beams on which rest both a lower roof extending above the heads of the seated congregation, and a higher clerestory above the central area. Because of the nature of ruins, this design is not completely preserved at any of the four sites. Strange suggests that the experience of "looking through columns" is the architectural signature of the synagogue and may be meant to replicate the experience of watching Jerusalem Temple rituals from the colonnaded porch that sheltered the Court of Israelites. Thus, the center of the room is bathed in daylight, while the people facing into this light on all sides are sitting in shadow.

In other words, the hall is built like a tank of light. Significantly, it is shielded from the sights of the surrounding streets, whose vistas and edifices were increasingly Hellenized and, later, Romanized. People collect in this tank-like area, with no apparent provision for segregation of the sexes. Religious services like those suggested by first-century texts could easily be accommodated in such a structure, as Strange points out. So could the various civic activities mentioned by Levine.

In effect, the "heart" or gate of the local community has now taken the form of a stone tank that collects and holds people and daylight, separating them from the throngs milling about in the streets and from the sights and shadows of the urban built environment. This pumping station facilitates the "circulation and grounding" of the people, their things, and their various activities. Its architecture has antecedents in Greco-Roman forms such as the odeion, the bouleterion, the basilica, and even the triclinium and the amphitheater, adjusting for scale. Some of those secular forms direct people's vision at one another across a central space, while others focus all eyes in the same direction toward one end. But none produces the visual effect of looking from shadow into light through columns. None "catches" and contains people, light, and what people do in the light in quite the way achieved by the first-century synagogue design. This form is a hybrid of available Greco-Roman elements, shaped by the requirements of the indigenous idiom of circulation and grounding. Our "archaeology of mind" finds something to understand in the material ruins.

Neither system nor process

What I have called the indigenous logic of the first-century BCE Hasmoneans does not "automatically" produce their synagogue architecture. When we practice a "cognitive archaeology," an archaeology of mind, we must leave aside the categories of cause and effect, which were the stock in trade of an earlier kind of archaeological investigation. The 1960s and 1970s were the heyday of a movement called scientific archaeology, or processual archaeology, or even "the new archaeology." Its research practices tried to identify causes and effects in social processes that would operate analogously to chemical, geological, or biological processes. Generally, the causes found were environmental factors, such as climate, terrain, productivity of the soil, disease vectors, and so forth. Human initiatives that responded to those factors were treated as if they were "effects." Behavioral responses were termed "adaptations" and were treated like dependent variables that followed necessarily upon the impact of the environmental causes. A good explanation was deemed to be one that arranged environmental causes and behavioral effects into a tidy system. A systemic relationship that had been discerned in one situation might have predictive value when applied to another situation in which the environmental situation was similar. Systems theory extended into sociology and economics. On the basis of many discrete cases analyzed by the same conceptual tools, grand models were built that were intended to make it possible to classify all human societies into a finite number of types of adaptive responses to a finite variety of configurations of the environment.

The general theory of society as system or process, and the particular application of this way of thinking in processual archaeology, share at least two technical faults that limit their usefulness for interpreting the sort of phenomena that interest us here: spatialized habitations of the Galilee. First, human behavior tends to deviate from perfect compliance with any systemic rule that might be formulated. This is so because human beings follow rules in a strategic, game-like way, rather than in the way that a dropped rock follows the law of gravity. Humans tend to have their own interest in view, and they tend to devise creative new ways to take advantage of the material conditions that they encounter in order to further those interests. Second, in their strategic, game-like responses, humans tend to anticipate possible futures and to project plans for things that do not yet exist. Those ideal plans cannot be "causes," in the scientific sense, because they literally do not yet exist at the time the behaviors occur for which they would have to be the causes. If the behaviors were truly "effects," then they would have to happen after the enactment of the states of affairs in view of which the behaviors themselves have been initiated. Human intentional behavior may depend upon causal factors, but it is never entirely determined by them. Therefore, human responses cannot be entirely predicted on the basis of prior environmental factors.

For example, the kinship practices that we have examined cannot be accounted for as caused effects. The acknowledged religious laws of caste operate not as causes, but as incentives for negotiating marriages so as to maintain the possibility of rhetorical defense of the caste of one's household in the future. This incentive works only to the extent that everyone acknowledges the reality of the caste structure and agrees to the prerogatives that it grants. The laws of caste supervene upon the biological laws of human reproduction. Births are biologically caused, but Israelites are created over the course of many ancestral generations. In another example, water is delivered causally to homes in Romanized cities through the engineering of the gravity-fed aqueducts. But the social character of the water depends upon religious meanings that are symbolically flouted by the aqueducts, but that can be repaired through the ingenious rehabilitation apparatus of the *miqveh* plumbing. This repair is by no means a caused effect. If we want to understand what was going on, we must resist the impulse to seek simple causal explanations.

Human responses are meaningful only when we can compare the actual behavior with the range of possible, expectable behaviors. One response has been chosen from a range of options. That range is determined by a set of commonly recognized relational meanings, which I have been calling an idiom or a grammar or a logic, and which other theorists call the principles of organization of the community in question. This common template of meaning is what contemporary cognitive archaeology seeks to uncover. In the case of first-century Galilee and Judea, we have seen that the idiom is formed from the interplay of containment, grounding, and circulation of fluid elements in the social world.

The earlier processual socio-economic models unfortunately discounted the significance of human creative choice. The premise that social systems respond automatically to pressures from the environment is a premise that obscures the dynamics of cultural realities like caste and kinship. But the designs recovered from ancient ruins and ancient texts indicate that people strategically built and used the structures to manage their affairs according to the idiom of circulation and grounding. With this logic they imparted meaning to their everyday choices.

On this basis, archaeology can be an interpretive retrieval of human motivations and creative decisions based on values that were culturally meaningful. This is of utmost significance for our understanding of the Galilee of Jesus. Roman colonization occurred precisely as Herodian disruption of the indigenous circulation patterns. It was resisted in the same idiom. Those resistances were formative for early Judaism and for the Jesus movement, in contrasting ways.

▪ ▪ ▪

In this chapter, evidence from religious texts has strengthened the impression that circulation and grounding were basic metaphors used by the people of ancient Palestine to make sense of their experiences. We have observed motifs analogous to those found in the built environment and already introduced in the last chapter. Containment, release, and re-direction are the capabilities built into the design of the house, and these functions were also used for understanding the land of Israel itself. Certain elements were understood to have "grounding" and "flow-correcting" powers in relation to other elements, but nothing was absolutely grounded or static independently of other elements in the pattern. People, their productivity, and their ideas were understood to be "fluid" in various degrees and respects. Two motion patterns in particular seem to serve as paradigms for all the others. Materially, the house appears as the basic architectural form. People, food, and other commodities flow from house to house. In the realm of human relationships, maintenance of caste through marriage is the basic defining mechanism. Lineages flow together in correct kinship patterns. These two paradigms join in the patrilineal residence, the house whose threshold admits and releases brides.

This template of meaning is not our own accustomed template. However, it is intelligible because we have the same kinds of bodies that ancient Palestinians had, and they moved as we do. What is strange to us is the notion that nothing is stable all by itself. For our part, we tend to think in terms of definable and self-defining status. We imagine that we can change status by moving between social locations, then we imagine those "locations" as if they were stable as well. It is difficult for us to conceive the notion that patterns of motion are all that constitute those locations.

In social theory, this deficit of imagination shows itself in essentialism. An essentialist claims that there is such a thing as a status regardless of the historical events that defined it and continually define it. For example, the categories of "woman" or "peasant" or "honor" have all been treated this way at times in the literature. Essentialist theories lose sight of the role that analogy plays in translating between ancient Palestinian terminology and contemporary Western terms. To be sure, there is a material basis for the analogy. Female human beings in the first century were physically quite like women today, with the same physiological capabilities and needs. First-century farms were worked by people whose ties to the land resembled those of modern peasants in many respects. But there were differences as well.

The attempt to model ancient Galilean society in terms drawn from the indigenous socio-economic organization of Palestine itself is not an end-run around the problem of analogy. Rather, it foregrounds this problem. Our model explicitly proposes that motion through built designs can re-constitute a formal system whose terms are pre-linguistic in an important way. The articulations or physical motions through space do not rely on culture or language; rather, languages and cultures arise from them. The analogy that we mean to foreground is the creative analogizing impulse that funds this rising. This is an intra-cultural analogy of structure, not an inter-cultural analogy of function. Our premise is that analytic questions can be framed in terms drawn from Israel's built environment and from the world of meaning that was erected there. Before pursuing this premise, we will discuss alternative social models of first-century Palestine in the next chapter.

4 The Trouble With Models

CULTURAL MEANINGS MATERIALIZE IN THE LANDSCAPE and in the indigenous economy. But first-century Galilee had no purely indigenous economy left after centuries of military and economic interventions by successive waves of colonizers. If its landscape had ever expressed the integrity of an indigenous culture, that time lay far in the past. The built environment had become an on-going quarrel between the demands of empire and the resistive responses of the land's people. Sometimes shouted and sometimes whispered, this argument in stone deployed the Israelite idiom of grounding and circulation against Hellenistic Mediterranean idioms of centralization and marginalization.

In this compromised land, how did Galilean society organize and continually reorganize itself to feed people and to produce the goods and services they required? How did empire tap into those activities and squeeze a "surplus" out of the colonized land? Those who study Jesus historically would like to know about these matters, for the economic terrain is a key component of the context in which Jesus' words and deeds make sense. The relevance of economic conditions in Galilee for any adequate understanding of the teachings of Jesus has been amply demonstrated in the recent work of Seán Freyne, from which some constructive elements of the following discussion have been taken.

This chapter will argue that a spatial interpretation of Galilee, couched in terms of the indigenous logic of circulation, supplies something that is lacking in all three of the predominant "modeling" strategies listed in the last chapter: economic-conflict models, gender-ideological conflict models, and honor-shame models. None of those earlier modeling programs has been able to show how human beings, including Jesus of Nazareth, were able to exert individual and

61

collective agency by means of their common built environment, through competent and creative use of their common spaces. None has taken human bodies seriously enough: as mobile agents who build for access and control, who trespass, who devise short-circuits and detours, and who move through real spaces strategically.

The proposal that is taking shape in this book is that a basic idiom of circulation and grounding expresses itself in various architectural forms in ancient Galilee. The architecture operates recursively. To inhabit it reinforces the perceptions of relative stability and fluidity that were built into the architecture originally. Habitation practices are adaptive with respect to the pressures of colonization. But adaptation is no mere automatic self-reconfiguration of a physical or social system. It is a strategy, a rational and purposeful initiative. Gendered strategies of collaboration and resistance were being pursued in Galilee during Jesus' lifetime. These strategies operated effectively in the economic dimension although they were not limited to economic issues. They left traces in the landscape that can be empirically recovered and reliably interpreted.

Any claim to understand the phenomena of resistance to empire is premised upon the possibility of our being able to interpret the built environment and read the meanings that are written in it. The ancient architecture is best read by moving through it—physically if possible, but at least in imagination. This reading can be a somatic following of the pathways inscribed in the earth. Nothing of this kind is possible with the other available social models of ancient Galilee. Moreover, as we shall see, some current "social science" approaches to historical study of Jesus invoke blind causal forces and so exclude the possibility of innovative social agency. Other approaches describe agency only in essentialist terms. Some current ideological approaches require that the ancient people take our places instead of allowing us to visit theirs. They superimpose alien conceptual structures on the Galilee of Jesus, much as the ancient colonizers erected alien architectures upon the land.

In making a spatial approach to Greco-Roman Galilee, I propose that we allow ourselves to be led bodily through its built environment, guided mentally by the logic of grounding and circulation, which appears to be the organizational principle of indigenous Galilean mind. Research as a program of following the ancient pathways is an attempt to understand the meanings of first-century Galilean society on its own terms. It is not a new modeling; it is a discernment of the ancient modeling. This discernment will always be partial and incomplete. Much will remain alien and opaque. But more will become clear. The principal instrument for this research is the mobile human body. We as twentieth-century investigators share the condition of bodily mobility with the ancient people, just as we share the conditions of hunger, fragility, desire, fear, hope, and other somatic experiences.

The fragile, mobile, and minded human body is the one basic cross-cultural universal. It is what lets us understand the occupied land of Jesus, despite the remoteness of ancient Galilee from our own environment. Therefore, bodily phenomena such as mobility, including mobility's cultural modulations into distinctive practices for bride-giving or grain distribution or political assembly, take precedence over texts. Practices of textual production should be interpreted for their congruence or dissonance with other somatic practices. The content of any text is not to be confused with the world as such. Any written content was just a little worldlet that fit within the complex of pathways of the built environment where it was produced. Perhaps it served projects of managing or deflecting the paths of people through that environment. But no text was a self-sufficient environment unto itself. No text was a perfect reflection of its world.

Hypotheses are not data

Given the priority of bodily habitation practices, we can still turn to text-based research programs for further information about ancient Galilee and the practices of its inhabitants. While claims of "cross-cultural validity" for explanatory models should be regarded with caution, prudent use of comparative data can greatly enhance our understanding of the material conditions of life in first-century Galilee, its economic organization and cultural practices. There is a crucial difference between comparative and deductive research programs. Indigenous responses to imperial urbanization may be detected through comparative research guided by relevant parallel cases; they should not be sought through deductive research that imposes synthetic cross-cultural explanatory models.

Models are epistemologically powerful tools when they are properly used. To model is to (1) analyze, (2) analogize, and (3) hypothesize. We will consider these three steps in sequence, illustrating them through recent applications of an economic-conflict model, the so-called Lenski-Kautsky model. But first let us recall where that model comes from.

Gerhard Lenski was a sociologist whose 1966 book *Power and Privilege: A Theory of Social Stratification* spurred developments in Jesus studies in the 1990s. John Kautsky is a political scientist much influenced by his grandfather, Karl Kautsky, who pioneered the application of Marx's and Engles' theories to the social sciences and the humanities.

John Kautsky's 1982 book *The Politics of Aristocratic Empires* offers insights that can add nuance to Lensky's account. Together the two works have been taken as something of a short-cut to simulate a "cross-cultural anthropology" in Jesus studies. This simulation unfortunately bypasses the work of contemporary cultural anthropology, where neither the Kautskys nor Lenski has attracted much of a following.

There is a troubling reason why the *socio-political* conclusions of Lenski and the younger Kautsky have been adopted in Jesus research as if they expressed *anthropological* verities. It has to do with the perceived opposition of "nature" to "culture." This spurious opposition is constructed on the false assumption that anthropology accesses human nature in its pristine, pre-cultural, pre-civilized state. Thus, a model that purports to be "anthropological" is claiming access to natural processes through empirical examination of necessary interactions between human animals and their environments. Such a model would represent laws that would operate independently of human discretion. It would claim to be "cross-cultural" by virtue of being prior to and foundational for any particular culture at all. Working anthropologists today would not make that a claim.

Nevertheless, such an anthropology may indeed be possible, as the *philosophical* investigation of those common basic conditions that render human beings prone to cultural expressions and initiatives at all. This philosophical anthropology would, among other things, establish the grounds for the possibility that twentieth-century human beings could follow and at least partially grasp the meanings of first-century human beings. But it is a mistake to take a generalized socio-political model that was built out of numerous empirical observations and promote it to the status of such an *a priori* anthropology. Let us now review the three steps by which the Lenski-Kautsky model is applied, bearing in mind its character as a generalization from observed societies, not a set of natural laws governing the relationships into which humans are bound to enter whenever certain environmental conditions obtain.

(1) IN THE *ANALYTIC* PHASE OF SOCIAL MODELING of the world of Jesus, categories are imposed upon the data of observation. Those data usually are texts, but need not be. The texts are taken to reflect in some way the social phenomena that are of interest to the investigator. The analytic phase determines aspects of the phenomena to be either states or processes; that is, it breaks them down into parts comprising a system. The states are arranged into temporal sequences linked by arrows of causality, and the processes are clustered together into functions. Any system must have a finite number of discrete functions, and will tend

toward homeostasis through the reciprocal regulation of feedback loops amid those functions. This much is what systems modeling introduces into the observed social phenomena—*a priori*, that is, without regard to the particular society that happens to be under investigation. The systemic character of all societies is simply assumed. Thus, the data are not entirely "given" at all, for they are constructed analytically through the application of conceptual tools. And after data have been analyzed, that is, fit into a modeled system, it is easy to forget the ways in which any particular "datum" has been given and gotten.

(2) THE *ANALOGIZING* OR COMPARATIVE PHASE begins when names are assigned to the states, the processes, and their functional groups. The names are general labels that have already been in use in other models; labels such as food production, education, defense, government, inheritance, kinship, and so forth. These labels serve to pick out functions that resemble functions already identified in other societies. The causal patterns that structure the functional clusters may also be recognized as resembling those operating in other societies. This generates a typology, a set of kinds of structures: market economy, agrarian empire, feudal state, and so forth. In comparative study, data derived from the society under investigation are sorted out and interpreted into patterns like those patterns already discerned and named in societies that are well understood.

(3) THE *HYPOTHESIZING* PHASE has to do with the collection of further data. When an ancient society is under investigation, preliminary data may suggest that this society resembles some other particular society that is already well known, or some particular variety of social organization exhibited by numerous other well-known societies. Knowledge of those known patterns of social organization allows investigators to focus their subsequent work of data-gathering. It provides a context, a source of questions, and a range of expectable responses against which to assess the data that come in from the particular society under investigation. For example, if it is known that an increase in women's opportunities for paid employment is associated with a decrease in the birth rate in many societies that have been thoroughly studied, one can frame the hypothesis that a similar correlation will be detected in the data for a society just coming under investigation. Beyond this heuristic use, hypotheses can be used to extrapolate data where none are available. Then the hypothesis, which is no more than a good guess, turns into a tentative claim. Since ancient societies offer us much less data than living ones do, historians and archaeologists

may fill in the blanks in their data by referring to one or more modern societies that resemble the ancient one in several known respects. The similarities detected through comparison among the known features warrant an assumption that other features would also be similar, if only we had the means to discover them.

When Jesus historians speak of the Lenski-Kautsky model of socio-economic organization, they are referring to a conceptual tool that makes such comparisons easier. Lenski produced a typology, that is, a handy list of a few general kinds of social organization, with a range of values for certain characteristic functions within each. Those categories and average values are useful for interpreting first-century Galilee. For example, in the absence of evidence to indicate what portion of the population in first-century Galilee belonged to the artisan class, J.D. Crossan may guess that the figure was about five percent, based upon Lenski's finding that this proportion holds relatively constant in comparable societies whose demographics are more reliably known. We are justified in relying upon such guesses unless there is some reason to suppose that a unique cultural factor came into play in Galilee, such as Herodian-Roman economic development and urbanization. In that case, the expectable proportion of artisans in the population would be higher than Lenski's average for other agrarian empires.

But such a model-based guess is not a fact; it is a hypothesis for scientific investigation. The proportion of artisans in the population, initially estimated on the basis of an appropriate model, should then be submitted to empirical testing through examination of evidence from texts and from the archaeological record in Galilee. The model as such gives us no "data." The model is merely suggestive; it piques the imagination. It bears fruit in Crossan's profound and compelling portraiture of Jesus as a Galilean who worked for a living and who hated religious power-brokering. But such portraits, no matter how religiously satisfying they may be, do not excuse us from the scientific duty to inquire and thereby to confirm or correct them.

A further helpful use of political-economic models is to prune back unwarranted claims about a given society, claims that go beyond their evidence. For example, the Lenski-Kautsky model enables Crossan to argue effectively against any claim that the relationship between Galilee's city-dwellers and its farm workers must have been one of mutual benefit. A rather subtle line of reasoning supports this objection. Not the model itself, but the concrete historical cases from which the model was built, are what provide Crossan with the contrary evidence to cancel the necessity of the alleged beneficial relationship between city and countryside. In fact, there have indeed been analogous but better known societies in which aristocrats exploited peasants and gave nothing in return; these are contrary cases that cancel the necessity of mutually beneficial relations but not the possibility. Thanks to Crossan's invocation of the model, this claim is now removed from the realm of taken-for-granted necessity, and placed in the realm of hypotheses that need to be confirmed or canceled through examination of evidence. The possibility remains that Galilean farmworkers had mutually beneficial relations with city-dwellers. Data must still be collected from the archaeological record and the textual record in order to pare down that possibility to slim or nil.

Moreover, when we go to the archaeological record for data, we must be willing to reframe the data-gathering questions themselves. For example, we cannot be certain that farmers and city-dwellers were indeed two distinct groups *in Galilee,* simply because Lenski or Kautsky treated them as two discrete and non-overlapping populations in various other societies. Did Galilean peasants spend no time at all in cities? On the contrary, judging from the Tyrean coins commonly found in the ruins of their houses, it seems more likely that indigenous Galileans devised a variety of commuting arrangements for daily or seasonal employment in the new cities of Sepphoris and Tiberias, while expatriate city-dwellers could walk out to the countryside for agricultural labor or other business. Then can they still be classified as "peasants"? One must take care not to force the evidence of Galilee into the mold of Lenski's ideal type, the "agricultural society," or into Kautsky's "commercializing society."

In summary, the generalized model adds no evidence; it simply makes the comparable cases easier to find and to juxtapose with the ancient society under study. This brings us to the question of the creeping essentialism that lurks within the ambiguity of the phrase "cross-cultural anthropology." On one hand, this phrase is benignly redundant, for all anthropologists "cross cultures" as they seek to explore points of contrast and similarity among diverse peoples. On the other hand, to assert "cross-cultural" validity for a social relationship can connote "universality," in the sense that the relationship must now be taken to be a constant and necessary factor in every culture. Critical anthropological practice guards vigilantly against naturalizing its research apparatus by extending the status of "cross-cultural universal" to such things as economic and sociological models.

Genuine universals are few in human societies. Even categories such as "peasant" or "the economy" or "the family" are ethnocentric, which is to say that different peoples define themselves through the distinctive ways that they construct these realities. For example, virtually all known societies organize the assignment of labor and personal identity through some sort of gender system, usually in connection with other coordinated and locally constituted systems such as class or kinship or race or age. Gendering, then, is one of the few genuine cross-cultural constants. Ironically, the supposedly cross-cultural Lenski-Kautsky model takes no account of the universal human denominator of gender.

But gender is not sex. What constitutes a "man" or a "woman" in a given society cannot be known *a priori* through any cross-cultural model; it must be discovered case by case through empirical investigation. The practices that constructed gender and kinship in Roman-era Israel could be wielded politically as well. The reckoning of kinship was the idiom in which political power was negotiated. Yet it has commonly been assumed within Jesus studies, as well as in Palestinian archaeology, that no information about gender and kinship practices can be recovered from the archaeological record, and very little from the ancient texts. It has been assumed as well that political and cultural resistance to imperial occupation left few traces in the landscape. Even Richard Horsley, who asserts that Galileans must have been defending an indigenous culture of their own through their resistance to imperial urbanization policies (Horsley 1994: 124–5), nevertheless concludes that "when looking for evidence of Galilean popular culture in the first century, we come up empty." This pessimism is surely owing to a defect in the Lenski-Kautsky model, which overlooks practices of kinship, gender, and inheritance that were key elements of traditional village life in the Galilee. It takes a spatial reading of the landscape to disclose the logic of kinship, the logic of circulation and grounding, and to expose the strategies of adaptive resistance for our understanding.

Misplaced suspicion

Jesus historians have been reading sociology too reverently and texts too suspiciously. As I have argued, we have been methodologically seduced by the hope that "social science models" can reveal universal causal laws enabling us to patch gaps in empirical data. The other side of that hope is an inordinate doubt running rampant in the hermeneutics of ancient texts. This brings us to the second variety of modeling that requires critical assessment here: gender-ideological conflict models.

Hermeneutics, the art and science of interpretation, has undergone complicated development in the philosophical literature of the last two centuries. The phrase "hermeneutic of suspicion" was coined by Paul Ricoeur in 1965 to characterize the interpretive work of Marx, Nietzsche, and Freud. Unlike earlier theorists, those writers drew meaning from expressions—whether texts, actions, or patterns of social organization—by regarding those expressions as symptoms covertly caused by another hidden reality, rather than as straightforwardly intended messages. The interpreter's task, according to this view, is to discern the hidden forces whose conflict is producing the troubled features on the surface of the text. Reading becomes diagnosis.

Materialist interpretation in the tradition of Marx is predisposed to find those hidden conflicts in the form of class struggle. In this respect, materialist interpretation of phenomena in the ancient world "models" those phenomena after the class struggles that emerged in capitalist economies of the nineteenth and twentieth centuries. According to such a marxist-materialist model, the conflicting interests and initiatives of the different factions in an ancient society would be matched up with analogous relations in modern history that are better understood. Several decades ago the classicist G.E.M. de Ste. Croix suggested such a correlation. He applied Marx's model of class struggle to Greek literature, and elicited from it a social description of an economy based on slavery. But de Ste. Croix was careful to stop short of identifying the Hellenistic and Roman imperial administration of Palestine as a historical instance of a trans-historical category, "class struggle." He merely asserted that certain resemblances existed between ancient Palestine and those societies where class struggle had been a well-attested factor. Thus, de Ste. Croix avoided the methodological mistake of exporting data from the ideal model into the ancient society under consideration.

A hermeneutic of suspicion is practiced today by Elisabeth Schüssler Fiorenza in her feminist hermeneutical research into New Testament texts. The hidden conflict that she seeks to diagnose is not class struggle, but the oppression of women by men of the powerful elite. Unlike de Ste. Croix, who practiced a carefully comparative and heuristic method of interpretation, Schüssler Fiorenza treats oppression as a trans-historical factor that is instantiated in every society. This historical constant, imposed as a universal law, states that women are always oppressed and always offering resistance to oppression. The universal oppression of women, and their resistance to it, are epistemologically analogous in Schüssler Fiorenza's arguments to the thesis of perpetual class struggle in so-called vulgar marxian social analyses. She has proposed the ideal category of "wo/men" to include oppressed and marginalized men along with all women (1995: 191). On this view Jesus is one of the wo/men (p. 89), who constantly struggle against their social oppression. In Schüssler Fiorenza's research program, perpetual struggle between the genders is not an empirical finding, much less a generalization induced from textual and material culture. Rather, this struggle is posited as an explanatory principle held to be beyond the reach of any empirical challenge whatsoever.

Used heuristically, this thesis of women's oppression and resistance can indeed disclose hitherto unnoticed information and configurations of meaning in the New Testament texts and other ancient documents. That is, it imparts intelligibility, hints at missing data, inspires effective portraiture, and destabilizes previous conclusions about the necessary status and role of women in ancient societies. What Schüssler Fiorenza explicitly disallows is the crucial scientific use: the framing of hypotheses to be confirmed or disconfirmed through empirical research.

But if the scientific use is disallowed, then this feminist hermeneutic is useless for archaeologists and for others who are attempting any sort of inductive or empirical study of ancient Galilee. Indeed, Schüssler Fiorenza explicitly rejects contemporary empirical historical research as positivist and "kyriocentric," that is, complicit with pervasive oppressive structures of social domination by elite males today (1995: 9, 73–74, 87–88, 156, and 108–9; 1992: 79–96). Naturally, this rejection is not maintained consistently throughout her work, which is a historical project of impressive productivity in its own right. One hopes that this methodological anomaly will eventually be resolved by Schüssler Fiorenza herself.

The rejection of scientific or empirical historical research into Jesus and the Jesus movement by a number of feminist scholars seems to stem from their theoretical orientation toward literary theory and discourse studies. That methodological choice, in turn, rests upon the mistaken and unexamined assumption that texts comprise the entire universe of evidence. If that assumption were correct, then the built environment, too, would be a text. (And I would be wrong to hold that, on the contrary, texts are no less artifacts than the built environment is.) But if everything that exists is a text of some kind or other, then so are our descriptions of the habitation practices housed in the architecture, and so are heuristic models like the Lenski-Kautsky model discussed above. Every description and every model becomes just another text; there is no point to maintaining the distinction between data and model.

Obviously, there can be no social science without the distinction between the data and the models that are used to constitute the data. The means by which this crucial distinction is maintained in feminist archaeological practice have been examined by Alison Wylie, whose findings are discussed below. This distinction is not eroded by the recognition that all data are (in part) determined by the models through which they are produced. Science is possible because data are (in part) not determined by the means of their production.

But the foundational assumption itself is faulty. Besides texts, we have a wealth of material evidence for reconstructing ancient Galilean social practices. Nor can this evidence simply be reduced to text. Walls and windows and roads and wharves are not text-like. They are not random-access devices, as texts are. They permit only a narrow range of comings and goings. Their physical solidity does not permit users to enter or exit at any point they may please. They cannot be easily cut, copied, or pasted into other contexts. These physical structures demand sequential following, as narratives do, but they do not permit the breadth of tropes and transferred reference that text permits. In all these ways, they repel inscription and they therefore require interpretation by other than textual, literary means.

Suites of evidence

The human body, with its physical needs and limitations, is bound to material conditions quite closely. Texts proper are produced through material technologies that are themselves seated within walls and dependent upon material supplies of papyrus, ink, and human scribal power to push the pen. The built environment imposes conditions of distance and propinquity. In spite of this, or perhaps because of it, material things can always be turned to uses other than those for which they were first built. To read the built environment is to read its functions and dysfunctions, its uses and its creative, resistive misuses. The indigenous gender and kinship strategies that we are seeking to understand were waged on the ground, amid the buildings.

If the only evidence we had were that deriving from texts, then obviously we would have no extra-textual way to choose which of several texts yielded a more adequate representation of the past. In that case, one could simply choose to favor the texts that promoted some liberating project in the present. This is the choice embraced by Schüssler Fiorenza and by a number of other feminist scholars.

But in fact, a wealth of extra-textual evidence is indeed available. Therefore, we are quite able to test and thereby to confirm or disprove the tentative conclusions drawn from an examination of text-based data facilitated by some social theory, whether marxian or feminist-liberationist or scientific-processual. This is not to say that "pure facts" will somehow become available so that we can check our deficient "theory-drenched facts" against them. Rather, the alternatives are: a thread of facts spun from one kind of evidence and dyed with one theory (which feminists of all stripes rightly reject) versus a fabric of facts woven of threads from many kinds of evidence and spun out through various social modelings (which feminist empiricists accept). The "fabric" will be logically stronger than the "single thread." Its strength comes from the complex corroborations among data that have been produced through theories that are independent from one another, from the investigator's interests, and from the fields of evidence themselves.

What I call logical strength is termed "security" in the literature of science studies, which is a growing interdisciplinary specialty that draws in part upon classical and postmodern philosophy of science. An illustration may help to clarify this point. Archaeologists today rely upon arrays or "suites" of evidence. Three different and independent bodies of theory support, respectively, the dating of pottery shards, the identification of certain road construction techniques as Roman, and the linkage of long-term climatic processes to the deposit of soil layers in the earth. In other words, these three sorts of evidence, though thoroughly drenched with their background theory, are all steeped in different and independently derived theories. Therefore when Douglas Edwards and Thomas McCollough argue for a second-century dating of the monumental paved road in Sepphoris, they invoke each of those background theories to interpret one field of evidence: the configuration of materials excavated in two squares at the site. Thus they avoid vicious circularity in inferences. Furthermore, Edwards and McCollough go on to correlate their tentative conclusions with inferences deriving from other fields of evidence, such as ancient texts telling about the reigns of Trajan and Hadrian, and the contemporary texts telling about the finds of other archaeological excavations. No single thread of inference is conclusive; however, the fabric that they weave is very strong. Wylie (1995 and 1996) describes this strength as the convergence of many evidentiary lines upon one coherent model.

Postmodern pessimism about the possibility of establishing historical facts, like that espoused by Schüssler Fiorenza and some other feminist interpreters of ancient Galilee and Judea, is owing both to their exclusive reliance on literary theory and to their apparent unfamiliarity with the science of archaeology in general and with feminist archaeological practice and theory in particular. Archaeology does indeed provide evidence, independent of the ancient texts, that will either corroborate or contradict the textual claims about events and structures in past societies. Through this convergent use of many lines of evidence, new archaeological data continually spur revisions of explanatory models like the Lenski-Kautsky typology and the marxian diagnosis of ubiquitous struggle between opposed pairs of social classes.

Moreover, as Alison Wylie's fine-grained epistemological studies have shown, contemporary feminist practice in archaeology is establishing a middle course between and beyond the two extremes of positivism and constructionism, where so much of recent historical scholarship has run aground. *Positivism* reduces all phenomena to what can be measured, quantified, counted, calculated, and made to yield necessary predictions about future states of affairs. It allows only causal logic, and therefore cannot account for its own formulation (for one does not embrace positivism as a caused effect of any observed phenomenon). *Constructionism* reduces all reality to descriptions formulated with terms from arbitrary symbolic networks and serving the interests of those who formulate them. It states that all knowledge is relative to the social perspective of the knower, so that facts can be neither shared nor checked (but it absolutizes this very statement and exempts it from that rule, of course).

As a historian of the science of archaeology, Wylie (1995, 1996) shows how the discipline has visited each of those extremes several times already in this century. In the most recent swing of the pendulum, the "new archaeology" of the 1960s and 1970s in North America aspired to value-free, rigorously scientific and "objective" data collection. Its practitioners regarded past cultures as mere autonomically equilibrating systems that just adapted blindly to environmental influences such as topography, climate, and food supply. Those adaptations were understood to be natural processes governed by laws that could be discovered; in other words, they could be "modeled." The research program of this *processual* archaeology was explicitly positivist and deductivist. It aspired to be a science that could generate hypotheses from its models and then get to work confirming them. Failed hypotheses would lead to adjustments in one's model, enabling the model itself to evolve gradually toward the epistemological status of a cross-cultural universal—an ideal never attained in practice. Having modeled social processes in this way, processual archaeology could deduce explanations of its data from them. (Lenski's 1966 sociological model is geared for this same sort of positivistic research program, and was expounded contemporarily with it.)

However, as Wylie remarks, this method did not work for some of the most interesting cases in archaeology. Factors such as the uniqueness of a given culture or the unpredictability of a spontaneous human initiative often become the key to understanding the human past. But cultural uniqueness and individual initiative are the very factors that in principle must elude deductive explanation, because they cannot be deduced from universal explanatory models. While processual archaeology was producing diminishing returns, advances in general social theory by the early 1980s spurred an alternative methodological proposal: *postprocessual* archaeology. This movement went to the opposite extreme from the positivism of processual archaeology, embracing instead a "constructionist" position with regard to archaeological data. On this account, the past is produced in the present, through a vicious circle of inquiry in which the data are largely or even entirely determined by the questions that the investigators ask and the models they employ, as well as by the investigators' own social locations and political commitments. From an extreme postprocessualist position, the quest for scientific rigor undertaken earlier by the "new archaeology" now appeared to be not only futile, but sinisterly complicit in a project of promoting the interests of today's elite classes. (Proponents of postprocessualism in archaeology draw on the same trends in literary theory that inspire the *a priori* rejection of historical Jesus research by some feminist scholars today.)

But Wylie detects a turn toward a more moderate mediating position in some recent statements by representatives of postprocessualism. This turn is being led by practice, not theory. Feminist archaeological practice has disclosed that data are not entirely determined by the interests, hypotheses, and models that investigators have brought into the field and the lab, as the postprocessualists contended. Quite simply, Wylie shows, it does sometimes happen that material uncovered in the earth surprises us and disconfirms our expectations. This is precisely what could not happen if postprocessual constructionism were correct, for then we would never disconfirm our hypotheses.

As Wylie suggests, the practices of feminist archaeology are currently leading the way toward a resolution of the stand-off between positivism and constructionism in archaeological method. The key to this advance has been a recognition of the length and complexity of the inference chains that tie the reconstructed picture of the past onto the raw excavated earth. Because so many sorts of material and textual evidence are available for examination, these inference chains are multiple and they can stabilize one another. Thus, historical inferences that could not be supported wholly upon texts, or wholly upon skeletal remains, or wholly upon material culture, become much more reliable when many lines of reasoning converge from several different kinds of evidence.

Feminist archaeologists, then, for the most part have shunned the relativism and constructionism that many feminist scripture scholars and theologians have adopted from literary criticism. Evidence for reconstructing women's lives is not as scant in the archaeological record as it seems to be in biblical and secular Greek texts. Thus, there is less temptation for archaeologists to resort to extrapolating data from sociological or ideological models. However, there is a dire need to correct those models when they omit gender, a principle of economic organization in all known human societies that was a key factor in the assignment of civic and nutritional prerogatives in first-century Galilee.

Mirrors are not windows

We turn now to a research program in which gender indeed has been an important consideration, in the third sort of modeling that must come in for critical assessment here: the honor-shame model and the "social science approach" to New Testament studies in which it is deployed. Bruce Malina, John Pilch, Jerome Neyrey, and their colleagues have adapted the findings of Mediterranean-area anthropology into a general thesis. They hold that the key organizational principle of first-century Galilean and Judean society was the opposition between honor and shame, continually negotiated in speech and behavioral practices geared to maximize honor. This thesis in effect proposes an archaeology of mind, pursued in ancient texts but guided by hypotheses derived from mid-twentieth-century anthropological studies. If this thesis is correct, if the negotiation of honor and shame was the common idiom of social expression in the Galilee of Jesus, then I must be mistaken in my contrary claim that circulation and grounding comprised that idiom. Therefore, it is vitally important to my argument now to examine how the thesis of an honor-shame society has been advanced.

The methodological similarities between these two rival theories are striking. Both Malina and I seek to articulate a fundamental syntactic structure that was taken for granted by the ancient people even as they invoked it routinely in their everyday interactions. Both Malina and I draw upon the field work and theories of anthropologists. Proponents of honor-shame anthropology in New Testament studies have confined their investigations to textual materials, for the most part, but there is no reason why this idiom should not be sought in architectural and landscape expressions as well. Indeed, the massive Herodian construction projects and the geopolitical uses for which they were designed surely lend themselves to interpretation as honor-enhancing initiatives.

Nevertheless, the difficulties I see with the honor-shame proposal are twofold. First, its proponents have imported this idiom into the first century from the twentieth, importing as well a set of technical problems with the derivation of the terms. Second, the avowedly "Mediterranean" character of the grammar of honor and shame makes it highly problematic for Galilee, which was a culturally mixed and conflicted society in the first century. This is readily apparent in the very fact that Herodian initiatives in social engineering happen to fit the description of honor-shame negotiations so well; for Herod was trying to *Romanize* Galilee. Herod the Great and his son Antipas were deliberately re-making the Galilean landscape and mindscape in order to render them "Mediterranean." Mediterranean meanings such as the honor-shame calculus were overlaid upon indigenous practices. Resistance to that forcefully imposed imperial re-design is one of the most important factors that we would like to understand in connection with Jesus of Nazareth and his movement. But we defeat this project at the outset if we simply assume that first-century Galileans shared the cultural grammar of the Mediterranean, or that they easily adopted it during the Roman occupation. After all, as Seán Freyne has pointed out, Galilee did not even have a Mediterranean coastline in the first century.

The construction of a so-called Mediterranean "area" in the anthropology of the 1960s and 1970s has been seriously called into question by subsequent research. The question is whether there are sufficient grounds to consider the linguistically and religiously diverse peoples who reside around the Mediterranean Sea today as one homogeneous cultural group. Are there any "Mediterraneans" among them? Do the majority of individuals find the grammar of honor and shame to be a meaningful template for framing their everyday projects and relationships? And if so, does this proclivity to negotiate honor mark them out as different from surrounding peoples and from the rest of the world?

Those questions have received negative answers in the critical literature after about 1980. The Mediterranean area, as an anthropological construct, does not embrace all the cultural groups that live near the Sea. Most notably, Balkan and Israeli societies were left out of the original field studies upon which the thesis of pan-Mediterranean familiarity with the categories of honor and shame were based. Moreover, anthropologists are increasingly wary of the tendency to emphasize those traits that are most familiar to the researchers in their own culture. As it turns out, negotiations for honor and shame have been recognized as quite a common practice among people with cultural roots in Western Europe, and in particular, among ambitious academic practitioners like anthropologists. Thus, the organizing principle of honor-shame negotiation turns out not to be at all workable as a defining characteristic of those societies that reside near the Mediterranean Sea in the twentieth century.

And even if it were, we would still face the difficulty of showing that this twentieth-century idiom had persisted unchanged from the first century. It is quite true that folkways and organizing principles tend to replicate themselves among indigenous populations even during periods of political upheaval and economic stress. But in the last two millennia, the Mediterranean has seen the development of Greco-Judaism into Christianity as a cultural force, the expansion of Islam, Crusades and trading excursions from the West into the East, the rise and fall of several sea-going European empires, and most recently, two world wars. All of these entailed the movement of peoples as well as ideas across the Mediterranean region. This is not to say that these upheavals certainly obliterated whatever organizing principles might have been in play during the first century. But the burden of proof lies upon those who wish to claim that first-century Galileans thought and organized their affairs by exactly the same logic as post-World War II Italian or Arab villagers do.

The anthropologists who first articulated the honor/shame distinction sought to preserve differences of nuance among cultures and among individuals within cultures. That which is labeled "honor" by Western anthropologists can differ drastically from place to place around the Mediterranean, yet all of these different kinds of honor seem to correlate with aspects of male gender definition that happened to be shared by researchers and informants. This coincidence was noted by feminist readers of the ethnographic record. The honor-shame sensibility resonates so strongly with Euro-American gender values that it must be suspected of being an ethnocentric projection of the male researchers who proposed it. The scheme emphasizes values that the anthropologists happened to hold in common with their informants.

Moreover, the English terms "honor and shame" are but a rough approximation of the various indigenous terms that they are meant to interpret, and they apply in dissimilar situations. Perhaps, then, it is only the poor translation of many different indigenous terms into one English word that has made "honor" appear to be a Mediterranean universal. "Hospitality" has been proposed as a more apt general label than "honor" for classifying the diverse practices observed. "Vulnerability" has been proposed as a better term than "shame" for some discursive practices among Bedouin people in the region.

Our social polarities are not theirs

Since it has become increasingly difficult to use the honor/shame construct to interpret even *contemporary* Mediterranean societies with confidence, we should hesitate to apply it to phenomena in the *ancient* world. Furthermore, the ease with which this binary pair binds itself with other conceptually opposed pairs of objects should give us pause. "Honor" is often cited in Jesus studies in connection with gender relations, or even as a cipher for the prerogatives of masculine gender, uncritically understood. In many instances, explicit gender analysis proves to be more illuminating than interpretation in terms of honor and shame. Gender, like the anthropological notion of honor, is not a static quality that one simply possesses. It needs continual maintenance through everyday practices.

In our world, those practices consist largely of bipolar confrontations defining maleness against femaleness, as two opposed statuses. But if we simply presume that the first-century Galilean practices of gender maintenance were identical with our own, then we will have imported twentieth-century categories into the first century. This will make it impossible to find empirical evidence of the indigenous practices through which kinship was maintained, and with kinship, gender. Lacking data on indigenous gender-maintenance practices, we will then be unable to begin to detect or understand transgressive or resistive practices.

There is no reason to suppose that ancient Galileans constructed the same binary pairs that we do. The very bipolarity of the notion of "honor versus shame" reflects a modern Western logic, like that of the oppositional pairs "public versus domestic" and "culture versus nature." In each pair, the former term codes as "male" in our own Euro-American idiom, while the latter codes as "female." This observation alerts us to an ethnocentric bias that may well affect our interpretations of societies that do not make this association. In other words, we must compensate for our own tendency to think in terms of one grand opposition between a privileged public realm of honor, culture, maleness, production; and a denigrated domestic realm of shame, nature, femaleness, consumption.

Aristotle, of course, distinguished *polis* from *oikos*. But it was Levi-Strauss's conceptualization of "nature versus culture" that led to the mistaken belief that "public space" is a universally available and intelligible category of description. The public/domestic distinction, though commonly invoked in contemporary popular anthropology, recently has been contested on both theoretical and empirical grounds. Its basic but mistaken assumption is that all human societies both understand and enforce a distinction between exactly two spheres: a public realm where important affairs are transacted among members of different kin groups, and a domestic realm where inconsequential matters are taken care of within a kin group. Furthermore, these realms are identified with physical spaces and governed by different rules. Human activities divide up neatly between them. The public realm is supposedly the place of culture and creativity, while the domestic realm belongs to nature and necessity.

Against this nest of assumptions, the theoretical criticism has followed along familiar poststructuralist lines. It has been pointed out that the binary pairing creates a value and a disvalue, reductively defines the latter in terms of the former, and tends to force the data to fit the categories. The empirical criticism of the domestic/private distinction has been even more devastating. Field anthropologists report that this construct cannot be used reliably to generate productive research strategies or to interpret their data. In the archaeological record, one cannot always identify an excavated space as either "domestic" or "public" on the basis of the tools and furniture found within it. One must first know how an activity was understood, the scale of the activity, how it fit into marketing arrangements, and so forth. Activities such as spinning, calligraphy, butchering, winnowing, and so forth, could be characterized as more "public" or more "private," depending upon a range of other factors, including the gender and the kin status of the people doing them. The supposedly "natural" association of female gender with domestic space appears to be particularly tenuous. There are contemporary traditional societies in which the gender of a place can shift with the time of day or the season.

The bipolar reciprocal construction of the notion of "honor and shame," along with its close association with these other opposed categories, renders it liable to the same sorts of criticisms. Proponents of "honor-shame" as the indigenous cultural idiom of ancient Galilee must demonstrate that the landscape, the elements of the built environment, and the activities pursued there will all fit unambiguously into negotiations of just this distinction. By comparison, the spatial idiom that I have proposed is not a binary opposition at all, but a composite of two scales: greater or less perceived fluidity for each item of the material culture, coordinated with greater or less perceived potential to ground and redirect other items. Moreover, these polarities were not transferred to the first century from twentieth-century exemplars, but were derived inductively from first-century material remains corroborated by texts nearly as ancient.

One further note of caution should be sounded. As with the economic-conflict models, there is a right way and a wrong way to use the thesis of honor and shame and the related construct of patron-client relations. The right use is comparative and heuristic. When similarities are observed between contemporary societies around the Mediterranean and the society of Jesus, then we are justified in formulating a hypothesis that the similarities might extend into behavior in the ancient world that have not yet been found in any sort of evidence. The hypothesis is a good guess, but it requires confirmation independent of the honor-shame thesis itself. The wrong way to use the honor-shame thesis is to export data from the twentieth century into the first. This would be to treat the honor-shame and patron-client grammar as a kind of natural law that "goes with the territory" of the Mediterranean geography and persists despite historical changes.

Recent discussions of patron-client relations imply that these are transhistorical universals: one-size-fits-all descriptors of a structure that either is or is not present in a given society. This premise is invalid, for it treats Galilean relations as a real instantiation of an ideal structure, rather than as one side of a comparison with a similar real society from an era when we have fuller information.

▪ ▪ ▪

In this chapter, we have seen that applications of any generalized socio-economic model to first-century Galilee must be tempered by four considerations. Modeling must include all relevant factors, such as gender and kinship. Modeling must address particular indigenous conditions, such as the impact of colonization. Modeling must function heuristically rather than as a source of spurious data. And modeling must allow for historical agency alongside of and even counter to the pseudo-causality of systemic evolutionary forces. The more we learn about Galilee, the less we need rely on analogy with other societies to generate interpretive approaches. We certainly should not rely upon them for data. It is now possible to begin to frame our questions in terms drawn from the indigenous socio-economic organization of Galilee itself and from the projects of the people who lived and worked there in the first century.

5 Material Landscapes to Be Read

THE WAY IN WHICH HUMANS INHABIT their environment is resourceful, ingenious, and purposeful. As we saw in the last chapter, that is why it takes an "archaeology of mind" to understand the material remains of ancient societies. Wherever human beings have lived, the architectural, organic, ceramic, and lithic remains present patterns that were not just put there by purely "natural" causes. Autonomic processes operating in biological or sociological systems do not account for the landscape of the Galilee. That landscape is a mindscape.

A material mindscape tells us about the choices that formed it. It shows us that human beings have made selective use of the materials at hand, in light of future objectives. But those objectives had to be framed within the limits set by the materials at hand. Each choice leads to a material alteration of the environment; and in turn, every new building or facility or item of equipment will suggest additional options for both intended and unintended uses. Thus, "adaptation" is not a purely physical process. Human adaptation is creative response. It has strategic, teleological, goal-directed dimensions.

In this chapter and the next, we will see how the Galilean landscape figured into a series of adaptive responses that by the third century CE were shaping some of the principal institutions of Judaism. The Judaism of the Mishnah and the Talmud, which became mainstream Judaism as scholars know it today, is in many ways a cultural achievement built up out of resilient responses to Roman occupation of the land. The Israelite idiom of "circulation and grounding" produced new expressions in a new and challenging situation. Given the present state of archaeological, literary, and historical scholarship, it is not yet possible to present a sharply defined chronology indicating exactly what institutions emerged at what time and in what order. But we can understand the dynamic of challenge and resistance from the material remains that we see. The mainstream Jewish adaptations examined in this chapter and chapter six establish a context. Contrasting proto-Christian adaptations in the same context are considered in chapters seven and eight.

An occupied land

The surface of Galilee today retains traces of the activities that people pursued there: ancient roadways, aqueducts, theaters, granaries, dining halls, orchards, homes, basilicas, synagogues, and factories. This cultural and economic landscape was occupied by people in motion, people carrying things and ideas to various destinations. Galilee itself worked with this fluidity, like a grand machine for channeling or withholding, concentrating or separating, introducing or extracting, mixing or distilling these mobile items. Galilee moved things by design, and aspects of the design can be recovered and understood from the landscape today.

The Galilee that interests us is that of the Roman period: from Herod the Great, who came to power in 37 BCE, through the middle of the fourth century CE. The language of international business and imperial government throughout this period was Greek. During these four Greco-Roman centuries, the land sustained no single enduring design, but underwent multiple partial *re*designs and repairs. It supported a built environment that was dynamic, changing, and contested. The cultural and economic landscape, already colonized by Judeans, was colonized anew by Romans. Imperial policies intervened as a real factor in the material and cultural environment. Galileans adapted to ideology and trade pressures from across the empire.

The Roman period can be characterized as one in which Galilean social institutions underwent repeated ruptures through cultural and economic trauma. An evolutionary view of history is not adequate to understand such a period. Cultural practices were confronted repeatedly with novel and challenging circumstances, for which solutions had to be rapidly cobbled together. The flow of historical time in Jewish history seemed to hit a series of turbulent cataracts. Galilee had been forcibly annexed to Hasmonean Judea during the administration of Alexander Jannaeus at the beginning of the first century BCE. Hasmonean administrators built fortified outposts overlooking important trade routes, and they promoted the economic and legal integration of Galilee into a larger Israel. Herod the Great soon took over from the Hasmoneans. As a client of Rome, he built cities including the Mediterranean port of Caesarea. When Herod died in 4 BCE, his kingdom was partitioned, and a revolt in Galilee was crushed with Roman military assistance. The province was assigned to Herod's son Antipas, who first built up the city of Sepphoris and then established a new capital, Tiberias, on the western shore of the Sea of Galilee. Demographic shifts accompanied the establishment of those cities, and there were additional influxes of refugees after the destruction of the Jerusalem Temple in 70 and the banishment of Jews from the holy city in 135. The third century brought drought, famine, plague, and monetary inflation.

Galilean adaptations to traumatic political and social events in the Roman period are still evident in the landscape. But they are difficult to interpret because they occurred in several successive waves. Just before the Romans, the Judeans had put their mark upon Galilee. For two or three generations, starting about 100 BCE, Judean administrators representing the Temple state had governed Galilee from fortified settlements on hilltops all across the province. The Hasmoneans, who represented Jerusalem's high priestly families and also had cultural and trade ties with Jews in the Western and Eastern Diaspora, seem to have built the first synagogue structures in Galilee and to the east in the Golan. Their outreach to the Galileans was in some sense an attempt to win hearts and minds over to the Judean version of Israelite religious thought and practice. They promoted pilgrimage to Jerusalem and the payment of tithes to the Temple as well.

The Hasmoneans did not build cities. Jerusalem was their city, and it could not be cloned. When Herod took over, what he took control of were their fortified towns and some of the agricultural estates and the industrial complexes that they had established. Herod added urban institutions, with their distinctive architecture: the basilica, the public baths, and so forth. Ironically, the Judean colonizers then became the colonized. The former targets of indigenous resistance became resisters of imperial power themselves, but in a mode of prudent collaboration that served both Herodian interests and those of the Jerusalem-based priestly aristocracy.

Roman imperial intrusions show up in the landscape in structures such as the rectilinear design imposed upon cities to implement Roman urbanization policies. Indigenous cultural resistance shows up, for example, in the maintenance of a separate and ritually pure water system after Roman aqueducts brought plentiful, wholesome, and convenient Roman water into neighborhoods of the city of Sepphoris. However, as post-colonial studies of colonialism in the late twentieth century indicate, it may not always be possible to distinguish cleanly between an "imperial intrusion" and an "indigenous resistance," especially in artifacts produced several generations after the initial colonial establishment. In contact situations, the indigenous people may adopt imperial forms in some contexts or at some scales, while indigenous forms persist in another context or at another scale.

Like the British in India in our more recent past, Roman administrators cultivated indigenous collaborators. By the time those collaborators had grandchildren, imperial institutions had became indigenized into the culture in many respects. The Roman presence, together with Mediterranean culture generally, could then be taken to be the natural, ordinary state of affairs, by people who were born and raised after it was imposed upon Galilee. But this would have happened in the generation after that of Jesus.

The cultural products of people living in such a situation are inevitably hybridized, but in different ways and degrees according to the character of their contact with representatives of the occupying administration. This means, for example, that the texts produced in Roman Palestine must be read in the context of Hellenistic literature, of which they are a part. This is recognized by most interpreters of Josephus and the New Testament, which are Greek texts. However, the Mishnah also is the literature of a colonized and compromised people. It displays Greek loan-words and patterns of argumentation, assimilates Jewish customs to Roman laws, and presumes that Greco-Roman lifestyle accessories and housing patterns are in place. This literature, foundational for Christianity and Judaism, respectively, is a literature produced in accommodation to colonization, often by the collaborating class, growing out of the fissures in society and seeking to patch them over.

The Mishnah comes from a later "wave" of adaptation to Roman occupation than the Gospels do. But the Gospels, as Greek texts, come from a later adaptation layer than that of Jesus. They do not give us his own words and concepts directly. The date of his birth indicates that he may have been of indigenous Galilean stock, or he may have come from the elite family of a transplanted colonial Hasmonean administrator or from an intermarried lineage. Jesus was born very close to the time when Roman military forces had besieged and ransacked the city of Sepphoris. Thus, his own resistances and adaptations to the imperial occupation of Galilee may have been addressed to Hasmonean or to Herodian administrators, or both. Or they may have been targeted at the Herodian regime but couched in terms taken from the Hasmonean version of the basic Israelite idiom of circulation and grounding. If we can determine more exactly how Jesus used the available cultural idiom, in the version that it came down to him, then we may enhance our understanding of his teaching. The landscape holds important clues to the mindscape that Jesus inhabited.

Reading as following

The interpretation of the social and economic landscape of colonized Galilee is sometimes characterized as a task of "reading." If the land is like a text, then how ought one to "read" it and the archaeological record that it contains? On the other hand, if texts are but one kind of artifact, while the inhabited landscape is another, how do we coordinate our reading of the built environment of colonized Galilee with our reading of its textual artifacts: the Mishnah, portions of Josephus, the sayings of Jesus, the architectural inscriptions? These issues have been addressed in various ways. The options for coordinated reading can be classified into three categories: reference theories, critical confrontation theories, and recursion theories. In this book I am proposing a fourth, synthetic option: virtual or actual bodily following.

(1) REFERENCE. In this approach to reading Galilee, the texts are taken to refer straightforwardly to the land. They are "about" events that simply "took place" somewhere in Galilee. The texts claim correspondences to material culture insofar as they mention various items that may in fact turn up in the earth; for example, scythes, perfume bottles, walls, coins, courtyards. Written texts are epistemologically privileged by investigators as the most reliable means of access to the realities of the past. This stance has been criticized as an "interpretive hegemony" of texts over the physical remains. It asserts dogmatically that past events really occurred just as recounted in the texts, for it assumes the absolute determination of the textual references by those events. The events supposedly caused the texts to be written just as they were. Archaeology's function, on this view, is to match up written words with dusty things. It tries to corroborate and illustrate the facts already communicated in the texts.

(2) CRITICAL CONFRONTATION. With this option, texts and archaeological evidence are equally privileged as sources of information. Both are "to be read." Reading is understood to be a more or less straightforward decoding of information. The same formal codes are presumed to apply to textual and material artifacts alike. Yet in addition, texts are regarded as having rhetorical and ideological capabilities that

are lacking in the landscape and artifacts in general. Thus, texts alone are to be read "with suspicion," as potentially deceptive or ideologically bent, and therefore thick with hidden meanings waiting to be teased out by hermeneutical procedures. Material remains are regarded as innocent, truthful, and relatively transparent. The assumption is that, inasmuch as things were deposited accidentally and not on purpose, their arrangement can be explained fully just by identifying causal factors. Nothing other than the "natural" forces of geology and marketplace economics is thought to have been at work in the configuration of the landscape. Thus, the material remains may be summoned, like irreproachable witnesses, to disclose and impugn the tendentiousness of the texts and of religious authorities who endorse them. Architecture and domestic implements may be regarded as offering a truer account of the past, and even as having functioned in the past to teach people how to behave. Thus, our interpretation of them today simply resumes their original straightforwardly informative and formative function. In short: texts may deceive, but material culture tells the truth and does so in a universally accessible language.

(3) RECURSION. With this approach, neither texts nor any other material remains are presumed to communicate straightforwardly and innocently. Both texts and other artifacts are read with appropriate hermeneutics of suspicion first, and then those tandem readings are critically correlated. Furthermore, the interpreters take into account their own position within a tradition and their own susceptibility to the persuasive power of artifacts and texts. Artifacts are active. When they were placed in use in antiquity, they were already subtly persuasive and were being "read" by their users right from the start. It is this ancient reading that archaeologists today should examine, and that task entails identification of the specific mechanisms for the encoding and decoding of meaning in space. Moreover, archaeologists should expect to encounter "resistive" readings of various sorts. Both texts and artifacts, including the landscape, may well have been strategic interventions in the negotiation of social relationships, whether for the sake of maintenance or for change. Mark Leone and his archaeological colleagues describe artifacts as "agents": potent vectors for the cultivation of virtues and viewpoints in the population. Even archaeological investigation and reporting produce non-innocent textual artifacts that are strategically powerful in the service of various academic and political enterprises today. Items of material culture are contagious. To use them is to let them use us. They write their meanings into the patterns of our lives.

(4) BODILY FOLLOWING. Aspects of the first three methods suggest a fourth, somewhat synthetic approach. It makes no distinction between texts and the other built elements of the environment in terms of their semantic potential. All artifacts belonging to a culture are expressions framed in a common cultural idiom. We understand them when we acquire that idiom, which is a kind of grammar or template for the production of meanings. But this idiom is not an ideal abstract pattern. The substance of any such idiom is some habitual practice accessible to the mobile and fragile human body. To understand is to follow, either virtually or really. "Following" is temporally sequenced emplacement. When reading texts, we follow virtually along a line of narrative or argument or instruction, according to the genre of the text. When understanding things and spaces, we handle them or walk through them to experience the real possibilities that they present, sequentially and materially.

This is not to say that we must displace someone else in order to occupy a space and appropriate its vantage point for ourselves. Those whose spaces we are seeking to understand are already far removed from us in time. Moreover, places are intrinsically capable of multiple occupations and they admit a range of habitation patterns. Some spaces enforce different kinds of movement for different kinds of people, and through this enforcement, impose the designs of those very differences upon their bodily practices. There is no understanding such spaces and things through mere verbal descriptions. The material requirements and enablements of the places and things must be experienced. Their meaning is their use. And once built, they lend themselves to uses that exceed those which they were first designed to serve.

A literacy of space

Greco-Roman Galilee was a rhetorically effective cultural landscape. The "reading" and the "writing" of the landscape—or more precisely, the continual re-reading and re-writing of it—required a distinctive literacy of space and movement. The landscape constructed and inculcated certain social realities by managing the movement of water, foodstuffs, labor, and lore, along with numerous other things. In this management of flow, we see the mechanism through which the landscape communicated, taught, persuaded, encouraged, dissuaded, inspired—in short, was read. Spatial constructions are keys to interpreting the textual construction of certain social realities that come down to us in our religious traditions and that remain quite powerful today. Among these social realities are two that have received increasing attention from historical archaeologists: ethnicity and gender. Let us consider these in turn.

(1) ETHNIC IDENTITY. The quest to uncover the national past is a powerful and praiseworthy motivation driving archaeology in Israel. Everyone wants to discover Jewish cities, Jewish architectural forms, Jewish artworks and artifacts. But archaeologists must first determine what "Jewish space" looks like in the ancient ruins. They must show how Jewishness can be securely identified in material culture, particularly in the landscape.

For archaeology these are scientific questions, and they are not easy to answer satisfactorily. On one hand, inscribed Hebrew letters and decorative motifs such as the menorah bespeak the intention of ancient builders to construct and furnish a place "Jewishly," to house aspects of an intentionally Jewish way of life. On the other hand, in the Roman period in Galilee many Jews wrote Greek or Aramaic, used Hellenized names, and behaved "Jewishly" in places adorned with secular and heathen cultural themes, places built with colonial interests in mind.

In Galilee, or in the cities of the Empire, how did people recognize Jews, and how did Jews recognize one another, beyond their circle of friends and acquaintances? The visibility of expatriate Jews in communities throughout the empire is indirectly attested by textual references of various kinds: mentions of their taxability, their expulsions from Rome, their ability to locate one another when traveling to distant cities. Sometimes it is supposed that circumcision made Jewish men conspicuous in the urban public baths. Yet people in Roman baths did not usually bathe nude like the Greeks. In any case, the behavioral cues that made living Jews visible to one another are no longer directly visible to us in the archaeological record.

To "behave Jewishly" in colonized Roman Galilee must have had something to do with maintaining identity while moving through a built environment designed to gobble up indigenous culture, wealth, and labor into the imperial maw of worldwide trade. As far as we can tell, spatial isolation within the city, or from the city, was not the strategy for cultural and religious survival chosen by the majority of colonized people in Roman Galilee. We do not find urban enclaves (ghettos), nor has anyone yet excavated a village unpenetrated by Greek and Roman goods and services.

What is found is something much more ingenious. Excavators see evidence that ancient colonized Galileans were working on the very same question that perplexes today's archaeologists: "What is it to be Jewish, really?" The efforts of the ancient inhabitants of Galilee and

Judea to address this question, in their own particular context, are what produced the texts and the architectural features that in turn produced Judaism and provided for its reproduction. So it might be said that archaeologists find "Jewishness" by finding the instrumentalities for producing it.

Those instrumentalities or templates cannot be understood in a static frame. They are not determined according to some eternal and transcendent pattern. They operated across time, transgenerationally. For example, a burial inscription memorializes someone's service to the Jewish community. Such inscriptions have been found in Galilee. Or, the municipal archives at Sepphoris keep track of ancestors' marriage contracts; these archives do not survive, but are mentioned in rabbinic texts. Both of these examples illustrate ways of securing Judaism in the past, that is, in the past as perceived by a first-century Galilean. On the other hand, when rabbinic texts specify requirements for valid marriages and for relations within marriage, they are providing for a Jewish future. Shaye Cohen has shown that the principles for assessing Jewish identity and caste were adjusted by the framers of the Mishnah so as to conform to Roman laws determining personal status and inheritance.

Thus, backward-reaching and forward-reaching templates for *making Jewishness* can be discerned in the archaeological record, just as they can be excavated from ancient texts. Their elaboration at just this period surely is owing to the challenge of the colonial situation, a situation in which every traditional geographical and social border was pierced.

(2) GENDER. The quest to uncover the roots of gender oppression is also a praiseworthy and powerful motivation in archaeology. Recent advances in the archaeology of gender and caste in other parts of the world have not yet been incorporated into the planning and reporting of excavations in Israel. However gender is increasingly considered in the interpretive discussions subsequent to excavation. One example is Peskowitz's provocative study of the co-construction of gender in rabbinic texts and in material culture. As we have seen, this work contrasts representations of women's labor with the economic realities of women's and men's work in one selected trade, that of textile production. Peskowitz argues that femininity was defined through the cultural icon of the good woman who spins and weaves at home. Even corpses were accessorized with spindle whorls in their coffins.

Peskowitz means to read the spindle whorls "with suspicion"; that is, she astutely identifies their rhetorical use to assign meaning to women by connecting individuals into the symbolic system of gender at a specific location. Besides being tools, then, the whorls are words in a language.

They are the adjective "feminine." If so, then the language that is the ancient Jewish gender system has separated economic worth from the connotation of "feminine." What is womanly is private and therefore invisible in the economy. Peskowitz terms this semantic event the "decommodification" of women's labor. The power of the gender semantic is so great that it can accomplish this ironic assertion of women's economic insignificance through the very same artifact, the whorl, that produces women's substantial economic contributions.

This reading of rabbinic texts is theoretically critical and sophisticated. But the spindle whorls register in the analysis primarily as textual content. Their real and socially potent physical use, though described, is not taken seriously enough. Because Peskowitz settles for a naive reading of materials as if they were mere texts, her critique reaches only to an imputed ideological dimension of the gendered relationship. On that view, the whorl functions as a physical word but takes its meaning from a nonphysical formal system: the ideal symbolism of gender that is also encoded in the rabbinic texts. Thus, Peskowitz regards the rhetorical decommodification of women's work in the rabbinic texts as a guilty denial of oppression by the oppressors. She finds that this decommodification is accomplished semantically through the rabbis' spurious claim that women's work is valueless, advanced by the very men who are profiting nicely from that labor.

That well may be. But surely the whorl has significance within a physical system as well: the imperial infrastructure that extracts wealth from Galilee by means of edifices and roads cut into the Galilean landscape. For full spatial literacy, should we not read the whorl also in terms of its material economic function? The technology of weaving appropriates women's time and labor for production of textiles, for export, and for military tribute. It turns womanpower into imperial wealth and might, as it turns fiber into thread and thread into cloth. From the perspective of spatial management, then, the tools of the textile trade bespeak the *commodification* of women's labor, because they extract the benefits of women's labor from their village kinship circles and drain it off into the imperial economy. Now the full irony of the overlay of rabbinic ideology upon economic reality comes into view. The textually produced *decommodification* of women's labor, established by Peskowitz, cloaks the actual *commodification* of it required by the colonial administration.

A more comprehensive account of the interplay of ideology and space, empire and resistance, must press on beyond ideology critique. It must examine the connections between the rhetorical estrangement of women from their labor, on the one hand, and the material colonial extraction of the fruits of the women's labor away from themselves and their kin, on the other hand. The more comprehensive inquiry will actually provide a more satisfactory answer for the narrower investigation of gender relations as well. Ancient gender relations were not a closed self-referential ideological system, and certainly not a system running on the sheer desire for power over women by men. The assumption that human relations can be reduced to struggles for power underlies programs of cultural analysis inspired by the work of Michel Foucault. Such analyses rest on a twofold fallacy: that a desire for power accounts for itself, needing no further justification, and that the many things that human beings actually desire all are reducible to power. On the contrary, while negotiation for power of various sorts can be an aspect of gender, gender systems can and do express many other kinds of quests as well. Desire for power is not self-evidently the ultimate explanation of all social transactions.

Gender is part of the indigenous kinship system. In traditional societies, that is in societies not organized as states, kinship is an instrumentality for assigning personal identity and for managing labor and its fruits. For comparable cases, we can look to the kinship practices in African societies studied by the anthropologist Karen Brodkin Sacks. Sacks found that the reckoning of kinship was the means of directing the benefits of each person's labor to someone else, and conversely, the means of assigning responsibility for the welfare of each person to someone else. It attached lineages to lands, offices, and prerogatives. In other words, kinship provided the comprehensive "social safety net."

This is precisely what is disrupted with the advent of the state. In the case of Galilee, that means the advent of Hasmonean administration, which diverted labor and land out of the traditional kinship arrangements while leaving them otherwise intact, followed by the advent of Herodian and Roman administrations, which escalated that diversion in order to support large-scale urbanization and the expansion of international commerce.

Thus, if the rabbis reassert certain kin-based dependence relationships, this effort could plausibly be read as calculated resistance against colonial market pressures. In that context, to criticize the rabbis for repressing the prerogatives of individual women is to miss the point, anachronistically. The "individuality" of women, and that of men, was produced for the convenience of empire. Constructions of gender are affected whenever there is traumatic disruption to other social or natural systems such as agriculture, government, the economy, or the environment. Yet in turn, gender can be deliberately and skillfully manipulated so as to have an effect on other systems.

In the colonial context of Hasmonean and Herodian Galilee, gender constructions were a vehicle for constructing Judaism. The material traces that they left were geared to work trans-generationally. Gendered uses of artifacts secured a Jewish past, as when spindle whorls were placed in coffins to assert the productive femininity of the deceased. They also worked to secure the future, as when prospective brides learned the use of the *miqveh*. There's no such thing as "women's space" or "women's work" to be found in the archaeological excavations. What shows up instead is the acute salience of the double question: "What is the womanly way of being Jewish; what is the manly way?" There seem to have been no other ways to be Jewish.

Contact and adaptation

Roman power was projected onto Galilee, through the client ruler Herod Antipas, by cultivating indigenous collaborators, by manipulating the economy to draw off commodities and other resources for Roman projects, by relocating families from villages to urban areas, by occasional military incursions, and by diverting international travelers to the new tourist attractions at Tiberias after 20 CE. Economically, it was not the case that "before urbanization" there was a "surplus" of produce and industrial production just lying around in barns and warehouses of Galilee, as the Lenski-Kautsky model seems to suggest. Surplus had to be created through reorganization of labor, and that entailed an upheaval of residence and kinship patterns. The establishment of cities required massive labor displacements, first toward Sepphoris during Jesus' childhood, then to lakeside Tiberias when he was a young man.

The establishment of Tiberias made a huge difference in the human and commodities traffic across lower Galilee. The Lake was already ringed with harbors, permitting easy connections among the three seaside territories: on the northeast, the Tetrarchy of Philip; on the southeast, the Decapolis; and on the western shore, the Galilee. Magdala in Galilee had shipyards, fish-processing facilities, and export businesses. Fish products went out to world markets, probably by ship to Bethsaida or Capharnaum on the northern lakeshore, joining the Via Maris road and turning either west toward the Mediterranean ports of Ptolemais and Caesarea, or east toward Damascus and Babylon. There were substantial populations of Jews and other consumers in both directions.

When people in the Eastern diaspora wanted to visit Jerusalem, they had a choice of routes but they had no reason to cross Herod Antipas' territory, until he built Tiberias. The new capital city, with its lovely waterfront and the gleaming royal palace perched on the leafy cliffside, could be seen across the Lake from the old Hasmonean town of Gamla in the Golan (the hot, arid, dusty Golan). It was an inviting sight to travelers stopping there and at the other waystations in Philip's territory and the Decapolis along the way to Jerusalem. Herod made Tiberias a tourist gateway into the Jordan Valley and Eretz Israel. This enhanced his international prestige among influential citizens of the eastern diaspora. Galilean friends of Antipas, his "retainers," could rub elbows and make business contacts with the wealthy travelers from Damascus and Babylon whom Antipas entertained at Tiberias.

Only a minority of the resident populations of Tiberias or of the former capital, Sepphoris, were comprised of newly arrived foreigners. This leaves aside the not unimportant question of the criterion for counting someone as a "resident" of the city. Is the place of residence to be defined as the place where one sleeps, or eats, or works? These could easily be three different structures; and the practice might vary with the season. Many people would have come in to the cities from the countryside to do the service work that cities needed. People who stayed in the villages could still undertake textile or food or craft production for city markets. Service and tourist industries would have sprung up. Although village industries were kinship based, in the cities it could easily happen that non-kin groups worked and dwelled together. The upheaval in social and economic relationships offered novel opportunities, and we may imagine that people took advantage of them. We may imagine this *as a hypothesis* on the basis of comparison with other societies where experience with imperial contact evoked both accommodation and selective resistance. The hypothesis required gathering and interpretation of further evidence from the archaeological record.

The hypothetical picture of how the cities disrupted social practices in Galilee is based in part on comparable examples of imperial contact with indigenous peoples in other times and places. For example, the Spanish conquest and occupation in the Americas is analogous to the Roman occupation of the Galilee in some respects. The "contact archaeology" that studies it is a relatively recent project in Americanist archaeology, sharing some interests and techniques with feminist archaeology of gender. The *conquistadores* were military men who had to be housed and fed by the resources of the land that they had conquered. When their dwellings are excavated, the furnishings of the sleeping and administrative spaces tend to show continuity of design with those of Europe, while their kitchens have implements resembling those of contemporary Native American dwellings. This indicates that the Spaniards used the services of indigenous people who knew how to obtain and prepare local foods and did so using technology that was familiar to them.

Further ethnographic research suggests that those people were women. Thus, early colonial contact between Spanish and Native Americans occurred most frequently as a gendered contact between conquered women and male conquerors. Therefore, Spanish cultural influence initially was mediated to Native society primarily through those women workers. The European Conquest meant that some Native women had the opportunity, such as it was, to work outside their homes and make a living apart from their kin groups. But the physical intimacy of domestic service also promoted the spread of bacterial and viral diseases from the Spanish to the Native Americans, who lacked immunity. By contrast, in places where contact occurred in brief meetings for trade among men (such as Newfoundland, Labrador, and the St. Lawrence River), disease spread much more slowly. This indicates one way in which gender can be a significant variable in colonial contact.

It seems likely that indigenous Galileans, women or men, entered domestic service in the urban households of Herodian bureaucrats and their collaborators. How can we determine whether this was the case? The record of such service might be sought as a "culture frontier" between the kitchens and the other areas of elite urban homes, just as one finds in Mesoamerica and in the Pacific Northwest. If indigenous Galileans were cooking for Romans, then pots, ovens, foot-traffic patterns, and garbage deposits in and around the villas of Tiberias and Sepphoris would resemble those associated with Galilean village housing more than those associated with urban villas elsewhere in the Mediterranean.

Archaeologists are far from being able to test this hypothesis. It has not yet been established whether there is a distinctive material signature for Galilean village cookpots, ovens, or food processing. Present practice in Galilean excavation establishes dates for common potsherds, but does not further classify them as to village or urban provenance. If indeed the shards do not vary from city to village, then that finding itself will support the hypothesis that no foreign help was imported and local villagers were employed as urban cooks. Whether those cooks returned home each night is another question.

The distribution of pots across Galilee from production centers at Kfar Hanania and Shikhin has been established by David Adan-Bayewitz. More precisely, he established that the clay of which the pots were made had come from sources near those villages. That finished pots were transported, and not raw clay, is something that he had to infer on the basis of the presence of "wasters" (misshapen and rejected pots) at Kfar Hanania and Shikhin, along with the obvious difficulty of transporting soft wet clay. What was the social mechanism that accomplished that distribution? Adan-Bayewitz and others have concluded that the pots were carried by traders in a commercial network of some kind.

This is plausible. But the distribution of potsherds could also be accounted for by a migration of people. Perhaps Kfar Hanania and Shikhin were famous for their excellent cuisine; perhaps villagers from there were wooed away as cooks, and took their equipment with them to their new jobs or to catering businesses that they established in the cities. But there seems to be no support for such a presupposition in rabbinic texts. On the other hand, maybe pots went with brides to their new homes. In that case, the shard distribution would constitute a trace of persistent patterns of bride-giving, perhaps following matrilines.

Another example of historical inference based on ceramics comes from Aztec society. At several late prehispanic sites in central Mexico, Brumfiel was able to detect variations over time in the relative frequency of spindle whorls and cooking pots, as well as in the ratios of large to small whorls and of pots to griddles. Ethnographic analogy indicated that weaving and cooking probably were jobs done in households by women. Brumfiel also knew that large whorls were used to produce coarse maguey fabric, small whorls to make fine cotton, and that cloth was one important medium in which tribute was paid to Aztec conquerors. The archaeological record indicates a change in the amount and kind of textiles produced at the point when the Aztec state expanded. Moreover, before expansion there was an inverse relation between weaving and agricultural production across various sites, suggesting that women would do more of one or the other kind of work, depending on local circumstances. Thus, when women were compelled to produce cloth for tribute, this took them away from agricultural work in some localities. Elsewhere, Brumfiel finds, after Aztec expansion the cotton production held steady, maguey cloth production dropped, and agriculture apparently intensified. She postulates that in this case, the reallocation of women's labor was a rational, chosen response to the marketing opportunities presented by the growth of cities. This interpretation is borne out by a rise in the ratio of griddles to pots. Griddles are used in producing dry portable food (tortillas) that could be carried away from home. Yet, tortillas are more difficult to make than stews in pots. Thus Brumfiel infers: "One of the effects of Aztec dominance was to draw labor away from the household context; women's work in food preparation subsidized this labor mobilization" (1991: 241).

This finding suggests some questions about the Hasmonean/ Herodian horizon in Galilee. If Roman urbanization induced people to commute to cities for work, did cooking practices also shift in order to provide the day laborers with portable food? Or did retail food shops in the cities offer different kinds of food than was available in the villages? Did village women perhaps make portable confections at home for sale in the cities? We need better information on the kind and frequency of ovens and pots in use in the villages before urbanization and after. Such information can support inferences about labor displacement.

Caste and nutritional privilege

Nutritional variations across time can also be read from skeletal remains. Grasses and legumes in the diet contribute carbon and nitrogen to bone formation, respectively. The ratio of isotopes of carbon and nitrogen in skeletal remains, therefore, can indicate the proportion of maize to beans in the diet. (However, a high proportion of carbon might also indicate that one ate the flesh of animals that had fed on grasses.) In an analysis of human bone from Peru, Hastorf found no difference in the isotope ratio between male and female skeletons dating from before the Inka conquest. Afterwards, however, male skeletons contained a higher concentration of the carbon isotope than female skeletons. This was interpreted as evidence of different diets after the conquest. The Inka consolidated their power by extracting a tribute of corn beer from conquered peoples and then distributing the beer to the male workers and soldiers who had been detached from their villages and enlisted in Inka projects. In Hastorf's interpretation, then, Inka political reorganization in Peru meant that more of the maize and meat was allocated for consumption by the male workers serving the Inka. Apparently, women had to produce more maize beer for tribute. Accordingly, they had to find something other than maize for themselves to eat.

In Palestine, caste entailed nutritional prerogatives. Was this merely a legal fiction, or did priests and levites really have greater access to grain and meat? Those components of the diet leave a distinct chemical signature in bone. Therefore, it is possible to map the consumption rates of meats or grains, and to make some correlations with the circulation of agricultural tithes across Galilee and Judea. At the very least, skeletal studies can produce information about the general level of health of the population and the kinds of deficiencies and diseases from which people suffered in the villages and the cities.

For Israel, however, large-scale studies of human bone present special problems. There are religious prohibitions against disturbing ancient graves. One hears that large collections of skeletal remains are now in storage awaiting study; but very little is ever published. In any event, the sex of skeletal remains cannot always be reliably determined, especially for children's skeletons and for partial and badly preserved remains. Skeletal studies are labor intensive and high tech; and the sample must include many individuals for statistical significance.

Nevertheless, an intact skeleton can disclose a great deal of information about someone's life and activities. For example, the number of births can be estimated from marks on the pelvis. Heavy lifting and walking up hills leave their traces on long bones. Various kinds of hand work will mold the finger bones in distinctive ways. Hours spent laboring at the loom would show up on the long bones of the arm, and some kinds of fiber processing would mark the teeth. If imperial contact altered the labor patterns as drastically as the evidence suggests, then there should be a distinct change in the frequencies of occupation-linked traits among female and male skeletons before and after the first century. For example, a longitudinal study of arm and shoulder bones might indicate that more women became weavers to produce military cloaks, which were one form in which Roman taxes were paid.

Architecture is the variety of ancient material culture that receives most attention in Israel. But excavation of public buildings now needs to be supplemented with more work on ordinary dwellings in both cities and villages, as well as examination of the roadways that linked them. For colonial America, excavators have been able to trace matrilineal kinship networks through the continuity of design of the greenhouses in which orange trees were cultivated at the grand plantation houses along the Chesapeake Bay. The secrets of designing successful "orangeries" apparently were handed down from mother to daughter, aunt to niece, as Weber has shown. On the Chesapeake, raising oranges was merely a prestigious hobby for the ladies of the leisured elite; nevertheless, a similar research strategy could help to profile the transmission of economically significant technologies among working families in ancient Galilee. Houses, generally speaking, were sites for industrial and agricultural production whose benefits accrued to the male lineage identified with the house. Nevertheless, variant technology could come into the house along with a bride or a non-kin worker.

Conversely, if the needs of the cities and the needs of imperial markets brought about a shift in production patterns, then a destabilizing "ripple effect" would impact traditional labor and kinship practices. As we have seen, the indigenous patrilineal household was regarded as a "container" that "grounded" the living "fluids" (caste, labor, food) carried by "mobile containers" (women). The idea of the patriline took material form in the village house with its finely engineered door-frames and sills for selectively admitting, retaining, and releasing the people, activities, and commodities of the household. If the house itself could not keep the empire out, then we may expect that people adapted to maintain the capability of "grounding" by enforcing certain kinship and gender practices more vigilantly, or by other comparable means. For example, as Cynthia Baker has shown, a polemic arose against "women weaving in the marketplace" in order to reassert gender control in an era when local control over commodities was being eroded.

In Roman times, another kind of house begins to be mentioned in the rabbinic sources. The *beit midrash* or study house—literally, a house of interpretation—has no distinctive architectural form yet discovered. Only one physical trace has been found, an inscription from Daburra in the Golan, excavated and identified by Urman. Textual sources indicate that the studyhouse had a door to restrict admission, was owned by or identified with a particular male teacher, was dedicated to the particular use of studying Torah, and was recognized in the neighborhood as such. Presumably, the edifice was large enough to accommodate the teacher and some learners, and had furniture to support them and whatever texts they might need to unroll. It was not the synagogue. It may have been a room within the dwelling of the rabbi associated with it.

Unlike the synagogue, the rabbinic studyhouse was indeed gendered space. Only men could enter. In fact, it was within this edifice that boys became men, *halakhah* became a male expertise, and Torah study became a male prerogative. The notion that studying is a religious activity probably originated in Africa. As Griffiths argues, Egyptian Jews likely adapted the combination of worship and study from their neighbors. In Palestine, the emergence of the studyhouse as an institution and an element in the built environment is part of the evolution of "rabbinic Judaism" and occurred after the time of Jesus, as the role of the rabbi was taking shape. Yet the various voices that speak in the Mishnah may well represent individuals, interpretive traditions, and even factions from the first century or earlier.

Although no distinct architectural form for the *beit midrash* can yet be described, we must come to grips with the fact that, at some point during the second century and perhaps as early as the first, the Torah started to need a house. That is, Torah itself was perceived to be in need of a means to maintain or restore its "grounding." As Selkin has shown, texts from diverse Roman-era communities in Palestine exploit the philological and metaphoric affinities between water immersion and "immersion" in correct interpretation. Early Jesus traditions reflect a discourse in the same idiom but opposed in important details. The housing of Torah appears to be a strategy to prevent pollution of one's *halakhah* by the *halakhah* of other "sects" or interpretive factions. It might be objected that the plurality of voices and opinions is the very essence of the rabbinic discourse recorded in the Mishnah. However, that plurality is safely in the past by the time the text is compiled. The text achieves closure in ways analogous to the house. The earlier free flow of argumentation ceases with the promulgation of the authoritative text. Interpretation now is channeled inside a secured and named studyhouse, and along lines defined by the textual agenda.

Architectural enclosure, male gendering, and privatization are all components of that process. While Torah continued to be studied, interpreted, and taught outside of those special enclosures, even in the open air, and certainly in the synagogues, something was changing. The land was pierced by empire and its various circulation patterns were increasingly disrupted. Symbolically, the architectural forms of the synagogue and the "house of interpretation" are resistive responses to the built environment of Roman power.

The paradigm of this occurrence is yet another new architectural form, which we have already considered, the *miqveh* or ritual bathing tank. Ritual bathing is prescribed in Leviticus; but ritual baths are not found before the Hasmonean period. Archaeologists must ask why Judeans and Galileans started to build these pools at just that time. What led some people to decide that their previous arrangements for purification had become inadequate? Jewish water architecture seems to have been an answer to the provocation of Roman water architecture: to the aqueducts, the public baths, the decorative pools, and the running water piped in to industrial installations. Those material improvements in the quality of urban life were enjoyed by all; still, they constituted a symbolic affront to the indigenous cultural patterns of "transmission and grounding."

All of that Roman water sloshing through the urban built environment now multiplied the physical opportunities to contract ritual impurity. It also multiplied the rhetorical opportunities for elaborating and developing various *halakhot*. Rabbinic rulings reflect a heightened concern with the management of purity, responding to a situation of increasing physical and symbolic danger that life fluids might "flow the wrong way." What does it mean if *miqva'ot* are found in nearly every first-century house in the Sepphoris acropolis? It may mean that the residents routinely incurred ritual impurity every day when they visited the municipal baths, but just as routinely grounded themselves in the right kind of water when they returned home to a Jewish house.

Significantly, the *miqveh's* grounding power depends on its having the right kind of water supply: "living water," not "drawn water." The rhetorical construction of this distinction did not occur, in all its complexity, until Judeans were confronted with Roman waterworks. Roman aqueduct water cannot be used in a *miqveh*, at least not without first being rectified or revived by mixing with a sufficient amount of "living" water. Aqueduct water was deemed to be a kind of "drawn" water. Although this may seem counterintuitive to us, the copiously flowing aqueduct water was regarded as more similar to water dipped out from a cistern in a pot, than to water flowing in a river. The aqueduct had "contained" the water in settling pools and regulated its flow with valves, before allowing it to flow down through a city by gravity. On the other hand, rivers and rooftop rainwater collection systems are alike in that they passively catch what drops from the heavens to the ground: "living" water. This distinction between "drawn" and "living" water had to be rhetorically constructed and maintained.

The character of the geological water cycle makes it an apt natural symbol for the divine covenant by which the Land of Israel was constituted as holy. Water pours down from the heavens onto the earth, where it produces crops and can also be caught in stationary containers that are both grounded and grounding. Or, it can circulate in mobile containers, but that circulation must be monitored and corrected ("grounded") when necessary. The relative uncertainty of rainfall and cisterns symbolically represents the people's dependence on the providence of the heavens for water. Enter the Herodians, with superior Roman technology. Israel had had sophisticated underground wells and water channels for centuries, but the Romans built tall, visible aqueducts that reached out to far-off mountain springs and quenched urban thirst without regard to season or drought. Caesarea sucked on Carmel; its harbor walked out onto the Mediterranean Sea. Herod secularized and subdued the water. That is, the Roman client ruler profaned water by removing it from the ideal realm of Covenant governance.

Roman civil engineers probably did not recognize the full symbolic impact of what they built. Perhaps their water architecture was well meant as a straightforward boon to the health and comfort of everyone. Galileans and Judeans of all castes used city water and appreciated its benefits. But paradoxically, this use may have spurred the elaboration of the alternative, separate, and symbolically resistive water system known to the Mishnah, other rabbinic literature, and the writers of the Dead Sea Scrolls. Interest in matters of ritual purity and regulations for its management expanded during the period of imperial urbanization. Sectarian differences grew up around water practices; and in turn, distinctive water practices became important markers of sectarian identity. The origin of the *miqveh* as an architectural form should be placed in that context. The *miqveh* was a technology of symbolic resistance, designed to correct the disruption of the circulation patterns for "fluids" (water, food, caste, labor, ethnic identity) and "containers" (women, men, pots) that the Romans had wrought: symbolically with their aqueducts, and quite materially with the various displacements of labor and commodities mandated by imperial taxation and trade.

Finding the Galilee of the Mishnah

Herodian policies and public works disrupted the circulation of labor and resources in Galilee. Under Roman occupation, the material hardship for the people was considerable. But it is the cultural stress that evoked the most creative strategies of resistance, adaptation, and survival. The architectural forms of the synagogue and the *miqveh* used the idiom of "grounding" to achieve a symbolic refusal of Roman light and Roman water. Besides these architectural expressions, there were also distinctive practices and rhetorics that enacted cultural resistance to Rome even after political and economic resistance had become futile. The practices and rhetoric of the Jesus movement were among them. Early rabbinic discourse and the texts and institutions of nascent Judaism must also be placed in the context of colonial contact, and read through the indigenous idiom of circulation and grounding.

What does resistance look like in the archaeological record? We must train our imaginations not to picture a clear line in the earth, with "Jewish" materials on one side and "Roman" on the other, or with "peasants" on one side and "aristocrats" on the other. The frontier of resistance is multidimensional and subtle. Models of binary opposition can be of only limited use for interpreting such a frontier. In contact situations, the borders run through every institution and location in the colonized land, and even through families and individuals. The village is no longer an indigenous enclave; but neither is the city a purely Roman intrusion. Rome and Israel saturate one another. The bodies of the indigenous people continually traverse every geographical demarcation, and their souls become borderlands.

Moreover, we the anglophone archaeologists are scholars with "borderland souls" as well. We cross into a land where we were not born, and then we attempt to read it through our polyglot western intellectual heritage. In that crossing, we walk in the footsteps of the Romans. As Antipas built Tiberias for tourists, so Western archaeology builds history parks at sites like Qatzrin, Gamla, Sepphoris, Qumran, Herodium, and Masada. Two of these, Qatzrin and Sepphoris, feature reconstructed houses with areas designated as dining rooms. They are curious places.

Sepphoris, in Galilee, shows off a Roman-era villa with an impressive mosaic on its triclinium floor. Catwalks let visitors lounge over railings and gaze at the beautiful image of a woman's face, but the scaffolding hides the serving pathways where slaves brought in the fine foods for the ancient elite diners. Qatzrin, in the Golan, welcomes visitors into the rustic "House of Rabbi Abun" featuring a "multi-purpose family room." Those identifications are entirely without warrant; the various people who lived here over several centuries probably used the room for livestock or crafts, not for family dinners. At both sites, the fantasies of the present have been projected into the past. Yet, visitors come away with the impression that they have "been there" and seen history as it really was.

Archaeological history parks provide visitors with an opportunity to engage in the sort of interpretation that I have called bodily following in regard to the reconstructed past. Visitors "feel like" they have walked through the past, as it really was. This sort of following can be highly deceptive when those who built the park have contrived to conceal its constructed character and the displacements in time and space that support the archaeological displays.

The State of Israel is developing a system of archaeological parks where its citizens and international visitors alike can visit restored ruins from various periods in the long and rich history of the land. This effort provides a wealth of cultural information, while displaying the means by which the information was recovered. Israeli parks exhibit information about the methods of excavation and inference through which the ruins have been brought out of the earth and into view. A visitor can arrange to volunteer in the work of excavating and recording data, because many of the sites are still being dug.

In the United States, Colonial Williamsburg is perhaps the most familiar example of an outdoor history park. Its visitors stroll through restored buildings of a pre-Revolutionary, pre-industrial town. They witness demonstrations of crafts and everyday activities, performed by actors in period costumes. But, as critics of Colonial Williamsburg have pointed out, "the American past" that you walk through in the reconstructed town lacks indentured labor, African slaves, disease, and other elements that were integral parts of the town's seventeenth-century life. Nevertheless, your bodily experience of touching and moving through the town is what makes the display seem convincing and "real." Two landscapes are superimposed in the history park. Or rather, the twentieth-century construction conceals its own selectivity by claiming to be merely a transparent window into the landscape of the past.

You can walk "everywhere" in Colonial Williamsburg and see "everything." But your feet and eyes are being detoured away from certain historical realities nevertheless. This carefully structured tour of the past lays down a screen for future understanding and behavior. The persistence of this template for subsequent learning and doing will continue to determine what is possible for the users' feet, eyes, and hands in history as we live it.

Selectivity and detouring are not the only troublesome features of the park. It can also amplify any structure that the past may happen to have in common with the present, making that structure seem to be "natural" rather than built. This sort of contrived familiarity operates persuasively in the two reconstructed "dining rooms" in northern Israel.

At the archaeological site, you are given to understand that archaeology is strictly scientific. The descent into the earth must be a journey into the past "as it really was." The somatic experience of walking or crawling through the ruins on your own hands and knees, together with the rhetoric of scientific discovery, make the constructed character of the landscape fade away out of awareness. The claim to perfect scientific transparency conceals two mechanisms of this epistemic portal: selective detouring, and the naturalization of constructed factors through amplified resonance between the past and its present display.

These warp mechanisms operate in the "dining rooms" of the partly reconstructed dwellings at the two Israeli history parks. One is an upscale urban villa at Sepphoris, which was a Roman colonial city in the third century when this house first was built. The villa's dining room is properly identified as a *triklinē* or "three-coucher": a room furnished for diners to sprawl upon couches along three walls of a rectangular space. The mosaic floor indicates how the room functioned. A squared-off U-shaped area along three sides is paved only with plain white tesserae because it was meant to be covered by the couches.

The rest of the floor, a T-shaped area fitting into the U, is richly decorated with scenes from the myth of Dionysos and would have been visible to the diners. There is a strikingly beautiful image of a woman's face worked into a medallion in the mosaic at the spot where the diner on the central couch could enjoy looking at it. This mosaic, discovered in 1988, has been called "the Mona Lisa of the Galilee" by the excavator, Eric Meyers.

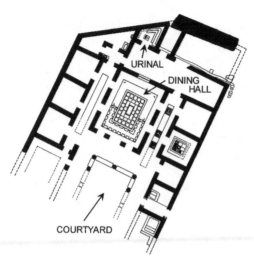

FIGURE 16: *Plan of the Roman villa at Sepphoris, after Meyers et al. The floor of the triclinium or dining hall is identified by the ornate rectangular mosaic, which includes a U-shaped white area marked for the placement of couches. People lounging on the couches could look out through the triple doorway into the peristyle courtyard. The dining hall was 5.5 by 7 meters, and its mosaic floor was crafted about 200–250 CE. The courtyard was 11 meters square, and the villa itself was 23 meters wide and at least 30 meters long.*

FIGURE 17: *Face in the mosaic floor of the triclinium on the Sepphoris acropolis, after Meyers et al. This face was the focal point of the gaze of the diners who reclined on the central couch.*

A *triklinē* was a banquet hall. As a Mediterranean cultural institution, the formal men's banquet is known to historians through textual evidence and numerous archaeological excavations throughout the region. The customs and the architecture of banqueting evolved over a period of nearly a thousand years. Ancient texts indicate that, generally speaking, women of elite families did not attend the *symposia* or drinking bouts that were part of banquet practices. But working women were there. They prepared and served some of the food. And as *hetairai* or companions-for-hire, some women reclined with the men and joined in conversation. Thus, one may regard any *triklinē* as gendered space of a particular sort: elite men met there for business and pleasure, assisted by working women.

The excavated architecture at Sepphoris confirms what the texts tell us: the reclining diners, facing into the center of the U, had to be served from the front and attended from behind. In the Sepphoris villa, the floor plan shows how banquet staff personnel had to come and go with food and drink in front of the couches. Just off the back hallway, there was a bathroom convenient for a personal assistant whose master needed to be taken there to relieve himself or wash up.

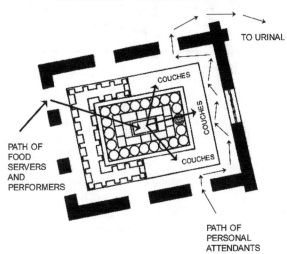

FIGURE 18: *The mosaic floor of the villa's triclinium indicates the placement of furniture and suggests how workers moved around it. As the elite men reclined on their sides, they faced inward. Food, wine, and entertainment were presented to them from the center of the room. Personal service was accessible from behind their backs, unseen until needed.*

But visitors to the site today cannot walk through the villa by the ways that those service personnel used. You cannot bodily follow the workers' movements. You do not notice, from the workers' perspective, how the leisure of the diners was provided for. In the museum space today, the mosaic itself now is established as the focus of attention. The room is kept dark. You walk around it on a raised platform with a railing. This platform interrupts and hides the "traffic flow" of the ancient servers' feet.

TRICLINIUM AS OBJECT OF ART APPRECIATION

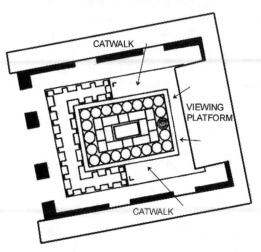

FIGURE 19: *Visitors to the triclinium in 1996 gazed down at the mosaic floor from nearly the same angle as the ancient party-goers. After the Roman villa at Sepphoris was enclosed as a museum display in the 1990s, a catwalk and viewing platform hid the pathways used by some of the ancient serving personnel. The mosaic is now presented merely as an aesthetic object. The catwalk obscures its ancient function as a template to organize the labor that made banqueting possible.*

The lighting, directed beneath the platform, illuminates the beautiful mosaics as you look down upon them. You may linger over "Mona Lisa" and contemplate her beauty, utterly detached from the exigencies of service in the villa. You are invited to fantasize about this lovely face. Who was she? Did she perhaps attend the nearby theater? There is time to ponder and enjoy as you lounge against the railing.

In effect, today's villa visitor is bodily put in the place of an elite visitor in the third century. Your gaze on feminine beauty replicates the gaze of an ancient male diner upon his *hetaira* or upon one of the serving women. At the same time, you are bodily prevented from replicating the gaze or the movement of any of the caterers, waitresses, entertainers, or attendants. The villa in the Sepphoris history park does not lie; but it tells a selective truth. The mosaic truly is beautiful. But the space of the dining room is still gendered in the twentieth century, and in quite the same way that the gendering was accomplished in the third. The ancient male diners' bodily attitude is offered today for students and other tourists to assume, as the correct and only access to the site. Although there are no couches today, visitors stand on a catwalk above and behind where the couches used to be. They still lean on their elbows and gaze down at the mosaic just as the ancient diners did. The catwalk covers the ancient serving paths, for the most part. Museum visitors position themselves with their backs to the service-access hallways and the bathroom. This puts the traces of ancient labor both out of sight and out of mind. Yet this is *the same space* that ancient working women knew differently, according to their different paths through it.

Another sort of gendering is at work in the reconstructed village house at Qatzrin in the Golan Heights. Synagogue excavations nearby indicate that Jews lived here in the third through the eighth century. The reconstructed house has been dubbed "the House of Rabbi Abun" after a name inscribed on a tombstone found reused in another building some distance away.

Unlike the Roman villa, whose display is designed to promote aesthetic contemplation, the village house at Qatzrin has been furnished by its curators to illustrate daily life in the era when the Talmuds were being written. Both at the site and in a popular magazine article, the excavators have been careful to specify what parts of the architecture and the furniture are "original," and what has been introduced on the basis of twentieth-century ethnographic parallels or from other ancient sites.

But several crucial conceptual imports to this site are not identified as such. First, the reconstructors assume that this building housed a nuclear family throughout the centuries of its use. The residents are imagined as a patrilinear, patrilocal kinship group. ("Rabbi Abun" literally means "great father." No alternative hypotheses are considered, in spite of textual and material evidence that people often shared houses with their workmates instead of, or along with, their blood relatives. Second, the areas around ovens are designated as "kitchens," the places where the women cooked. This presumes that all cooks were women and that cooking was done within nuclear families. In fact, textual evidence suggests otherwise. We read that breads and meats were prepared in different edifices, at different times, with different frequency, and by different sexes. Third, and perhaps most interesting, a large interior room of the house has been designated as the dining room or *traqlin*, "a multi-purpose family room."

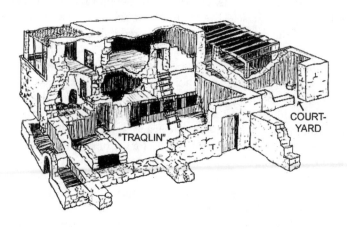

FIGURE 20: *"The House of Rabbi Abun" as reconstructed for the history park at Qatzrin in the Golan. From a drawing by Lura K. Teter, after Killebrew and Fine. The identification of the "traqlin" or triclinium is doubtful. The room measures 8 meters by 2.7 meters, and a ladder ascends from it to a sleeping loft. This house can be dated no earlier than 500 CE, but it is part of a residential compound that was inhabited in Hasmonean and Roman times and underwent repeated remodeling.*

The word *traqlin* is a loan-word from Greek *triklinē*. The Talmuds often mention events or conversations occurring in the *traqlin*, usually translated "dining room." Were there really dining rooms in ordinary village houses of the third through eighth century? Whether a traditional village dwelling would have a room entirely devoted to dining is an interesting question; but if it did, then there should have been a Hebrew or Aramaic word for that room. More likely, the term *traqlin* came into Hebrew when upscale Jews dwelling in Greco-Roman cities began to adopt the architecture and the social customs of the colonizers, for the Romans had a policy of co-opting the loyalties of the indigenous ruling class. In an urban Jewish home, a *traqlin* probably looked and functioned much like the *triklinē* in the Roman villa at Sepphoris: a spacious salon for gentlemanly entertaining. The very word indicates that the Mishnah and the Talmuds came from a class of people who were urbanized and were close associates of the Roman colonizers.

There is no scientific reason to designate the large room in the reconstructed village "House of Rabbi Abun" as a *traqlin*, much less "a multi-purpose family room." More likely this space served as a work-room housing some industrial tasks during most of the several centuries when the house seems to have been in use. At Qatzrin, the nostalgic provision of seemingly authentic period furniture and the tagging of various features with Talmudic allusions produce a resonance in today's visitor. You recognize familiar things there: kitchens for the women to work in, a bedstead for dear old "Rabbi Abun" himself, and a cozy "family room" where he gathers his brood together. It feels right; it feels as though you have been here before. Nothing here tells a lie; it merely prevents you from considering whether the people who built and inhabited this space might have meant it to house their shared labor rather than their kinship. Your hands and feet are deterred from exploring alternative uses of this house.

As with the history-park reconstructions of ancient Sepphoris and Qatzrin, so with the sociological and anthropological reconstructions that our scholarly imaginations visit while questing for the Nazareth of Jesus: the model can effectively conceal significant indigenous practices. The indigenous cultural terrain of Galilee can be falsified and utterly obscured if it is overlaid with a socio-economic conflict "model," or if it is glimpsed through the lenses of ideological interpretation or so-called honor-shame anthropology. Religious interpretations can be equally troublesome. The "dining rooms" of Sepphoris and Qatzrin have their Christian architectural analogues in the altars and communion tables of churches. The recently redesigned Catholic church at Nazareth, and the church now being constructed over "Peter's house" at Capharnaum, are two examples of modern-day architectural time machines designed to conduct visitors on guided tours of "the real past, just as it happened" amid the structures that now lie in ruins beneath them. All Christian churches, whether they are erected over a site in Israel or not, are built to be replicas of the event of the last supper of Jesus' life, as recounted in the Synoptic Gospels and Paul's letters. They are designed to work like time machines to transport people back into the remembered past and make that past real. Those who participate in the eucharistic ritual receive the somatic impression that they have been to "the table of the Lord." They are given to imagine that Jesus ate with his (male) friends around a table rather like the tables that they have at home.

In Galilean village dwellings of the first century, however, no dining rooms have yet been found that could accommodate such tables. Christian eucharistic practices, insofar as they are table practices, more likely have their roots in affluent urban villas equipped with triklinai. If one wishes to read a distinctive message out of the particular dining or feeding practices associated with Jesus of Nazareth, then one should first establish what food meant and how it was handled by everybody else from villages like Nazareth.

■ ■ ■

This chapter has explored the use of bodily following as a mode for interpreting material remains of the past. The literacy of space is referred to the pathways that people used as they traversed their built environment, together with the real and imagined trajectories of goods and values that wove their world. Considering examples from recent archaeology in the Americas and in Israel, we saw how motion made meaning. Motion, both real and virtual, is the key to recovering such meaning. Recovery differs from recursive reinscription. It does not occur automatically, nor does the process guarantee the success of the result. On the contrary, deception and illusion are constant dangers when we try to walk to and through the spaces meaningfully inhabited by our ancestors. Bodily following therefore requires critical awareness of intentionality as a factor operating both in today's scholarship and in the ancient world. The "objects" that we wish to recover from the past are the intentions of the ancient people, executed more or less effectively in the structures that they built, but often foiled or subverted by contrary intentions and resistive movements through those same structures.

Our recovery of early Jewish intentions and spatial practices continues in the next chapter, as we take a closer look at the engagement between Rome and Galilee in the centuries just after Jesus lived.

6 Spatial Management Strategies

IMPERIAL DESIGNS WERE INCISIVE. Some cuts merely divided; others channeled. This chapter demonstrates a practice of interpreting ancient designs by discerning how they worked. The chief questions that need to be addressed are these. What were the Romans trying to say and do by means of their architectural interventions in the Galilee? How did Galileans and Judean residents of Galilee respond? What material and rhetorical successes did each side have? By the time the Mishnah was compiled, in the early third century CE, do we have "two sides" related as staunch opponents, or do we now have uneasy partners cohabiting the land?

Hadrian reigned as emperor of Rome from 117 to 138 CE. Across Britain he built a wall from sea to sea, but across Galilee he built a road from port to market. Because the North Atlantic hostiles wanted nothing to do with empire, Roman policy in their regard was surveillance, vigilance, and separation. Hadrian's wall was a 73-mile elevated sentry walk for keeping an eye on hostile people. But the situation was quite different in Palestine. By the second century, many Galileans saw quite clearly the advantages of worldwide trade. Rome fortified their economic infrastructure for them. A strategic bypass along the ancient Legio-Acco road was laid down about the 120s, and it connected this major trade route to the heart of downtown Sepphoris' business district. The paved and colonnaded avenue crossing lower Sepphoris from southwest to northeast is thought to be a spur of this route. These contrasts notwithstanding, the wall and the road alike were incisions that left the scars of empire.

An item of material culture may promise one thing and deliver quite another, as the archaeologist Parker Potter has remarked. The road linking Sepphoris to the Mediterranean sea was supposed to bring the benefits of Roman civilization and commerce into the Galilean capital. Hadrian himself arrived by means of it to display his person and imperial power in a highly visible visit to the city about 134 CE. But roads run both ways. The covert function of the Roman roads, and of Galilee's complex connections into Roman world markets, was to siphon wealth out of the land. Roads had networked the Galilee from time immemorial, but the Romans resurfaced and graded them the better to accommodate wagons, which transport goods more efficiently than pack animals do.

More impressive even than the roads were the Roman waterworks. The establishment of Roman cities at Caesarea Maritima, Sepphoris, Tiberias, Gadara, Gaba, Hippos, and Bethsaida/Julias would require public baths. Caesarea's aqueduct brought fresh water to the seaside, while at Sepphoris two main channels running westward from the reservoir likely spanned the lower city, delivering spring water there and probably to the acropolis as well.

Americans run water mains underground. The Romans flaunted their hydraulics, with great stone arches leaping across valleys and through city neighborhoods in giant strides. Roman water at Sepphoris bounded up the hillside on huge lifting wheels, according to a rabbinic text (Ecclesiastes Rabbah 12:6), although no remains of that apparatus have yet been found. The visibility of those channels and machines was crucial to their social function. On a clear day, we are told, they could be seen from as far away as the lakeside city of Tiberias.

The rhetoric of water architecture had long been deployed for imperial persuasion in Palestine, starting with the Herodian dynasty in the first centuries BCE and CE. Herod the Great had built himself a little ocean in the Judean desert, filled up this toy from a branch of the Jerusalem aqueduct system, and staged mock sea battles there. He did this not just for fun, but to show that he had manpower and technology enough to waste on fun. The fortress Herodium, overlooking this nautical wonder, had its own independent water supply from winter rains caught in immense cisterns. Herod Antipas, raised in Rome and ruling in Galilee, was adept at the rhetorical use of water like his father before him. It was probably he who built the overhead aqueducts of Sepphoris, which must have been familiar landmarks to the rabbis in the circle of Judah ha-Nasi, framer of the Mishnah.

Water was at once a biotechnology and a technology of time. The urban management of water permitted large concentrations of population within the cities. Skillful utilization of storm runoff and of waste water enhanced agricultural fertility and supported groves of trees in and near the city. They provided aesthetic enjoyment as well as fuel.

Use of the city baths signified the Roman way of life. The practices of bathing gave structure to the daily routine of Roman citizens and their household personnel. People spent several hours at the baths: exercising, relaxing, grooming themselves, and doing business. Some cities had separate facilities for men and women; otherwise, women and little children generally attended the baths before noon, men between noon and nightfall.

The baths were staffed by crews of personal attendants, plumbers, engineers, and maintenance specialists, working in shifts. It has been estimated that a city's baths would employ a workforce third in size after those engaged in military administration and in construction. Their regular work hours and their occupational identifications organized their social identities. The workforce of the baths was only one of several industrial groups whose rhythms and methods of production were affected by the provision of Roman water. Textiles, ceramics, glassmaking, and tanning also could be upsized and regimented thanks to the availability of plentiful, reliable running water for the city workshops. In Galilee, the natural passage of time is marked by the alternation of two seasons: torrential rain and baking heat. Submissive to this divine time, traditional urban water systems had caught winter rainwater in copious cisterns, to be lifted out by hand or by animal power for the summer droughts. But now, seemingly contrary to divine plan, the Roman aqueduct ran independently of the season through the steady inexorable earthly power of gravity.

With roads and waterlines converging upon it, the Roman city itself was designed to connect these channels with neighborhoods. Streets were laid out in regular grids, with drains leading off into sewers. The grids defined blocks of *insulae* or multiple-family apartment dwellings clustered around courtyards. These dwellings did not necessarily house what we would term "nuclear families" or "extended families." In fact, their physical layout itself may well have contributed to the deterioration of traditional Galilean kinship structures as expressed in village housing patterns.

Urban dwellings, like village housing, served as workspace both for provision of food and clothing, and for craft production, agricultural processing, and business. Co-workers might live together, regardless of kinship. Traditionally in the villages, virtually all inhabitants would be at least distant cousins, each related and obligated to the others by several possible patterns of reckoning. In the city, this no longer was true, especially in Roman cities like Tiberias, which had been created by the forced resettlement of people from different localities. Moreover, traditional village housing was such that it could expand irregularly to accommodate family growth: a new daughter-in-law, a widow returning to her paternal home, a cousin's sons arriving to begin a business venture. But with the Roman urban *insula*, there soon was no more room to grow. The street grid had the tenements and neighborhoods tightly boxed in, and the walls did not support more than two stories. New residents, whether voluntarily or involuntarily occupying urban dwellings, found that traditional kinship connections in many cases simply could not be housed there. For lack of spatial realization, then, these relationships would have become less real.

Depending upon whether your village cousins had been a social advantage or a liability for you, the urban options for non-kin alliances could appear either as a family-eroding threat or as a golden opportunity. As alternatives to kin ties, the city offered novel architectural expressions of social identity and cohesiveness that could be chosen as a substitute for the cousin network. For example, the theater arranged its seating by social rank; various craft guilds sponsored their own baths; and the synagogue of one's choice might be that of one's geographical origins and/or business connections. In villages, one would expect business associations and craft-guild connections to form along kinship lines. In the Roman city, that need no longer be the case.

A city like Sepphoris was designed to be the economic interface of Galilee with the rest of the empire. The heart of the city was the basilica, a large hall in which the administrative, judicial, and financial interests of the empire were brought to bear upon the local community. Before there was a Roman basilica in Herodian Sepphoris, goods and services probably had circulated regionally among the towns and villages of the Galilee. People and produce also would have moved southward to Jerusalem at festival times, especially after the Hasmonean conquest. But then Roman cities were inserted like spigots to tap into those economic cycles and drain the system. One mechanism for this was taxation. Romans taxed the agricultural produce of the land, and they taxed commodities moving along the trade routes as well. Prominent local citizens were put in charge of raising revenues both for the imperial treasury and for local civic projects. They were held responsible for this liturgy or "people's service," and whatever they could not collect they had to make up from their own resources.

By the third century CE, this requirement was suppressing Galilean agricultural productivity in at least two ways. Some landowners abandoned their fields and fled in the face of insupportable tax debt. On the other hand, land was taken out of food production and used for raising sheep for wool, textiles being a better "cash crop" than wheat and oil, and in some cases being the required form of payment in lieu of severely devalued currency. This led to innovations in textile production, further altering the work patterns of both women and some men.

Taxation aside, the city was designed to interrupt the traditional local cycles of production and consumption. It extracted "surplus"—a euphemism for goods and labor that previously had been tied up at the village level. Seán Freyne has pointed out the cities, and the administrative functions that they brought to bear in Galilee, made commodities markets more efficient and boosted the economy of Galilee at a time when conditions in the empire at large favored these developments. But if we consider the construction and staffing activities mentioned so far, we can begin to appreciate the effect of Roman urbanization at the human scale. The Romans brought with them the plans for cities. They did not bring along all the workers necessary to cut and lay the stone, stoke the furnaces of the thermae, launder the bath towels, and weave the woolen cloaks for the infantry. Those people came into the cities to work from elsewhere in the Galilee and beyond. Significantly, they would have come from places where a kinship network insured that their general welfare would be provided for, to a place where their starving would diminish no one else's reputation. They came out of villages where the only way for wealthy people to enjoy the prestige of their agricultural surplus was to bestow it upon their poorer relations, into world market centers where "surplus" grain and oil now could be liquidated and transformed into material signifiers of luxurious lifestyle. Cities made consumption conspicuous. Moreover, in the cities the workers had to use wages to purchase food and clothing in shops, which entailed transportation and overhead costs previously unknown in village production. The relative ease of transport over the Roman roads brought Galilean urban consumers into direct competition with consumers in distant parts of the empire.

A further complication for Galilee was the manifold demographic and economic impact of the destruction of Jerusalem. Before 70 CE, while the Temple stood, a significant portion of Galilean produce went south to be sacrificed and eaten within the holy city during festivals, mostly by Galilean pilgrims on holiday. It may have gone in edible form, or it may have been redeemed and taken as money. Law and custom also required that specified portions of produce had to be given to the priests, the levites, and the poor. Only a few aristocratic families among the priestly and levitical castes lived year-round in Jerusalem; the others went there when it was their turn, for a week's service, about twice a year. Thus, before urban interference, tithes of produce had mostly stayed in Galilee for consumption by Galilee's local priests, levites, and poor people.

This system obviously helped to concentrate surpluses locally and regionally. It was disrupted by the abolition of Temple sacrifices and pilgrimage festivals, following upon the demolition of the Temple building itself. Afterwards, priests still retained their hereditary right to receive agricultural tithes, at a time when the roads opened up world markets for that produce while traditional strictures localizing its consumption had become impossible to observe. The wars of 66–74 and 132–135 likely enhanced the potential economic value of priestly kinship status, even while other kinship advantages were being eroded in various ways. Many priestly families emigrated to Galilee after Jews were expelled from Jerusalem in 135, and some were wealthy enough to buy land there. Small landowners in the first and second century were willing to sell, lured by the promise of waged jobs in the cities and not foreseeing the impact of the drastic inflation of currency that would befall their landless descendants after the middle of the third century.

Because it was there

Features of the landscape exhibit multiple layers of function. The roads, water lines, and city grids imposed upon Galilee both advertized and accomplished the Roman intention of bringing the benefits of imperial civilization into the province. These patterns were laid down upon the earlier template that the Judean conquest had imposed upon the land in the wake of the first-century BCE Hasmonean expansion, with the intention of unifying all Israelite territory under the Temple state. The successive material implementations of these two intentions—connecting Galilee with Jerusalem, and connecting Galilee with Rome—appeared on the surface to bring benefits to the land. But every gift had its price.

The impact of unification with Jerusalem may have been less socially disruptive than the subsequent Herodian makeover of the land. But the difference was one of degree. In the first century BCE, the Hasmonean administrators established hilltop fortified settlements in Galilee for surveillance of the highways. The housing units in these settlements were larger and more comfortable than those in the nearby indigenous villages. They seem to have had no marketplaces. But facilities for ritual bathing have been excavated at Yodefat and at Gamla in the Golan. The Judeans used cistern water in their settlements, but they also established the aqueduct carrying spring water to Sepphoris, which Herod Antipas and the Romans would later enlarge. Near their settlements are found comfortable villas, which may have controlled agricultural estates consolidated out of land previously owned by the Galileans who worked it. Industrial installations such as vineyards, olive oil presses, or the fish-processing facilities at Magdala produced commodities for distribution beyond the region. Building and running these enterprises would have drawn local labor away from traditional occupations. Apparently the Judeans introduced the practices of *ossilegium* burial into Galilee. The first identifiable synagogue buildings appear in Galilee and the Golan after the Hasmonean takeover.

This infrastructure made Galilee a satellite of Jerusalem. When Herod in turn brought the land of Israel under Roman hegemony, the Hasmonean installations were integrated into Roman marketing networks or converted to imperial service outright. Reviewing what has been said so far, the following chart compares the overt and covert effects of the chief elements of the Roman redesign of the Galilean landscape.

Herodian-Roman Landscape Strategy		
FEATURE	OVERT FUNCTION	COVERT FUNCTION
roads	import blessings of empire to Galilee: lifestyle enhancement through exotic cultural and material goods	apply pressures of world markets; produce becomes convertible to luxury goods; food leaves Galilee; labor redeployed to produce cash crops and exportable goods
aqueducts	improve hygiene and comfort, promoting greater population density and interaction	support new industries as incentive for labor to move to cities from land; display Roman power over the heavens and time
grid of urban streets and *insulae*	provide new residential neighborhoods, with good drainage	make kinship obligations and connections less visible and viable; geometric logic replaces logic of kin loyalties; move workers closer to where Romans need their labor
theater	entertain and educate city dwellers and visitors	introduce alternative cosmology and stories; assign social rank and affiliation through classified seating; promote fluency in Greek; open cultural windows to the world
basilica	provide a convenient central location for administrative and legal services and for market regulation	embody a bigger, stronger, more comprehensive regime for assigning obligation and identity, supplanting indigenous Galilean and Judean kinship practices

Clearly, the material effects emerging in the wake of modifications to the landscape differed alarmingly from the social promises that those innovations seemed to make. But analysis of material recursivity does not stop with a mere comparison of the overt and covert functions of the various spatial features of the urban landscape. It goes on to inquire how the indigenous people may have found ways to use the imperial built environment for their own purposes. It seeks to discern resistive uses of these spaces. Colonized people may devise various strategies of resistance, ranging from outright avoidance, to restrictive regulation, to incorporation of the new features into an updated version of their traditional spatial management systems. Moreover, colonized people don't always resist; they also collaborate to some extent with the colonial power.

For the collaborating class, imperial spatializations may efface the more traditional ones in part or in full. The next chart sketches some of the strategic indigenous responses to Roman modifications of the landscape; a fuller discussion follows.

Counter-Strategies of the Colonized

FEATURE	COLLABORATIVE ADAPTATION	RESISTIVE ADAPTATION
roads, opening world markets	land put to producing wool for taxes and export	avoidance of cities by villagers when possible; flight by estate owners
aqueducts, baths, urban factories	selective patronage of baths; move to occupations in urban crafts and retail	domestic *miqva'ot* for personal and industrial use; disparagement of "nonobservant" retailers
city streets, *insulae*; theater with three-tiered cosmos and segregated seating; basilica and urban market center	urbanization of the rabbinate; case law is developed to regulate relationships occurring in these venues	urban *bet midrash*: rabbinic schoolhouse re-colonizing urban space and time
Jerusalem Temple destroyed and overbuilt with a Roman temple	*miqva'ot* as defenses for hereditary right to tithes; the synagogue houses the official cult; sacrifices and localized consumption of tithed foods are abandoned	*miqva'ot* as defenses for purity of priestly kinship lines, with a view to restoring the Temple cult

This schematic comparison reflects three principles: that indigenous responses to colonization may be multifaceted and conflicting, that the distinction between resistive and collaborative spatial responses may be a matter of degree rather than kind, and that the passing of generations may modify and redirect the strategies of resistance and collaboration.

Roman roads and urbanization of the Galilee insured that, from the early first century onward, residents of the villages of the lower Galilee had opportunities to participate in the culture and business of the empire. Indeed, there were many incentives for them to do so. Yet it remained possible for individuals to withdraw aspects of their lives from the colonial spatializations and temporalizations produced first by the Judeans and then by the Romans. Like indigenous people in other situations of colonial contact that have been studied by archaeologists, Galileans could perhaps still manage their cuisine or their betrothals or their craft-apprenticeship practices according to traditional customs, while adopting Judean or Roman regimes for labor or for public religious observance or for the transfer of land and produce. Each sphere should be interrogated separately. Moreover, choice of which regime to follow might have varied according to season, or by age or gender. The archaeology of villages in Hasmonean- and Herodian-era Galilee has barely begun. It seems unlikely that the evidence will support the claim that villagers avoided the Herodian cities altogether, much less the Hasmonean fortified towns. More significant are the questions of which villagers went to those places, for how long, for what purposes, and with what immediate and long-term effects upon the indigenous patterns of village life.

At a slightly later period, roughly 70 to 200 CE, the rabbinic movement too was based in villages and seemed to be making its own detours around the Roman cities. The dispersion of rabbis among villages at this period made it impossible for them to promulgate a unified *halakhah*. Then, about the year 200, Judah ha-Nasi took the revolutionary step of relocating himself and his school to the city of Sepphoris. In some respects, this move was a concession to the realities of colonial existence and the inevitability of the cosmopolitan way of life. Thereafter, the Mishnah mentions rabbis in urban marketplaces and even in the baths as a matter of course. Any resistive avoidance of the city and its features has ended. But interestingly, some rabbis practiced spatial avoidance of synagogues; or, if they visited the buildings at all, they refused to pray there. The aspect of urban synagogue architecture that was offensive to those rabbis was the decorative figuration in the mosaics on the floors.

Establishing themselves and their schools in the urban environment positioned the rabbis to consolidate their authority and expand its scope. They effectively competed with the Romans for symbolic control of urban space and time, even while appearing to cooperate with them in the civil administration of urban affairs. Traditionally in Israelite theology, agricultural people had understood themselves to be owning and working the land in partnership with God according to the ancient

Mosaic Law. Now the urban streets, alleys, and *insulae* also became fields governed by Jewish law. For example, while residents sharing a courtyard might not be kin, a procedure is devised through which they can constitute themselves as a single household for purposes of sabbath observance. Furthermore, the rabbis determined that aqueduct water running through a common courtyard was not owned by anyone, and so could not be lifted on the sabbath; however cistern water was private household water and so might be carried on sabbath.

With a thousand little regulations like these, the rabbis took back the urban landscape. Symbolically, they re-colonized the built environment through which the Romans had first physically and psychologically colonized the land. Jews had lost Jerusalem and with it the possibility of celebrating festivals there together as one nation. But through reform of the calendar and the methods of calculating and announcing feasts, the rabbis attempted to synchronize national life. Rabbinic time resisted Roman time, not simply in the calculation of weeks and seasons, but more importantly in the manipulation of the future through the structure of finance, debts, and contracts. If you will, rabbinic Judaism mounted a nonviolent urban guerilla war against imperial space and time, from within.

The *amoraim*, or earliest rabbis, built a new kind of edifice in which to do this work: the schoolhouse or *bet midrash*. We have no specific information about the size or shape of these structures. Some supposedly were free-standing; others occupied rooms in homes or public buildings. The schoolhouse had a door and a doorkeeper, to whom students paid a daily fee for admission. This fee was to cover maintenance of the structure. The rabbi was not supposed to charge for his instruction, and rabbis supported themselves by a variety of trades and businesses.

This architectural innovation accompanied and facilitated the codification of the Mishnah. With it, a threshold was crossed here in several respects. The perceived competence of the rabbis was greatly expanded once it was housed in the urban *bet midrash*. Before 200, as Shaye Cohen has shown, the rabbis handled cases involving primarily matters of ritual purity and holy observances. Afterwards, they also exercised competence over civil matters such as marriages, the allotment of tithes, and disputes over ownership and use of property. Expertise in such business previously had been thought to reside in Jewish homes or with the elders and officers of the synagogue, whether village or urban. Thus, the rabbinic schoolhouse localized and concentrated the power to manage space: out of it came case law governing real estate transfers, travel, the maintenance of rental property, the shipment of agricultural produce, walls, boundaries, and courtyard relations.

The *bet midrash* also produced the means to manage time: regulations covering sabbath and festival observances, menstrual practices, loans, marriage contracts, and damages for injury resulting in loss of future earnings. This expansion of jurisdiction and consolidation of power was achieved partly through the rhetorical construction of the rabbi himself as expert and guardian of Judaism. It was both signified and accomplished by enclosing "the oral Torah" in a room with a door with restricted access. It was achieved, *spatially*, at the expense of discrediting other Jewish experts, such as mothers-in-law and farmers, and by gendering the voice in which the oral Torah would speak henceforth.

According to Dan Urman, the early rabbinic schoolhouse was architecturally separate from the synagogue as well as ideologically at odds with it. Only gradually would the two institutions merge. In the Roman period, Judaism does not yet express itself in the familiar European package where a synagogue is an institution with a rabbi, a study room, a prayer hall, and a miqveh.

Water as rhetoric

Like the *bet midrash*, the *miqveh* or ritual bath has an architectural history independent from that of the synagogue and shaped in part by Roman colonization. Also like the schoolhouse, the *miqveh* was to become a rhetorically powerful gendered space and an instrumentality for constructing gender relations in Judaism. The *miqveh* marked the taming and urban housing of a practice that otherwise was accomplished out of doors in wild water: in the sea, a river, or a spring. The evolution of the *miqveh*, in form and use, can be read as evidence of both resistance to Roman urban lifestyle and ingenious adaptation to it.

The basic function of the *miqveh* is to restore cultic purity to things and persons that have lost it, that is, have lost eligibility to participate in certain activities in certain places and/or with certain categories of people. Biblical requirements (Leviticus 11–15) were elaborated in the late Second Temple period to specify the design of the tank and the amount and kind of water needed for the bath. Ronny Reich found that stepped pools appear in great numbers in domestic contexts in and near Jerusalem, beginning in the middle of the second century BCE. Reich has also reported on larger water installations in industrial contexts that seem to have been used to insure the purity of oil or wine bottled for consumption in the holy city during festival times or by the resident priestly aristocracy.

Like Jerusalem itself, these industrial *miqva'ot* derive their economic significance from their cultic significance. The architecture asserts that purity regulations could be followed, and in fact have been followed, in the preparation of the product. This suggests that pilgrims and priestly families were two important "markets" for the bottled fluids. Those people needed to procure the specially prepared foods required by religious regulations connected with the sacred space of Jerusalem and the sacred actions that were performed there, according to the texts. Some industrial installations identified as *miqva'ot* have elaborate arrangements that seem to be designed to guarantee that vessels and persons emerging from the purifying waters will not accidentally touch those going down to enter the bath. Thus the architecture of the tanks is *rhetorical* insofar as its very existence was required in order to persuade buyers of the reliability of the bottling operation. This much is obvious, regardless of the complex problems of determining exactly who were attempting to observe purity laws, in which contexts, in which eras.

The overriding considerations in the design of the ritual bath are two: the kind of water supply that it uses, and the way in which that water is retained. In principle, the *miqveh* should be supplied directly from the divine hand—from rain, spring, or stream—without the intervention of any human instrumentality except that which passively catches and retains the water in a supply tank or in the bath itself.

This means that Roman aqueduct water as such is not suitable. Aqueducts are built rivers, with ingenious devices to hold back the water, let the sediment precipitate out, regulate the rate of flow, make the water run uphill by siphon, or lift it by machine. Roman fountains and baths manipulated water with a combination of gravity and pumps, producing effects that were aesthetically pleasing and hygienically beneficial. The Jewish population could have no moral or ethical objection to manipulation of water supplies as such. Water engineering at places like Megiddo and Jerusalem predated the Roman aqueducts by many centuries. The sheer hubris of the massive Roman hydraulics, supporting the lifestyle of the urban baths and theaters, may be the offensive note to which the *miqveh* become the counter-colonial antidote. The resistance built into *miqveh* practices is symbolic in nature. Poetically it reclaims the metaphors of rain and dew, familiar in the Psalms and the Prophets as vehicles for divine providential-salvific action. The urban *miqveh* simulates indoors a little of the wild, divinely managed hydraulics of the countryside, after that countryside itself has been subdued by gentile invaders and has had its substance tapped by their cultural practices and their global markets. The *miqveh* was perceived to be so potent that it could transform even aqueduct water by an ingenious mixture with living water.

Aside from their uses for expressing personal piety and for contradicting the secularizing rhetoric of Roman water architecture, the *miqva'ot* served a practical economic function. *Miqva'ot* enhanced the marketability of agricultural products and they figured into a system of managing labor. Reich suggests that workers at the bottling plants near Jerusalem were recruited from the doubtfully observant *'ammei ha-aretz* or people of the land, and were required to bathe when they arrived for work each morning in order to ensure their ritually correct status. The large, "industrial strength" pools excavated at several sites could accommodate this procedure.

The pools excavated at Sepphoris are smaller and occur in residences in the upper city. They came into use in Herodian times, contemporary with or soon after the founding of a nearby water-filtration installation that presumably was fed by the aqueduct and its lifting wheels. These houses were served by municipal drains and likely had aqueduct water. However they also had cisterns to store water collected from their rooftops during winter rains. We can no longer determine how the residents allocated their two water supplies. But there are suggestive parallels in Greek cities, where aqueduct water was favored for drinking while cistern water generally was used for household washing, for livestock, and for the needs of household industry. After use, "grey water" was not allowed to flow off into the sewers if it could possibly be reused. Greek bathtubs do not have drains, but at the foot they have little depressions in which water collects to be scooped out. But tubs of that kind have not yet been found at Sepphoris.

It would not be unparalleled, then, for residents of Sepphoris to have cisterns and non-drained stepped pools in their homes for light-industrial use: perhaps for textile processing and dying, ceramics, or spice and perfume preparation. Thus, the presence of a stepped undrained pool does not unambiguously identify a structure as the residence of ritually observant Jews. The two distinctive features of the domestic pools, their steps and their narrow but deep shape, can be accounted for as practical adaptations to climatic conditions. In very dry weather, the low surface-to-volume ratio of a deep pool minimizes evaporation. Yet, of course, the water does gradually evaporate throughout the dry season, so the stairsteps are necessary to provide access to the receding surface. In other words, steps need not indicate that people intended to climb down beneath the surface to immerse themselves. Likewise, cutting the pool into bedrock and covering or sheltering it are ways to keep the water cool and reduce evaporation; they need not be interpreted as provisions for modesty while immersing.

On the other hand, these Herodian-era domestic pools would comply with later rabbinic specifications for ritual baths. If they were indeed used in a practice of frequent ritual purifications, then we must inquire into the spatial implications of this use in the urban environment of Sepphoris. There are several levels to this inquiry. First, as with the bottling plants near Jerusalem, these pools could serve to enhance the *perceived* purity of a product intended for use in Jerusalem. Linens and woolens are one distinct possibility. For example, an ancient text known as the Infancy Gospel of James says that the young girl Mary was commissioned to spin and weave tapestry for the Temple in Jerusalem. Textiles and clothing may need immersion; see Ta'anit 4.8. Scribal industry is another possible use.

Second, the pools may be the boundary marker across which day workers must pass in order to shed the impurities of allegedly nonobservant village life before taking up the tasks of food preparation or craft production in the urban household. Third, the pools may be used to remove bodily impurity, particularly that accompanying menstruation. They would then form part of a technology designed to insure that heirs born in the household would escape suspicion of having been conceived unlawfully, by a *niddah* or menstruating woman. Thus, they would function to maintain "Jewishness" against threats from without and from within. From without, one's cultic status could be compromised by inadvertent consumption of improperly procured or prepared food. From within, the caste status of the household could be compromised by marriage to the daughter of a family that was careless in guarding the conditions under which conception was allowed to take place. For priestly lineages, this would endanger cultic status and the attendant economic prospects.

Ritual pools in homes seem to comprise part of a definition of Jewishness in which women constitute the permanent threat from within that never can be completely controlled. Women are always capable of adultery and of menstrual malpractice, and they can subvert the proper management of the home. The maintenance of kinship and caste requires the import of brides in each generation. But with each bride comes the risk that a defect in pedigree will enter the patriline. Therefore, bride-producers must have the means to offer rhetorical assurances that the girl knows how to manage a ritually pure household, wants to follow the rules of *niddah*, and will not commit adultery. No other guarantees besides rhetorical assurances are possible. These desirable and marketable behaviors cannot be *caused* by building walls for enclosure or baths for purification. The architecture itself must make a persuasive statement in stone that the girl has been raised right and will behave herself properly once married.

Textual evidence suggests that Sepphoris in early Roman times was home to families who married their daughters into priestly lineages, with alliances enduring for many generations. In several places the Palestinian Talmud mentions that Sepphorean women were exceptionally devoted to the Temple. Moreover, the resettlement of priests in Sepphoris after the destruction of the Temple makes better sense if the priests' fathers-in-law and maternal grandparents already resided there. This would be the case given a longstanding practice of bride-taking from the same matriline; that is, marrying boys to their maternal cousins.

The national hope of rebuilding the Jerusalem Temple made it vitally important to maintain the pure lineages of priests, insuring that there would always be a generation on hand to resume the Jewish cult. Just as the rabbis went to great trouble in the late second and early third centuries to remember and record every detail of the Temple ceremonials, they concerned themselves meticulously with guaranteeing caste status as well. Priests may not marry non-Jews, Jews of doubtful parentage, widows, divorced women, or victims of violence. The bride's family tree had to be certified free of any proscribed union for several generations back, and Sepphoris archived its marriage contracts so that bridal pedigrees could be thoroughly researched. Levitical lineage was carefully guarded as well, and a pure Israelite family tree was required for serving in many honorary civic positions, such as witnessing documents.

We may then plausibly regard Sepphoris as a recognized producer of high-caste brides. The Mishnah preserves a ruling that, when a town falls to a siege, all its women are rendered ineligible to marry priests (Ket 2:9). Sepphoris would have lost its bride crop once, in 4 BCE, when Varus took the city. Subsequently, in the revolt of 66–74, the fathers of Sepphoris avoided another loss by making a deal with the advancing legions. Their decision is congruent with the intention to insure that there would be priests for the future, by maintaining the eligibility of Sepphorean girls to conceive and bear them. This same intention is expressed in domestic ritual bathing facilities. Thus it might be said that the first stones for rebuilding the Temple were laid in the *miqva'ot* of Sepphoris.

An economic interest surfaces here as well. Independently of any hope for restoration of the cult in Jerusalem, priestly caste status carried the right to agricultural tithes. This would be a steady income that was sheltered from Roman taxation and protected from erosion by inflation of the coinage. Rome opened access to distant markets for priestly families, should it happen that they received more Galilean produce than their households could consume. Such families needed the right kind of brides if they wanted to maintain their entitlement to those tithes transgenerationally. Galileans reportedly were loyal to the religio-national tithing system. They willingly gave portions of their produce to priests, provided the lineage of the priests was securely established. Thus, priests' access to tithes ultimately depended upon their ability to mount a rhetorical defense of their caste status, especially their vulnerable matrilines. That defense was in part spatially and architecturally accomplished.

We see, then, that alterations to the landscape introduced by the Romans evoked various collaborative and resistive responses from the indigenous leadership of occupied Galilee. Those responses, in turn, altered the social realities of labor and gender management in the region. Once again, this can be indicated in schematic form and then discussed more fully.

Spatial Impacts on Labor and Gender Practices

FEATURE	LABOR DISPLACEMENT	GENDER DISPLACEMENT
roads, opening world markets	farms sold to absentee landlords; migration to cities; waged labor competes with distant markets for food	women and children tend fields in men's absence; women visit city for jobs or to sell produce and cloth; material "commodification" and symbolic "decommodification" of women's labor
aqueducts, baths, urban industrial shops	urban employment opportunities in service and manufacturing	increased social and industrial contacts among non-kin women
theater with classified seating; urban synagogues; basilicas	craft and geographical affiliations strengthened; kin identification weakened	women consume culture and religious discourse on an equal footing with men
urban rabbinic *bet midrash*	students leave home, take menial jobs to afford admission, and claim the tithe for the poor	"Judaism" becomes an expertise assigned to men; women lose competence in the ritual technologies of space and time
domestic *miqveh*	a threshold between "Jewish" urbanites and the "nonobservant" *'ammei ha-aretz* who work for them, assigning oppositional identity to each	the "threat from within" to caste status is foregrounded by this attempt to reduce it; basis of negotiation within marital sexuality

Our hypothesis is that connection with imperial world markets, through Roman cities and roads, encouraged Galilean farm laborers to move to urban jobs, producing the kinds of social displacements experienced in other urbanizing situations. But archaeology in Israel has not yet presented the kind of physical evidence that would confirm this. Such evidence as we have comes from reading the Mishnah and the Talmuds with an eye trained in economic and business analysis. The interpretive problem arising from the fact that these texts reflect and promote the interests of male household heads is increasingly recognized. Moreover, historical events can affect different sectors of society in different but related ways. Thus, this assessment of the spatial impacts on labor and gender practices is heuristic and is meant to indicate the kinds of correlations that might well be found.

The Roman alteration of the landscape increased the mobility of labor and commodified it. Men increasingly left the land for waged jobs in the cities. They now sold their labor, and at the same time they created a market for food, clothing, and housing. Women may have done likewise. But if women stayed on the land, perhaps more hours of their days now were spent in producing crops, textiles, and crafts. They may have visited the city markets more frequently, or they may even have commuted to regular jobs in town. "Commodification" of women's labor means colonization of their time. Industrialization, or the reorganization of society to promote efficient production at the expense of other institutions, could now tap into the hours that traditionally had been occupied with rearing the next generation, caring for parents, producing for home consumption, and/or social interaction with kinswomen. The city's markets and industries now had the power to take those hours away from those tasks, and channel them into production for distant markets. In itself this is neither good nor bad for women. However, it constitutes a real change in the gender system of the indigenous society. Aspects of that system were resilient enough to keep on replicating themselves at an ideological level in the face of real and far-reaching changes in the organization of women's work lives.

A spatial analysis highlights the probable social and cultural effects of workplace proximity for non-kin women, whether in single-gender working groups or mixed. In the shop it would become possible to form an identity and forge allegiances apart from one's family. But in an urban workplace one also lost the protection of a family. It is futile in Galilean excavations to try to identify "gendered space," if by that is meant rooms or buildings used exclusively by men or by women. While texts inform us that the rabbinic studyhouse was a men's house, we do not know what the *bet midrash* looked like, and furthermore we infer that not only women but most men as well were excluded from it. Similarly, texts inform us that the wealthier homes had women's apartments where men did not go; however, we also are told that old women, girls, and poor women did not have to remain inside those apartments, while male infants and little boys were at home there.

In short, architecture does not produce gender in any automatic or causal sense. It supplies the game board on which people, going by the rules of gender and kinship, produce novel plays. Their strategies sometimes even bring about alterations to the rules. The built environment provides for creative management of conflictive social relations. Sociological observation of those conflicts is not possible. However, contemporary ethnographic studies are suggestive. For example, the potential for using the *miqveh* in power negotiations between spouses is illustrated by the practices of a twentieth-century Israeli immigrant group. R. Wasserfall found that wives did not go to the *miqveh* unless and until "sent" by their husbands; but even if "sent," they might refuse or procrastinate. Thus, either party could apply psychological pressure to the other by delaying, advancing, or even forgoing the trip to the *miqveh* that was to signal the resumption of intercourse after menstruation. Wasserfall's women respondents associated the *miqveh* with the future health and welfare of the Jewish people.

In the Roman period, to maintain social identity amidst the spatial traumas of colonization, the gender system was both played and dynamically adjusted. Whether this meant that the burdens of colonization were allotted unequally between men and women must be decided on the basis of material evidence that has yet to be excavated.

Visualizing the contest for time

Empire extracted more than commodities from the Galilee. It took away time as well. Economic pressures redirected work hours away from local needs, channeling them into production and service for the sake of world trade and imperial administration. But Rome tampered with time on a grander scale, too. Highly visible Roman hydraulic power took control of water away from the heavens and the seasons, harnessing it by means of reservoirs and aqueducts. In cities the markets were geared to the festivals of the pagan Roman calendar. Rome's history overwrote all others. Having a national past and a national future was an indulgence not permitted to subordinated provinces of the empire. The present exigencies of Rome's imperial programs overrode national memories and dreams. In response, Jews redesigned gender and ethnicity counter-colonially, as means to re-take a Jewish past and a Jewish future from within the midst of the colonized present. As we have seen, material culture projected Jewishness into the perceived past and future, as a kinship woven in the regulated interplay of femininity and masculinity.

The spatial shock of empire upon the people of the Galilee consisted in their being forced to recognize that their region was a mere node in a worldwide network, rather than one pole of a world axis whose other pole lay just a few miles away in the holy city of Jerusalem. But Roman commerce opened a vista upon a universe, doing for the first century what Copernicus did for the sixteenth.

The visual tactic of pacification that the Romans used on Galileans was not conspicuous surveillance (as in Britain), but the dissolution of viewpoint induced by exposition of obscenely huge perspectives. Time contracted into presence, and the "here" dilated. The possibility of rapid contact with very distant lands threatens your sense of who and where you are, especially if exotic people from those distant places confront you daily in the urban commercial centers, eager to buy up and carry away the fruits of your land and your labors.

We have already reviewed some rabbinic strategies for reasserting symbolic control over time and space: sabbath regulations and distances, calendrical calculations, the laws of *niddah*. But there is also a visual dimension to the counter-colonial initiatives of early Judaism. They emerge in opposition to certain technologies of visibility built into Roman cities. These Roman visual technologies regulate urban behaviors by directing people's attention to certain material and cultural contents: by showing them things.

The Greco-Roman city is built for surveillance. Unlike modern "panoptical" domes, which look outward, Roman public architecture placed people so that their gaze was directed inward. In the theater people see imported dramatic productions, mimes, and orators; and more importantly, they see one another taking in those cultural products. The Roman dining room, too, is C-shaped like the theater. At formal meals the diners lounging on three sides of an open space are entertained by performers brought into the space from the open fourth side. (This contrasts with the older Greek dining practice, where the couches were arranged on all four sides of the room and the diners entertained themselves with their own conversation in that enclosed space.) Roman elite diners, like theater-goers, see one another consuming imported cultural fare. The city imposes other viewing opportunities as well: the colonnaded avenue for strolling and people-watching, and of course the markets and the baths. Visual intimacy with the bodies of strangers may have given Jewish men a new experience of their circumcision, a bodily mark that traditionally became visible only within the family circle at moments of celebrating kinship, family, procreation, and the future.

This visual colonization, enforcing alien perspectives on the far-off and the intimate, was not operative everywhere in the Roman city. Some spaces were closed to vision from and of outside: the hippodrome, the residential courtyard, the industrial workshop, the rabbinic schoolhouse (which cloistered the Torah), the cistern, the *miqveh* and its private water supply. Or more exactly, those spaces were visually closed while being pierced and tapped ideologically, economically, or socially, in intentional ways.

It is significant, then, that the architecture of the urban synagogue in the Galilee develops as an open C-shaped space where people can see and be seen, rather than as a visually closed but pierced space like the Temple. By late Roman times, synagogue buildings are designed to focus the reflection of people who place themselves around three sides of the room, to let them see one another seeing, and to make a cultural content available to them at the focal point of their gaze. What occupies the fourth wall in the synagogue is the Torah niche and the *bema* for reading and preaching. Thus, architecturally the Torah scroll is positioned to face the people in their C-shaped seating, closing their conversation circle. Unlike the rabbinic school house, the synagogue belongs to men and women alike. During the late Second Temple period, synagogues in the Land of Israel were multi-purpose community administration and service centers. They became places for scheduled public prayers and Torah reading only gradually, after the destruction of the Temple.

Synagogues were not designed to resemble the Temple. They focused the power of words, not sacrifices. Synagogues were analogous in structure to the Roman forms of the theater and the *stibadium*: a C-shaped space that produces vistas, and so both receives and dispenses cultural messages. The arc of the seating opens toward Jerusalem; and set into the floor at the focus of the seating, there are sometimes found zodiac mosaics. The zodiac presents reality in the broadest vista that it can possibly have: the stars in the heavens. The zodiac motif was imported from beyond the Roman Empire, from Babylonia. Its design reasserts divine order through a stable mapping of the seasons and their cycles of agricultural production.

The usual layout of a zodiac synagogue floor is a circle inscribed in a square. The circle encloses the pictures of the twelve star signs, arranged in a ring and correlated with the names of the months. The four corners outside it are occupied by female figures and fruits, which have been associated with four seasons. (This seems somewhat incongruous for Galilee, where there are only two major seasons; and the seasons in the mosaics sometimes are out of step with the star signs.) The deity is represented in a smaller circle at the hub of the wheel with the figures of the star signs around him, either feet in or feet out. In the zodiac mosaic, time stands still on the floor for people to gaze at it; time supports them as they walk across it.

This imaginative mapping achieves its stability by preserving the naturally differentiated annual phases of time, and also by naturalizing the civil calendar's cultural periodization of them. The zodiac's principle for organizing the year is sidereal, just as in the Roman and Byzantine civil calendar, whereas the Jewish liturgical year follows a lunar calendar, a calendar of months. Thus, the zodiac floor mosaic accommodates Jewish life to Roman time. But it does more. Spanning this floor, the synagogue building itself effectively traps secular imperial time with walls, contains it within the living circle of Jewish Torah reading, and makes it support Jewish business and community affairs.

This *architectural* co-opting of imperial time by the synagogue community and its mosaic floor contrasts with the rabbis' attempt to assert *liturgical* time control. Because lunar time cannot perfectly match solar/sidereal time (for full moon occurs every 29½ days), the religious year had to be adjusted occasionally to keep the festivals aligned with the agricultural seasons. In the Second-Temple period this had been done by intercalation. That is, the authorities in Jerusalem would sometimes have to add an extra month in the spring to slow down the religious year. Subsequently, the rabbis took over the management of religious time through the calculation of the festival calendar. Imperial administrators recognized the subversive potential of an indigenous alternative calendar, and during fourth-century persecutions the practices of calculating holidays and inserting the springtime leap month were suppressed.

Controlling the annual holiday calendar was a rabbinic strategy of resistance to the Romanization of time. In comparison, mosaic visualizations of time and deity upon the synagogue floors were also defiances of Roman time, even when in the mode of accommodating secular solar/sidereal months to religious lunar months.

Which strategy was the more "Jewish"? Do synagogue mosaics profane the sacred, as some of the rabbis grumbled, or do they decolonize and sanctify worldly reality? For the "spatial Torah" observed by the community that walks on time, such boundaries are permeable interfaces, reflecting the community's urban colonial experience.

■ ■ ■

This chapter has attempted to simulate a bodily following of some features of the Galilean landscape. We considered these features as strategic interventions implementing the complex reciprocal negotiation of colonization and resistance during Greco-Roman times. Imperial economic pressure was brought to bear through elements of the built environment such as roads, insular high-density urban housing, civic architecture, and aqueducts. Besides siphoning wealth out of the Galilee, these structures destabilized the indigenous management of labor and production through kinship networks, and played havoc with the spatial and seasonal symbolism of Jewish religious culture. Jewish architectural innovations that emerged at this era in the land of Israel, such as the *miqveh*, the urban rabbinic house of study, and the synagogue zodiac, should be read as adaptations offering symbolic resistance to the incursions of empire.

7 | Israel as Little Italy

WHEN JESUS WAS A BOY, the spatial resistances to Roman imperial presence in Galilee that we examined in the last chapter had hardly begun to take shape. Consolidation of a Judaism involving synagogues, rabbinic teaching authority, meticulous calculations of spaces and times, and the regular use of *miqva'ot* had not yet occurred. The Temple still stood and functioned in Jerusalem. Judean religious hegemony in Galilee was a relatively new development and was not securely established with all sectors of the local population. Judean civil authority had been overthrown several decades earlier by the Roman client king Herod the Great, who died about the time Jesus was born. Herod Antipas, who had succeeded his father as ruler of Galilee, was rebuilding the city of Sepphoris for his capital.

Jesus was born precisely on what might be termed the historical fault line between the Hasmonean expansion and the Herodian takeover, when the former colonizers of Galilee were undergoing colonization by Rome. He grew to manhood and discerned his own religious calling about the time that Antipas mediterraneanized the Sea of Galilee by building a new capital city on its shore.

To which of these factions did Jesus and his family belong? Were they indigenous Galilean villagers? Or was his mother, Mary, perhaps the daughter of a Judean administrator posted to the Hasmonean settlement at Sepphoris? Had she been one of the victims of violence during the Roman siege of Sepphoris in 4 BCE? Did the young man Jesus find employment in a lakeside construction project at Herodian Tiberias, or in the shipyards at the former Hasmonean facilities in nearby Magdala? In this chapter we consider some evidence that places Jesus within the Herodian sphere of influence, but affiliates him with the old Hasmonean-sympathizing Judean families in Galilee.

The name of another Mary, Mary the Magdalene, comes down to us linked with that of Joanna in a tradition about wealthy women who financed Jesus' operations, traveled with him throughout Galilee, and stuck around for the culminating events of his career in Jerusalem. Apparently the business details of promoting the gospel were handled behind the scenes by women whom today we would call managers or agents. They seem to have taken charge of Jesus' career, at a time when Antipas was developing the Lake region of Galilee as a tourist attraction, in furtherance of his geopolitical agenda.

Tiberias, in the 20s of the first century CE, was becoming an international commercial hub for the promotion of agribusiness and industrial expansion. Nearby Magdala was making necessary adjustments. Changes in the character of shipping on the Lake disrupted old alliances and opened up new opportunities. Contrary to pious belief, the friendship between Mary and Joanna probably was not the result of their prior separate encounters with Jesus as his clients or patients. Rather, circumstantial evidence suggests that common business interests first brought Mary and Joanna together and then led them to "discover" Jesus and promote his career.

The argument on circumstantial evidence is far from conclusive. But neither can it be dismissed out of hand. Geographical and political circumstances obviously cannot determine the course of a relationship between two individuals, Mary and Joanna. Yet, inasmuch as the gospel was a movement launched in real space and time, the events of its origin undeniably were influenced by geography and current politics. Although scant information about Mary and Joanna comes down to us, it is of the sort that permits some startling inferences.

Before considering what it means to place Mary at Magdala and Joanna in Tiberias—capital city of her husband's boss, the tetrarch Herod Antipas—let us begin with a simple question about the women whom all four Gospels associate with Jesus. A large group of women supporters is mentioned parenthetically, almost as an afterthought, by Mark and Matthew in the crucifixion accounts (Mark 15:40-1; Matt. 27:55-6). In Luke 24:49 the women are unnamed. Luke has first mentioned these women earlier in his narrative and has supplied their motive: they have been healed by Jesus (Luke 8:1-3). John also places a group of women at the cross (John 19:25), although he does not report that they supported Jesus' operations.

Why are these women *there*? What are they doing in the text? This "why" really has two levels. First, why was it that *after* Calvary, stories about women supporters were circulating in the Jesus movement? Second, why was it that *before* Calvary, certain women were supporting

Jesus? The first level is the "why" of a historical fact, for there is no doubt about the existence of the stories after Calvary. Those stories can be accounted for in various ways: as either straightforward memories, or theological constructions, or a mixture of the two. At this level, one might ask why only Luke mentions Joanna. A plausible answer is that Luke was most alert to the international scope of the tensions among Herodian and Hasmonean/Judean factions, and so either sought out or invented narrative elements such as the Herodian lady Joanna and the third phase of Jesus' trial, by Antipas.

However it is the second level of "why" that is most intriguing. Why were women involved with Jesus *before* Calvary? This "why" has to be investigated without having established beyond any doubt "the fact that" Jesus' activities were indeed financed and managed by women in general and by Mary and Joanna in particular. There is no way to secure that as a fact; we have to accept it as a premise. But if Luke's premise is true—the premise that there was a Mary from Magdala, that she associated with the wife of the viceroy of the tetrarch Antipas, and that together they supported Jesus—then geographical and archaeological information can be used to fill in some gaps in the puzzle of the origins of the Jesus movement.

Partners in management

Generally, the role assigned to the women supporters of Jesus in the Gospel texts is a function of location. In Galilee, they finance his operations. In Jerusalem, they witness the climactic events of his career: the cross, the burial, the emptied tomb, the appearances of the Risen Lord.

Accordingly, Luke yokes Mary with Joanna in the Galilean role of financial backer. (In Luke 8:2–3, both have been healed by Jesus and both use their resources to provide for Jesus and the Twelve.) Luke also partners Mary with Joanna to witness in Jerusalem: they inform the Eleven about the events of Calvary, the burial, and the significance of the emptied tomb. (While the polite convention of anonymity for the women is honored in the narrative of Luke 23:49–24:9, v. 10 discloses that the group has included Mary and Joanna all along.) Neither in Galilee nor in Jerusalem does either woman act alone. They are portrayed as partners in the midst of numerous women associates, both named and unnamed, as they perform first their Galilean financial functions and then their Jerusalem witnessing functions.

But Luke has associated each of the women with another group as well. Mary represents the lakeside town of Magdala, also known as Tarichaeae. Joanna is the wife of the chief of staff of Herod Antipas, tetrarch of Galilee and Perea. In the early decades of the first century CE, the Herodians and the Galileans were distinct and opposed factions in a tense and deteriorating political landscape. The Herodian dynasty came to power in 37 BCE with Antipas' father, Herod the Great, who out-maneuvered the Hasmonean leadership of the Jerusalem Temple-state, and who made at least ten strategic political marriages for himself. On his way to the top in Judea, Herod the Great had married Mariamme, the daughter of the Hasmonean ruling family.

When they betrothed Mariamme to Herod in 42 BCE, the Hasmoneans were in the waning days of a century of administration. Judean independence from the Seleucid Empire had been achieved through the popular revolt led by Judah "the Maccabee" 167–152 BCE, with the establishment of an independent Temple-state under Judah's brother Jonathan in 160 and recognition by the Roman Senate about 139 BCE. The Maccabees took over the high priesthood as well as civil power. Thereafter, the family of the Maccabees, called Hasmoneans, extended Judean control northward into Galilee and the Golan again after many centuries of Galilean independence from Jerusalem. The brothers of Judah "the Maccabee," Jonathan and Simon, were the first two rulers in the line of "Hasmoneans." The term Hasmonean came to apply to their administrative officers as well as their kin. Thus, by 104 BCE, about a century before Antipas and Jesus lived, the Hasmoneans had newly imposed the economic and political hegemony of the southern Temple-state upon the northern territories that previously had followed a decentralized form of Israelite religion.

The Judeans took over Galilee by force and they ran it through a network of fortified administrative centers, as Richard Horsley has persuasively argued in several recent works. That is, Judean garrisons were placed within line-of-sight signaling distance of one another at strategic locations: Sepphoris and Yodefat on opposite hilltops surveilling the Bet Netofa Valley; Gush Halav (Gischala) in the mountainous northwest along the route to the Mediterranean port of Tyre; Gamla in the Golan at the far northeast corner of their territory to monitor travel between Damascus and the Lake region; Qeren-Naftali above the northern Jordan River; Magdala on the shore of the Lake itself, and so forth. Through those towns, the Jerusalem administration projected power northward and extracted tithes southward, gradually effecting the integration of Galilee and the Golan into the Temple state. Judean officials and their families had to be stationed in the north to carry this out. Meanwhile, Judea extended its political hegemony south and east as well.

The indigenous Galilean society in which the expatriate Judeans took up residence already shared their basic religious orientation: to the laws of Moses (though perhaps not in written form); to the prophetic traditions (especially the Elijah stories); to the practices of festivals, sabbath, circumcision, almsgiving, and tithing (involving local cultic personnel); and to Israelite kinship customs (including the reckoning of inheritance and descent). The Galileans probably did not share the Judeans' enthusiasm for the Davidic capital, Jerusalem, or for the institutions of the Temple and its royal messianic cult. Galilean villages probably did not blanket Galilee but existed alongside settlements of other ethnic-cultural heritage, perhaps in an overall sparsely populated interior between Carmel and the lakeshore.

The Hasmoneans, although apparently well loved in Judea, lost their grip on this extended domain through a series of political mishaps in which they were outmaneuvered. In 42 BCE they attempted an alliance through marriage with the rising strongman Herod, who would become known as "the Great" because of his political and architectural achievements and who was already in favor with the Romans. At the time, the betrothal of Mariamme to Herod looked like a good solution. Herod was not Judean, but Idumean; that is, he was from a people who had been forced to accept circumcision and the Judean laws in his grandfather's generation.

It would be anachronistic to ask whether Herod or anyone else was "Jewish" at this time. The word *Ioudaios* means "Judean" in ancient texts like Josephus and the Gospels. Outside of Palestine, this term could be applied to anyone from Judea, Samaria, Galilee, Idumea, or even beyond, especially if the person observed sabbath and the festivals. Inside Palestine, the term was used more precisely, and regional variances in Israelite religious practices were recognized. In modern English, the term "Jewish" connotes a history of religious development that had not yet happened in the first century BCE. Judaism (or, Judaisms plural) was still in its formative period.

The offspring of the arranged union between Herod and Mariamme would be "legitimate" according to the laws of Moses, as interpreted in Jerusalem. The children would be the legacy of both Herod, with his imperial connections, and of the Hasmoneans, with their popular local Judean support. Mariamme did bear five children. Two of her sons grew to manhood. But Herod had ambitions beyond Judea, and in 29 BCE he had Mariamme murdered. He also murdered her young brother Aristobulus, whom he had appointed high priest in 35 BCE, as well as his own two sons by Mariamme, in 7 BCE. This brought an end to the Hasmonean dynasty and lineage as such.

Nevertheless, Hasmonean personal names continued to be associated with hopes for Judean independence, and many nationalistic Judeans named their babies John, Simon, Judas, Salome, or Mariamme. In a meticulous study of the frequencies with which particular names occur in ancient inscriptions and documents, Margaret Williams found that the Hasmoneans' personal names became suddenly much more common in first-century Palestine, while in the contemporary Diaspora they became less common. She suggests that this discrepancy might indicate that Diaspora Jews did not wish to associate themselves with the destabilizing nationalistic sentiments that were surfacing in Judea.

There were plenty of Hasmonean nationalists in and around Jerusalem, as well as in the far-flung administrative towns of Galilee and the Golan. Herod the Great nominally controlled those towns, with backing from the Roman Empire. But the Herodian administration had to deal continually with the Hasmonean faction, which included Jerusalem-based elite priestly families with extensive agricultural holdings, economic power, and (in Judea) popular support. Unsurprisingly, civil unrest broke out at the death of Herod the Great in 4 BCE, but was suppressed with help from Roman legions.

Demography and Galilean landscape

As we have seen, there were at least three identifiable social factions in the Galilee of Jesus' childhood: Herodians, transplanted Judeans, and indigenous Galilean villagers. Since this was the ancient Near East, individuals did not affiliate with these groups at will; rather, people were born into them, married into them, or, especially in the case of the Herodians, entered them in servitude and perhaps rose to positions of relative power. Who were these people? Let's take a closer look.

(1) GALILEANS were the portion of the indigenous population descended from Iron-Age Israelite stock. That is, they were villagers whose ancestors were overlooked for various reasons when the Assyrians deported most of the Israelite population in the eighth century BCE. In addition, there were probably roadside settlements in subsequent centuries by people of different backgrounds. There is insufficient evidence to support claims that Galilee was "empty" or "abandoned" from the seventh through the second centuries BCE. Indigenous Galileans farmed their ancestral plots of land; herded sheep and goats; produced wine and oil for local consumption; fished in Lake Kinneret (the "Sea of Galilee"); lived in villages; practiced trades such as weaving, pottery manufacture, or masonry; exchanged products with households in other villages by means of traveling peddlers or hucksters; and maintained their Israelite identity by following Mosaic

law concerning festivals, marriage, inheritance, and the distribution of produce to kin, to the poor and to local priests.

Speaking an Aramaic dialect, indigenous Galileans would have managed community affairs through traditional institutions like a circle of elder men or a network of senior women, each with its proper sphere of competence. Every member of a village could reckon himself or herself kin to every other member, through multiple lines of relation; the customary kin-based procedures for redistribution of commodities would be clearly recognized. The difference between the richest and the poorest member of the village could never be very great.

The archaeological signature of indigenous habitation sites has not yet been established. This lack has permitted the hasty conclusion, on the basis of surface pottery finds, that Galilee was unpopulated before the Hasmonean influx. An indigenous Galilean site would have to include traces of the villagers' cuisine, their manufacturing, and domestic architecture adapted to accommodate their complex extended kinship structures. There is no reason to expect that Galilean villagers built "public" community centers, whether for educational or political or economic or religious uses. Their "synagogues" were not buildings. They had no need of market squares either, for they had no conceptual means of defining anything as "surplus."

(2) JUDEANS in Galilee of the first century CE were the descendants of Hasmonean administrators, with connections to the Jerusalem aristocracy. They include some members of the priestly and levitical castes. They cluster in the areas around the former Hasmonean outposts, where they still have control over agricultural estates consolidated in the previous century out of small indigenous ancestral holdings. They regard the Galilee as a province in a land whose capital is Jerusalem. Even though political administration of the land was divided among sons of Herod the Great after 4 BCE, so that Jerusalem is no longer in political control of Galilee, David's city remains the religious capital for the Judeans in the north. They return there for festivals, and they maintain family ties with their associates in the south through intermarriage.

In the late first century BCE and the first decades of the common era, the descendants of the Hasmoneans are working out a *modus vivendi* with the new Roman-backed Herodian party. But resentment smolders. The transplanted Judeans harbor nationalist sentiments, and while collaborating with the Herodians they find ways to subvert and impede Herodian projects as well. They seek to undo the annihilation of the Hasmonean dynasty symbolically by naming their daughters after the last Hasmonean princess, whom Herod the Great murdered. The name "Mary," previously uncommon in Palestine, suddenly becomes popular just after the murder of Mariamme and her sons. Therefore, this name may serve as an index to families who support a return to Hasmonean-style Jerusalem-based rule and who oppose Herod, the emperor's man. If so, then the mother of Jesus probably came from a Hasmonean family or from nationalists who were Hasmonean sympathizers. Nazareth lay close within the orbit of the Hasmonean administrative outpost at Sepphoris.

The archaeological signature of Hasmonean habitation would contrast with that of indigenous Galilean villagers in some ways, but not in others. Their cuisine and their household equipment (pots and tools) would be quite similar, for they would have been locally acquired. But there would also be some luxury goods, such as imported fine ceramics. Their housing and its decoration would be larger and finer. Unlike Galileans, they might have *triklinai*, dining rooms furnished for reclining at formal meals. Traces of Hellenistic design are to be expected, since Hasmonean material culture in Judea was already influenced by Greek Mediterranean motifs in the first century BCE. As we have seen, *miqva'ot* or ritual baths are first found in Galilee and the Golan within Hasmonean-era settlements.

Hasmonean fortifications and housing in Galilee would be found beside or overlaid upon indigenous Galilean villages. The Hasmoneans, with their international connections, might very well have enlarged existing indigenous industrial installations in order to produce goods for export: fishpacking, oil and wine bottling, weaving. They needed warehouses, arsenals, and granaries. Galilean villagers, on the contrary, would simply store grain for the year in large jars in each household, to be shared with kin in time of need. They did not stockpile it. Large collection facilities like the vaults in the lower city at Sepphoris are an indication that taxation, foreign trade, or both have been imposed upon the land.

The Hasmoneans likely improved the roads somewhat as well. It makes sense to look for public buildings—"synagogues"—in Hasmonean sites, because of their administrative character and because the preexisting local indigenous social institutions of the villages did not belong to these expatriate Judeans or welcome them. With the Judeans also came the first need of organized and dedicated market spaces in the growing towns of Galilee, in order to provide for exchange of goods among people who did not regard each other as kin.

(3) HERODIANS were the officers of administration in the court of Herod the Great and, after 4 BCE, in the court of his son Herod

Antipas. They ruled on behalf of the Romans. They built in the Greco-Roman style: temples, theaters, market fora, colonnaded avenues, baths, hippodromes, harbors, roads, villas, stupendous mountain fortresses, swimming pools in the desert. Their kinship practices were opportunistic. The multiple intermarriages between pairs whom we would consider uncle and niece, or brother- and sister-in-law, were driven by geopolitical ambitions more often than by lustful whim. The same may be said for their interfamilial murders. They were inventive compromisers. Herod the Great had masons trained from the priestly caste so that he could Romanize the Jerusalem temple without violating religious taboo. Among his other architectural accomplishments was the harbor city of Caesarea on the Mediterranean coast. His son Antipas refurbished the inland town of Sepphoris as his first capital after 4 BCE. About two decades later, Antipas built Tiberias as an entirely new capital city on the shore of the Kinneret. At this period, the non-indigenous non-Judean population of Galilee also was growing, due in part to international commerce and to retirements from the imperial legions.

Herodians were thoroughly hated throughout Judea and Galilee as interlopers and as the agents of Roman power. Yet they were a fact of life. You could not beat them, but there were various ways of joining them and working out some viable accommodation. Intermarriage was one way. Although the royal Hasmonean attempt to forge a high-level alliance through betrothal eventually failed, still it indicates that brides like Mariamme functioned as more than passive pawns in the power game.

This brings us to a Herodian lady of the first century CE, Joanna. In Luke's Gospel, she is the link between the Herodians and the Jesus movement. This fact is largely overlooked in recent scholarship. But Ben Witherington remarks that the mention of Joanna, possibly the source for Luke's information, shows that the gospel has penetrated the court of Antipas. The obvious inference would be that Joanna herself was its agent.

If Luke is essentially correct about this connection, the reader is confronted with something puzzling. The wily Antipas very much wants to meet Jesus, but somehow he is prevented from seeing him. Luke asserts that Herod Antipas is interested in Jesus, whom he regards as an entertainer, and is even favorably disposed toward him. Yet Antipas' curiosity is thwarted, and Jesus is kept out of his clutches all the while that he operates in Galilee. Antipas does not get his hands on Jesus until Pilate, the Roman prefect himself, sends the prisoner to the tetrarch for trial in Jerusalem. (This is essentially Luke's version of how Jesus' career reaches its climax. In Luke 9:7–9, Antipas hears about Jesus' activities and his curiosity is piqued. In Luke 13:3 the Pharisees warn Jesus to flee because Antipas wants to kill him, but Jesus sends a taunt back to the tetrarch. In Luke 23:6–12, "Herod was delighted to see Jesus. In fact, he had been eager to see him for quite some time, since he had heard so much about him, and was hoping to see him perform some sign.")

Antipas earlier had no trouble detaining John the Baptist. The baptizer's name, John, is one of those favored by Hasmonean nationalist sympathizers. In fact, "John" or *Iōannēs* is the masculinely inflected form of the name "Joanna" or *Iōanna*. Indeed, Luke provides this John with Jerusalem connections and a priestly lineage on his mother's side as well as his father's (Luke 1:5–25, 57–63). Intra-caste marriage, like that which Luke attributes to John's parents Zechariah and Elizabeth, was a means by which the leading priestly families concentrated their power. Although Zechariah is not permanently resident in Jerusalem, neither has he married a woman of mere Israelite or Levite ancestry. This detail of Luke's story tends to corroborate the suggestion that Hasmonean sympathies prompted Zechariah's preference for the name John, which none of his kin had previously had.

Although Antipas easily seizes John, Jesus seems to have had a powerful and effective protector on the inside of Herod's court. Apparently he needed one, because Luke reports that Jesus' own attitude toward Antipas was rather foolhardy. If Jesus had a protector inside the Herodian inner circle, as Luke implies, most likely she was Joanna.

The fact that women were powerful and active in Antipas' court is further attested by the role of Herodias in determining John's fate. It is no less plausible that Joanna protected Jesus, than that Herodias engineered John's arrest and execution (Matt. 14:1–12; Mark 6:14–28; Luke 3:19). To anyone advocating a return to Hasmonean-style national autonomy, Herodias' breach of the marriage laws portended something much more disastrous than the waywardness of an ordinary woman. Herodias was the granddaughter of Herod the great polygamist and Mariamme, which means that her grandmother's grandfather had been the Hasmonean high priest Hyrcanus. But Herodias' own grandfather Herod, who had murdered her father, then chose to become her father-in-law as well by betrothing her to another of his sons (Josephus, *Ant.* 17.1.2.). Accordingly Herodias, descendant of the Hasmonean priestly line through the princess Mariamme, was married into the lineage of the *other* Mariamme: one of the series of out-caste women who had taken Herodias' grandmother's place as Herod's wife; Mariamme "the second," whose father had been installed in the high priesthood by Herod after he deposed the Hasmonean priestly line. In Herodias' children, then, royal-priestly Hasmonean blood would mix with that of usurpers of the priesthood. (In fact, this would be the lineage of the daughter who danced for the party-goers in Matt. 14 and Mark 6, a distasteful detail omitted by Luke.) Herodias later switched husbands—keeping the same father-in-law, interestingly enough. Offspring of this second marriage, to Antipas, would mix Hasmonean blood with that of the Samaritan mother of Antipas. Presumably, this prospect was even more offensive to nationalists who regarded the Hasmonean dynasty as the last hereditarily legitimate rulers of Israel.

Thus, the Hasmonean nationalists, the Herodians, and the indigenous villagers related in complex, conflictive, and sometimes collaborative ways in the Galilee of Jesus. The picture was surely much more complicated than can be summarized here. We must conclude, however, that the significant frontiers in that society were not drawn between "Jews versus Romans" or "aristocrats versus peasants" or "village versus city," conceived as simple oppositions. Those clichés are inadequate to the data.

Magdala and Tiberias

The Gospels provide little direct information about Joanna and Mary, the patrons of Jesus. But historical and archaeological sources allow us to make some inferences about what it meant to be "the wife of Herod's viceroy." We can also determine with some confidence what it meant to be known as being "from Magdala" in the first century.

Magdala lay on the western shore of Lake Kinneret, three miles north of Tiberias (the modern city, continuously inhabited since its foundation by Herod Antipas about 18 CE). Josephus calls it "Tarichaeae" after its famous export commodity, salt fish. *Taricheiai* are factories for salting fish, or for pickling, salting, or otherwise preserving any food. The verb *taricheuō* means to pickle or smoke food, or to embalm a human body. Salt would have to be imported in bulk overland to the Lake from the Dead Sea in Judea, and this connection would have been facilitated after the Hasmonean conquest of Galilee. In fact, a Judean family could achieve what we would call a vertical monopoly over the salt, the fish, the processing, and the shipping. A tower in this lakeside town could have been a smokestack or simply a landmark on the shore for the fishing vessels. The Aramaic name of the place likely comes from the word for tower, *migdal*.

The material remains of the first-century habitation at Magdala are scant, but they fit the suggested profile for a Hasmonean site. There was a small (18' by 21') colonnaded hall, later converted to a city fountain house, apparently. Textual references indicate that the city had a shipyard and facilities for processing fish. Josephus, a Judean of priestly caste, found sympathizers here when he was leading a rebel army against the Romans during the First Jewish War (66–73 CE). The picture of Magdala that emerges is that of a thriving busy town organized to support its export industry. If Hasmonean encroachment in the first century BCE had pushed peasants off their ancestral farms in the hills and valleys to the west, they could have found new livelihoods in Magdala as shipwrights, net makers, fishers, and fish packers. Not only was the Lake the source of fish, it was also the route for shipping jars of pickled fish across to the ports on the eastern shore that connected with trade routes going north and east to Damascus and on into Babylon. Coincidentally, the region is spectacularly beautiful, especially in the springtime.

As noted above, the name Mary was given to girls in the generation ahead of Jesus' as a nationalistic gesture of protest against Herod. The Hebrew name comes from the Torah, and is that of Moses' sister Miriam. In the Septuagint the name is spelled *Mariam*, with no accent and no inflection. Josephus adds the inflectable ending, *Mariammē*. In Latin, the name became *Maria*; in English, *Mary*. As Williams points out, the nationalistic overtone may not have been consciously embraced. The name may also have been increasingly coopted by the Herodians. One of the later wives of Herod the Great himself was named Mariamme, or perhaps took that name to ennoble herself and to reinforce Herod's elevation of her father to the office of high priest, which previously had belonged to the Hasmonean Mariamme's family.

Thus, Mary of Magdala may well have been old enough to be Jesus' mother. An older woman would have had greater status and greater freedom to travel. And this Mary must have traveled, for no one calls you "Magdalene" in Magdala. Significantly, this Mary is not called (in Greek) "Mary of Tarichaeae"—"Pickleworks Mary"—but is identified by the indigenous Aramaic name of the place. Later rabbinic texts refer to the town as *Migdal Nunya*, "tower of fish." So, why is "Mary from Fish-Tower" going abroad in Galilee? Plausibly, she is conducting business related to the export of salt fish. This occupation is well attested for women in early Roman Palestine. Herod the Great regularly did business with women who were wholesale suppliers of provisions. The names of three businesswomen were found at Masada on the labels of food containers in the fortress's massive storage vaults, as Hannah Cotton and Joseph Geiger have recently reported. In any event, the association of this Mary with Magdala is circumstantial evidence that her parents, who presumably named her, belonged to the well-to-do, Judean-sympathizing, anti-Herodian faction in Galilee.

Magdalenes had reason to shun the Herodians in the new resort city of Tiberias, planted just an hour's stroll down the beach from their harbor town. Hasmoneans arriving from Judea apparently had established themselves at Magdala about a century earlier and had expanded the village comfortably to suit their administrative and business needs. Assuming a common basic religious heritage and kinship customs between Judeans and Galileans, that transition may be imagined as a relatively smooth one, though there would have been economic conflicts and frictions over land ownership. But the foundation of Tiberias in 18 or 19 CE brought more drastic changes to the region's administration and its landscape.

Tiberias was erected from scratch and populated with involuntarily displaced peasants, artisans, traders, foreigners, and whomever else Antipas could grab. Why did he go to the trouble of building himself a spanking new capital on the shore of the Lake, when he already had adequate facilities in the beautiful inland city of Sepphoris? The answer is to be sought in the geopolitical ambitions of the Herodian dynasty in general and of Antipas in particular. Antipas controlled less territory than his father had. He lacked a Mediterranean port. The Jordan River was the eastern border of his northern territory, Galilee, and it was the western border of his southern territory, Perea. Antipas did not care about the land as such; he cared about how people crossed it on their way to and from Jerusalem. Jerusalem was a worldwide pilgrimage center, thanks in part to the magnificent Temple enlarged and renovated by Herod the Great. Travelers disembarking at Herod's new Mediterranean port of Caesarea—that is, those arriving from Alexandria, Rome, and other western imperial cities—were received and entertained in palatial facilities before proceeding on their journeys east overland toward Babylon or south to the Temple city by the coastal route.

But Antipas, unlike his father, did not control either Caesarea or Jerusalem. His capital, Sepphoris, was off the beaten path and apparently could not attract the elite imperial pilgrims approaching the Temple city from the west. And from the east, travelers arriving from Babylon and Damascus were bypassing Antipas as they entered the Decapolis region on the southeast lakeshore, proceeded down the eastern bank of the Jordan, forded at Scythopolis without entering Perea (Antipas' other territory), continued south along the river to Jericho and ascended westward toward Jerusalem.

To divert and capture this traffic, Antipas needed to give elite travelers a reason to sail across the Lake. He chose the site for Tiberias on the southwestern shore opposite the gleaming hilltop city of Hippos / Susita. At night the lights of Tiberias would shine out across the black water like those of Hippos, visible as far as Bethsaida and Capharnaum on the northern shore, according to Rousseau and Arav. The voices of party-goers could also be heard across the waters, disrupting the fishing.

Antipas built an attractive cliffside palace to entice elite travelers to tarry with him on the way to and from the Temple city. The remains of that palace have not been identified in the archaeological record; however the textual record indicates that it was decorated in the finest imperial style. At Tiberias, Antipas would be the first to greet elite Babylonian tourists on their arrival in Eretz Israel and the last to bid them farewell as they returned home. Presumably, more modest commercial and civic facilities—synagogues, perhaps—would accommodate travelers who were not quite important enough to be Antipas' guests at the palace itself. Besides the obvious gains in international prestige, this would open up opportunities for business contacts not just for the Herodians, but also for any local agricultural or food-processing interests astute enough to get a piece of the action.

Antipas also entertained at the palace of Machaerus in his other territory, Perea. Machaerus was just 30 miles from Jerusalem, and part of the journey was a pleasant cruise across the Dead Sea. Sea travel, even for just a few miles, was not only more pleasant than travel by desert roads; it was also stylishly "Greek" and "Alexandrian." In this respect, the cities of Caesarea and Tiberias had the maritime advantage over the sometime capital Sepphoris, with its one puny little municipal swimming pool.

Antipas was not the only one who wanted to influence the pilgrims coming and going along the Jordan valley. John the Baptist positioned himself and his challenge to Herodian authority right on the banks of the Jordan, astride the pilgrimage route. This confrontation was the context for Jesus' own baptism.

At Tiberias, Antipas would need to arrange entertainments for wealthy business travelers and their families. His staff, supervised by Chuza, would take care of this work. Since pilgrimage was a socially acceptable motive for women to travel along with their husbands, it is likely that Chuza's wife shared responsibility for arranging hospitality for entire families. This is all the more likely if Joanna had family connections in Judea, site of the Temple and its pilgrimage facilities, but Chuza did not. Chuza's name is known to us only in the transliteration that Luke gives us: *Chouza*. It is probably an Idumean name. Herod the Great was of Idumean heritage, and the region of Perea remained a power base for Antipas. Josephus mentions an Idumean deity named

Koze (*Ant*.15.253), and an administrative officer of Herod the Great, Costobar, is said to be from the lineage of the priests of Koze.

But "Joanna" is a nationalistic Hasmonean name: *Iōanna*, feminine form of *Iōannēs* or "John." The betrothal of Joanna to Chuza may have been arranged with the same sort of political intentions as the betrothal of the Judean Mariamme to the Idumean Herod one generation earlier. Joanna's marriage may have been intended to forge an alliance between an elite Judean family and one of the first families of neighboring Idumea or Perea.

We then have at least three quite plausible reasons for Joanna to come into contact with Mary Magdalene. (1) Both apparently were born into families with nationalistic Judean sympathies. Perhaps they had even been girlhood friends and their friendship continued during their marriages. (2) Joanna may have assisted Mary to make international business connections through the court at Tiberias. (3) Mary may have assisted Joanna in hosting elite visitors on tours of local sights such as the packing facilities at Magdala, or in pleasure cruises on the Lake. A fourth possible connection is suggested by Luke, who says that both Mary and Joanna were cured of illness by Jesus. There are hot springs at Tiberias. It is not unlikely that the palatial Herodian resort included something like a health spa (as at another Herodian complex, Machaerus in Perea, which Antipas often used). If Tiberias was supposed to be a place of recuperation for weary pilgrims, then a Galilean faith-healer would be an intriguing addition to the list of local attractions. Jesus, Mary, and Joanna may have first come together in such a context. If, as Luke reports, Antipas himself regarded Jesus as an entertainer and a quaint but harmless curiosity, that fact lends substance to this conjecture.

A Herodian double agent

If the first contacts among Joanna, Mary, and Jesus occurred in a material context such as I have described, this does not in any way rule out a subsequent and profound transformation of their relationship. On the contrary, it helps to solve one of the toughest puzzles in early Christian history: how a local Palestinian reform movement, with locally defined issues, began to spread beyond the Jordan and the Mediterranean Sea. The Magdalene and the Herodian lady are the only disciples we know of for whom we can plausibly posit international commercial and political connections. Before Calvary, the Gospels report, Jesus himself traveled beyond Galilee into the cities of the Decapolis and northward to Tyre and Sidon. While the women financiers are not reported to have gone that far with him, their money probably did, and they may have made arrangements for him with their local contacts.

For the international mobilization of the gospel movement to get going after Calvary, as it did, there had to be people close to Jesus who knew something of the world beyond Galilee. Joanna and Mary are the only figures in Jesus' immediate circle who did, according to the circumstantial evidence of their involvement with international trade and their contacts in far-flung Diaspora communities. These likely provided the bridge for the gospel to travel up to Jerusalem and out to the cities of the eastern and western worlds. No other hypothesis fits the archaeological, geographical, and textual evidence so well.

But that was after Calvary, which is to jump ahead in this story. Let us recall that, as stated above, the Gospel texts distinguish between the Galilean functions of the Jesus women and their Jerusalem functions. In Galilee the women bankrolled and facilitated the road trips of Jesus (Mark 15:40–1; Matt. 27:58; Luke 8:1–3). We have seen how circumstantial evidence allows us to fill in some details about the context in which this occurred—given the involvement of a Mary "from Magdala" and of a Joanna "wife of Herod's viceroy." Our reconstruction suggested that Antipas turned Lake Kinneret into a tourist attraction. Travelers from Damascus, Babylon, and points east now crossed the Lake to Tiberias, where the cliffside palace of Herod Antipas offered hospitality and a chance to mingle with Antipas' local clientele. The hospitality of the palace, and of auxiliary commercial establishments, would mean party barges, ferry boats, dinner cruises, water sports, and other floating entertainments radiating out from the docks and beaches at Tiberias. This was the first stop in the Promised Land for travelers making their way to Jerusalem for business and/or pilgrimage. The number of elite guests for whom these facilities were intended was not large. But the power of those elite few was considerable, and well worth Joanna's trouble to provide a cordial welcome and an interesting visit. They represented an opportunity for international trading connections that could plug Galilean industries into the Syrian, Babylonian, and other eastern trade networks, and cultivate prestigious international political connections for Antipas.

If the eastern visitors had commercial interests, they would want to meet local managers and tour the industrial facilities along the shore from Tiberias up to Magdala and on toward Capharnaum at the northern shore of the Lake. The Herodian hosts would want to include some local color in the business itinerary. They also needed to provide diversions for members of traveling families who were not directly involved in business. Jesus the exorcist, healer, and teacher fit the bill. We have no record that he appeared at Antipas' spa or at the palace. Jesus seldom made house calls (according to Mark 5:22–43 and par; Luke 7:1–10), although if he healed Joanna he must have encountered the ailing Herodian lady *somewhere*. We are told that people went out in droves to hear and see Jesus along the shore and in the lakeside hills. Five thousand are fed in Mark 6:34–44. If the exaggerated story is not pure hype, it may reflect an influx of visitors during tourist/pilgrimage season, when villagers would be prepared to sell food to outsiders (as expected in v. 36).

Antipas began his makeover of the Lake region about the year 18 CE. The flamboyant Herodian lifestyle provoked vociferous opposition from John and others during the following decade. Jesus bought into that opposition and signaled his agreement by undergoing John's baptism about 28 CE, shortly before John was arrested and beheaded, in the timetable suggested by John P. Meier. The question is whether Jesus' career began with his baptism and therefore was anti-Herodian from the start. This cannot be presupposed. The connection with Joanna suggests that, on the contrary, Jesus may have first functioned as an exorcist under the sponsorship of the Herodians, at least for a time.

When he eventually broke with his patron—"that fox," Luke 13:32—Jesus did not sever all his connections with members of the Herodian court. Luke's text provides an additional consideration that makes this possibility appear more likely. In Jerusalem, the Roman prefect Pontius Pilate seems to have recognized Jesus as Herod's kind of guy. By Luke's account (Luke 23:6–17), Pilate sends Jesus to Antipas for a mock trial. Antipas is delighted to see him at last; he expects Jesus to perform tricks. The entertainer will not entertain. Nevertheless, Antipas and his soldiers have some fun with Jesus, dress him up in gaudy clothes, and send him back to Pilate. This little exchange occurs in the currency of contempt for indigenous religious idioms, and by Luke's account, sharing it cements a bond of friendship between the Roman bureaucrat and the puppet sovereign.

We cannot here establish the historical reliability of Luke's account of the trial, in all its details. Our discussion goes forward simply on the stipulation that Luke's report is essentially correct: Jesus was taken for a Herodian protégé, or at least a Herodian subject, by the civil authority in Jerusalem. This brings us now to what I have termed the second or Jerusalem function of the Jesus women. In gospel hindsight, that is, in Christian religious perspective, the women's role is to witness the events of the crucifixion, the burial, and the emptied tomb. But in contemporary secular perspective, it seems that the task confronting Joanna and her associates was to keep an eye on Jesus and keep him out of trouble by keeping him away from both Antipas and the Judean religious authorities while in Jerusalem for the festival of Pesach.

Joanna, I have suggested, walked a thin line in Herod's court at Tiberias. Cooperating with local associates like Mary of Magdala, Joanna promoted the teaching and healing career of her protégé Jesus both among Antipas' clients and in villages and towns of Galilee and beyond. Antipas heard rave reviews about Jesus, but Joanna managed to prevent the two from meeting in spite of the tetrarch's curiosity. Perhaps she could have continued indefinitely to juggle Jesus' itinerary against Herod's schedule in Galilee. But Antipas and his court went to Jerusalem for the same festival at which Jesus and his male followers, for whatever reason, chose to stage the political confrontation that quickly brought his career to a close.

The suddenness of Jesus' arrest and execution took his followers by surprise. It happened so fast that they didn't know what hit them; therefore many commentators assume that the details of Jesus' trial were unknown to his followers. Some scholars discount the possibility that there was any trial at all, and most agree that the trial "transcripts" in the Gospels are later, theological reconstructions based on various passages of the Hebrew scripture. But this skeptical view leaves us without a way to account for the fact that the Jesus people knew that Jesus was being crucified at all. If Jesus had been snatched in the night, and even if Peter skulked along behind the Temple police and eavesdropped on the arraignment before the Sanhedrin, then Jesus' friends would not have learned that he was to be marched out to Calvary in the morning. They would assume, rather, that he was kept in custody by the Temple police to hush him up during the festival. The Sanhedrin could not carry out a death penalty. If indeed there were witnesses standing by the cross in the morning, then there had to have been someone sympathetic to Jesus on the inside of the Roman-Herodian civil process overnight.

But if no such process occurred in Jesus' case, or if it occurred but Jesus' friends had no inside connections, then Jesus' friends would not have learned of his crucifixion at all—before, during, or after the event. The crucifixion of Jesus lasted just a few hours. The chances are slim that one of his male companions—out-of-towners staying in unfamiliar accommodations in a city mobbed with visitors like themselves—accidentally happened upon the scene during that narrow window of opportunity while the execution was occurring. Afterward, the corpse was quickly removed (assuming the accuracy of the Gospel report that the execution was cut short because of the festival). It stands to reason:

as the hours went by, the longer Jesus' companions remained ignorant of his fate, the less likely they were ever to learn what happened to him.

Yet, they certainly knew about the crucifixion afterward. And, in all four Gospel accounts, they knew soon enough to be present during the crucifixion procedure itself. Specifically, in the Gospel narratives it is Jesus' women associates who show up at the cross in time to watch Jesus die. The plausible explanation for this is that Joanna spread the word to alert her associates after learning of—or perhaps witnessing—Jesus' appearance before Antipas.

In other words, given the evidence that we have, we need to accept the historicity of the Herodian connection if we are to account for the fact that Jesus' companions knew about the crucifixion at all, not just while it was happening. The short duration of the execution and the huge number of visitors in the city made it unlikely that one of the relatively few people who noticed Jesus being crucified, and who also bothered to learn his name, would accidentally have mentioned it afterward in the hearing of someone who cared. For all Jesus' companions might have known, he remained in the custody of the Temple police.

Joanna, as a Herodian dignitary, may have been recognizable on sight to soldiers of the Roman death squad. If so, she could safely approach the place of crucifixion. As a mobile and discrete informant she would be an asset to her husband's boss. Antipas had found Jesus innocent and entertaining, according to Luke, and may have been quite interested in obtaining a back-channel report through Joanna about what became of his reluctant wonderworker. Thus, it appears that Joanna's stakeout at Calvary yielded intelligence that she passed on officially to Antipas and unofficially to the friends of Jesus.

It is quite unlikely (though technically possible) that Jesus' friends received timely word of the crucifixion from the other group that apparently knew about it, the Sanhedrin. In all four Gospels we meet the figure of Joseph of Arimathea, who buries Jesus after asking Pilate to release the body to him while it is still on the cross. Could Joseph have been the insider who leaked word of Jesus' imminent execution? Joseph is presented as an officer of the Sanhedrin, which supposedly prosecuted Jesus before Pilate and before Antipas. Matthew calls Joseph rich; Mark says he was looking for God's reign; Luke insists he was righteous and dissented from the prosecution of Jesus; and John makes him a secret disciple and partners him with Nicodemus. But these appear to be implausible attempts to rehabilitate Joseph in order to account for the disciples' knowledge of the crucifixion; they are not supported by any other evidence of a sympathetic connection between Jesus and the Judean authorities.

On the contrary, the Sanhedrin had every reason to try to keep Jesus' supporters from hearing about the crucifixion during the festival, when there was maximum risk from civil disturbance. It is likely that Joseph of Arimathea, acting for the Sanhedrin, claimed the body in order to complete Jesus' "disappearance," and also to fulfill the provisions of Judean law in capital cases (as later reflected in Mishnah *Sanhedrin* 6.5). An executed prisoner's body was supposed to be kept in the custody of the Sanhedrin, in a special tomb, without the performance of mourning and burial rites, for one year until the flesh separated from the bones. The death sentence was then considered completed, and the bones were released to the family for proper mourning and burial.

The Sanhedrin was supposed to maintain a facility for entombing executed criminals. The court might very well wish to keep the location of the criminals' tomb secret, since families and friends ordinarily might not agree to forgo mourning rituals or to let the body rot so shamefully apart from the bodies of kin. Hence the curious detail in the Gospels to the effect that the Jesus women had to follow Joseph surreptitiously in order to find out where the tomb was and witness the burial (Mark 15:47; Luke 23:55). Had Joseph really been such a friend to the Jesus people, he himself could have witnessed to the burial and the location of the tomb. In any event, we have now followed the women through the first phases of their Jerusalem witnessing function: explicitly, to see Jesus hung on the cross and to see him buried; and implicitly, to see Jesus fall into the hands of Antipas and be sent back to the Roman prefect for condemnation.

The culmination of the women's witnessing in Jerusalem occurs at the emptied tomb, according to the narratives that come down to us. Having seen Jesus condemned, crucified, and buried, the women now see the significance of his death and life. It is they who bring the message of resurrection back to Jesus' male associates.

▪ ▪ ▪

This chapter has followed the movement of women before and during the career of Jesus. Names and associations with a specific city or town have allowed us to frame hypotheses about their kinship and their economic and political agendas.

From Calvary to this very day, anyone who regards Jesus as the Risen Lord is looking at him through the eyes of Mary, Joanna, and their women associates. Luke reports that these women knew Jesus in the early days and stuck with him after Calvary. Their relationship became faith, but may have begun as something else. We cannot look into their hearts, but we have taken a look around their world. Someone saw the possibilities and the needs of that world. Someone after Calvary saw that the words of Jesus deserved repetition not only as a variant of the *halakhah* circulating in Galilean and Judean villages, but also as a variant of the Stoic and Cynic *chreiai* circulating in the Decapolis and other secular cities. Someone facilitated the translations in language and in genre that brought the gospel out into western imperial society, as well as into the Syrian and Babylonian east.

To understand the gospel, it is necessary to understand the social mechanisms of its cultural translation and propagation. The distinctive interface of Galilean, Judean, and Herodian factions on the Magdalene-Tiberian lakeshore was the context for a friendship between two women, and through that friendship, was the prelude to the decisive events of Calvary and the emptied tomb.

8 Salting the Earth

AFTER CALVARY, PRACTICES OF REMEMBERING JESUS produced material, social, narrative, and theoretical expressions. Those expressions were fitted to the colonized and compromised situation of Palestine and the eastern Empire where the paleochurch took root.

The term "paleochurch" designates the community that reorganized itself after Calvary to continue the work of Jesus before the Gospels were written down. The paleochurch is older than the New Testament texts, for it is their source. In this chapter, the question to be examined is whether we can find evidence of resistance to oppressive imperial practices among those early communities, and if so, whether we can determine just what sort of resistance it was.

This inquiry has to be launched against the tide of opinion. The prevailing consensus in exegetical and theological scholarship today holds that the communities of Jesus, both before and immediately after Calvary, were radically egalitarian and that they embraced a mission of liberation from oppressive social structures. That opinion is mistaken, as we shall see.

Liberation is a profound theological theme in the Hebrew Bible. Its primary spatial expression is the Exodus, the crossing of the oppressed Hebrew people from slavery in Egypt to freedom in the land of promise. Moses led them across the Red Sea, and they never went back. This story has empowered other oppressed peoples, such as the slaves in early nineteenth-century America. A theology of liberation discerns and celebrates the ways in which God still leads people out from oppressive situations toward horizons of possibility for fully human life. Liberation means spatial separation and escape. In ancient times the people of Israel defined their community as that people who had been liberated from bondage in Egypt and now served only the God who had led them through the perils of water, desert, and mountain to take over the land of Canaan.

This is surely a compelling theological vision. But it was not the vision of the early Jesus constituencies. They defined themselves quite differently. To be sure, the exodus pattern was well known to the Jews of Roman Galilee. Motifs lifted from it have been worked into some of the literary compositions that became the New Testament, such as Matthew's parallels between Jesus and Moses as lawgivers, or Mark's paschal interpretation of Jesus' death. But there was a time before the churches dared to improvise on Torah in such terms.

More importantly, the spatial deployment of the Jesus event simply was quite unlike an exodus, a "going out." Jesus' first followers knew that there was no escape, no place to go to get away from the civil and personal evils confronting them. They had to figure out how to live in a landscape compromised by colonial oppressions. They would seek and find God's kingdom precisely in the midst of that. The Kinneret was not designated a Red Sea, nor the Galilee an Egypt. There was no thought of attempting a Moses-style exodus from the bondage of Roman occupation toward a new space of freedom.

Instead, paleochurch practices were symbiotic with Roman power. This was deliberate, by design. Jesus' followers used the metaphors of salt and leaven to describe their stance toward imperial power. They understood the gospel to be both corrosive and preservative like salt; it was to be infectious, expansive, and profane like leaven. These metaphors express a theology of digging in and staying put, an ecclesiology of infiltration rather than escape and conquest. It is vitally important for today's churches to consider this early ecclesiological option, for it is older, more primitive, more radical, and yet more adaptable to our own political situations than "liberation theology" is.

The argument of this chapter is made in five steps. It begins by clearing up the confusion between real and metaphorical space-talk that has hindered our understanding of the paleochurch's deployment across its indigenous landscape. Second, it debunks the claim that disciplined historical inquiry must be positivistic, oppressive, and therefore useless to any progressive political program. Those two moves set the stage for a presentation of the theology of subversive cohabitation that can be found in early parts of the Gospels, where there is no "discipleship of equals," no ecclesial democracy, and no impetus toward liberation from patriarchy. Fourth, the coping tactics of the Jesus movements are compared with resistive adaptations to Roman imperialism that were developing at the same time in mainstream early

Judaism, which were discussed above. The chapter concludes with the suggestion that "to salt and to leaven" are canonical ecclesiological directives to be followed not by slavish imitation, but rather by creative analogy in Christian confrontations with present-day empires, if the churches are looking for the kingdom that Jesus was talking about.

Spurious spatializations

To say that Jesus was a historical person is to say that he lived and worked *somewhere*. Roman Galilee was a real place. Roads crossed it. From the northeast, the route from Damascus and Babylon funneled merchants and tourists into the Kinneret region. About the year 20 CE, as we have seen, Herod Antipas built his seaside capital city, Tiberias, on the southwestern shore of the Kinneret to attract those wealthy and well-connected travelers into his territory on their way to and from Jerusalem via the Jordan valley. The Lake already had thriving industries ringing it, such as the shipyards and fish-packing plants at Magdala. Galilee exported foodstuffs and textiles throughout the region and the world. There were fortunes to be made when Roman administration introduced worldwide market efficiencies, but the cost was the realignment of traditional small-scale village relationships as imperial cities drew labor away from the land.

The physical configuration of villages, cities, trade routes, and nutritional resources comprising the Galilean landscape must be understood before we can understand how Jesus went looking *there* for what he called God's kingdom. Unfortunately, it is easy to develop a bad intellectual habit that prevents us from taking the real space of Galilee with due seriousness. We talk about space figuratively, in various metaphors borrowed from materialist literary theory, and those figures have become so familiar that we may forget they are only figures of speech. The real spaces do not work like the literary figures.

Take, for example, the notion of "discursive space." Since Heidegger, it has become customary for theorists to describe the event of reality-recognition as an "opening up" of a space of disclosure. Habermas' theory of communicative action calls for the establishment of a democratic "public space," where all concerned parties may freely communicate and negotiate their interests. Such "spaces" do not open up automatically, but must be deliberately established. The protocols of communication constitute the "space." Fair enough; it is an apt metaphor. Yet it must be borne in mind that *physically* open spaces do not automatically result in unimpeded information transfer. Moreover, disclosure and communication can also be "opened up" (figuratively speaking) under conditions of confined and restricted real space, and even under conditions of real physical absence. The myriad connections of the Internet are only the latest illustration. The figurative "opening" of conversations in tight spaces may coincide with, and may even require, closures and exclusions of various kinds.

Another example of a spatial figure is the Greek term *ekklesia*, which designates the paleochurch in the texts of the New Testament. It connotes a calling out, a gathering together. The image is one of selection, displacement, and establishment of a new physical propinquity. This term was commonly used to designate secular political assemblies in which people met to decide various matters of common concern. The ideal of democracy, forged in ancient Athens, requires citizens to meet in a self-governing assembly. Participation in such an *ekklesia* at Athens was restricted both socially and physically. Socially, only free male property-owners were allowed to participate. Physically, the assembly was limited by the size of the physical enclosure, the reach of the human voice, and the distance people could travel in order to take part. It is conceivable that the intention to belong to an *ekklesia* might outweigh physical barriers to someone's actual presence there. On the other hand, historically, the church quite soon transcended *ekklesia*. The paleochurch's intention to scatter and diffuse across the empire was literally the antithesis of "ecclesial" gathering. For example, the spatial sundering of *ekklesia* is mandated in the "Great Commission" of Matt 28:18–20 and in the diffusion of information and personnel after Pentecost, Acts 1:8.

Exodus, already discussed above, is a third spatial motion metaphor. To escape, you cross over from one place to another. Physical distance separates and insulates you from the evil that is left behind. Thus, the exorcisms of Jesus are not "liberations," technically speaking. The demon is evicted from the body of the victim, but the victim does not go anywhere. Moreover, liberation from the bondage of sin is not a theme of the teaching of Jesus or of the Gospel narratives; it is a Pauline metaphor, in which "distance" stands for time. The "before" state is the religious ideology of Jewish law, as Paul saw it. The state of liberation is freedom from the law; that is, Torah, villainized to suit Paul's rhetoric. Today's so-called liberation theology extends this Pauline metaphor, aspiring to put an end to oppressive conditions: not by physically exiting, but by politically vanquishing certain evil economic and social structures. The incongruity built into this metaphorical use of the "exodus" motif is that one tries to "get away" from evil temporally without being able to move away from it physically. Liberation is proclaimed while evil circumstances are quite plainly still here. This liberation is not real. It does not materialize, but is supposed to subsist as the invisible engine propelling historical events toward some always future goal.

Contemporary social theory invokes a fourth spatial metaphor, *colonization*, to describe cultural appropriations or "displacements" engineered by a dominant group. Real, historical colonization occurred in space. That is, people from one land went into another land, where they altered the landscape to siphon off wealth. The colonizers dominated both in the material realm and in cultural affairs. Colonization produced secondary real displacements for the subjugated people: emigration, migration of labor, urbanization, homelessness, and so forth. Real physical goods were caused to circulate in new patterns, and wealth flowed away from the colony to the colonizing country. Roman imperialism, therefore, was a reality that was spatially deployed.

To be sure, cultural distortion accompanied and facilitated these real displacements. Rome achieved cultural hegemony by granting concessions to a class of collaborating indigenous client rulers. Thus, the Herodian princes were raised and educated offshore with the sons of elite Roman families. Antipas went away from Palestine to learn how to be Roman, and he came back to redesign Israel's landscape as a little Italy. During his administration, as we have seen, Lake Kinneret became another Mediterranean Sea, with shipping routes presided over by Antipas' new tourist attraction Tiberias, a little Ostia. From the Kinneret, the Jordan valley led tourists and merchants to Jericho, gateway to Jerusalem, just as the Tiber led from the port of Ostia inland to Rome. John the Baptist's effective opposition to this Italianization of Israel was spatially deployed as well. John situated himself astride Herod's little Tiber and used its very water to signal repentance—literally, "turning back"—for the tourists and business travelers making their way between Tiberias and Jerusalem. Jesus' own baptism by John signaled his disengagement from the colonial Kinneret industrial complex, in which Jesus may well have been participating as a shipwright. Colonization and colonial oppression in the real world are always embodied in material features such as these. Oppression as a subjective or psychologically felt experience is devoid of meaning, if it lacks reference to transactions in real space.

A fifth spatial metaphor commonly misused today is that of *social situation*. In real space, an individual human being can occupy only one place at a time and can see only the objects that are relatively nearby around her or him. Physical vision is both enabled and limited by real location. This "standpoint" determines knowledge and praxis. Metaphorically, empirical knowledge is somewhat like vision, and one's distinctive demographic peculiarities are somewhat like a location on a grid defined by all possible human variations. Thus, it can be said metaphorically that knowledge itself is both enabled and limited by social location. That much is clear. However, equivocation and nonsense creep in when we confuse the properties of real space with those of metaphorical, epistemological space. While *real* distance inhibits communication, people can and do understand others who *metaphorically* occupy very distant social spaces. Empathy does not require that one displace the other, or move into the space of the other. Conversely, understanding is not guaranteed by similar or identical social location. All of which indicates that knowledge can transcend perspective. If epistemological space were real space, we would indeed be trapped in relativism with no hope of reaching consensus. Scientific historical claims would then be nothing but attempts to achieve arbitrary hegemony for one's own view, simply because it is one's own. But epistemological space is not real space. Empirical knowledge is secured to *a priori* rational structures that are the common heritage of all human beings, wherever they happen to be and no matter how they came to be there. Knowledge is possible apart from "standpoints," and there are some profoundly important truths that are not "situational."

The argument against any "liberating praxis" on the part of Jesus and the paleochurch has had to begin with the foregoing critique of these metaphorical equivocations about space. Unless a clear distinction is made between real and figurative space, it is futile to try to investigate the interplay between the two or appreciate the resistive practices deployed by the early church. The next section pursues and challenges the implications of the relativistic epistemology that stems from perspectivalism and spatial equivocation.

The possibility of knowing history

Much has been written in the last decade about "the historical Jesus," that is, the profile of Jesus of Nazareth before Calvary as it can be drawn through critical cooperative study of the textual and material evidence available to us. Oversimplifying for the sake of argument, one might say that there are currently four theological options represented in the literature, which might be summed up as follows:

(1) *The Gospel portraits are substantially reliable* and can be taken more or less at face value. This is the position of conservative mainstream and fundamentalist Christianity.

(2) *Profiles of Jesus are mere ideological constructions*. We are free to portray him in any manner that furthers the interests of our community, just as the canonical evangelists did. "The name of Jesus" has always been elastic enough to cover innovative interpretations. It is still up for grabs. This assumption, either expressed or implied, is the foundation of liberation theology in general and of the widely accepted theology of "critical feminist biblical interpretation for liberation" whose premises were criticized above in chapter four. Surprisingly, the same assumption is shared by the American Catholic theological establishment. Many theologians today hold that the historical facts of Jesus' life are largely unknowable, and when knowable, are largely irrelevant to faith.

(3) *Scholarly consensus can be achieved concerning some important aspects of Jesus' career and message, though not all*. That consensus should confront and override the non-scientific memories of Jesus, particularly the cultic and devotional memories. This is the contention in public communications from the Jesus Seminar. It also expresses the stance of many biblical scholars in the academy.

(4) *Remembering Jesus occurs authentically in various places and practices,* among which are liturgy, charity, teaching, and healing, as well as disciplined study of the Gospels. Scholarly historical investigations of who Jesus was and of how he was remembered by the paleochurch comprise a vital component in the contemporary discernment of who Jesus is. This is the position of Catholic and Orthodox Christianity.

Which of these options, if any, did the paleochurch follow? Not (3), since the recovery of information about Jesus had yet to become an academic project. Not (1), or the paleochurch would have assembled a New Testament canon with only one gospel, not four different accounts which conflict in numerous details. If (2), then the paleochurch would be redesigning Jesus and his message ad lib as it went along, in whatever way best served the needs of the moment. But this seems not to have been what happened. We are left with option (4), and the hypothesis that, from Calvary onward, the wonders wrought and the words spoken "in the name of Jesus" were intended to have some real historical continuity with him and his practices, even as they creatively adapted to changing circumstances.

There are two reasons for optimism about the possibility of acquiring reliable information concerning the intentions and practices of the paleochurch: the breadth of evidence that is emerging, and the depth of analysis made possible by contemporary critical social theory. As we have seen, there are evidences of several kinds. There are ancient texts: the canonical books of the New Testament as well as other first-century religious and secular writings. There are also material remains: the landscape of Israel and the ancient Near East, artifacts, architecture, and floral and faunal traces of ancient dietary and labor patterns. There are comparative anthropological and socio-political data. And to assist in the collection and analysis of all that evidence, there is a repertoire of social theory. The blindly reductive "systems theory" of the 1960s has given way to more subtle postprocessual and recursive cultural analyses in archaeology. Moreover, the professional practitioners who undertake those scientific historical analyses now are drawn from a wider sector of society than ever before.

These are developments of the 1990s. Biblical scholars trained in the 1960s may not be taking them into account when they indict all historical investigation as necessarily positivistic, or when they charge that all data are produced arbitrarily from social-scientific modeling. As advances in archaeology become more widely known, the claim that historical study is necessarily positivistic and patriarchal will be seen to be without merit. Historical study can be conducted non-positivistically and non-patriarchally. The information produced by such study is indispensable for responsible theology.

Paradoxically, ideological rejection of the very possibility of objective historical data has gone hand-in-hand with the importation of anachronistic principles and concepts into first-century Galilee, especially in feminist reconstructions. There is a certain logic to this paradox. If nothing from the first century constrains our description of that era (that is, if the evidence can fit equally well into just any scenario that we might contrive), then we may as well make up a universal law from which to deduce a portrayal of first-century practices. We may as well assume that women are oppressed always and everywhere, and that they always resist oppression. Then we can syllogistically (though spuriously) deduce the statement that first-century Galilean women were oppressed and resisted oppression. This deduction can become the hermeneutical engine that pumps out convenient descriptions of paleochurch practices to overwrite the evidence. In the midst of the cities of the early Roman Empire, we would then be free to find the democratic polity described in fourth-century BCE Athenian texts, or the ideology of liberty, equality, and fraternity espoused in eighteenth-century Euro-American texts. Plato's Athens, Paul's Ephesus, James's Jerusalem, Voltaire's Paris, Jefferson's Virginia—their texts would be interchangeable.

No matter how exhilarating such an ideological interpretive project may feel to its practitioners and consumers, it obviously cannot forge a theological consensus within the whole church or a scholarly consensus within the academic community. Only some factions can accept it. But that is not the most telling indictment of this project. More problematically, it silences the voices of women and men in the first-century. This hermeneutic of idealist deduction obliterates the words of Jesus' first witnesses. The campaign to find "democracy" and "egalitarianism" in the paleochurch drowns out those indigenous expressions in which its members actually named, reflected upon, and propagated their practices. "Salt" and "leaven" are two of those indigenous critical namings, as the next section will show. We can indeed understand what the paleochurch was trying to say, but only if we listen without hastily assimilating their imagery to anachronistically imposed categories of liberation, equality, democracy, and so-called open discourse.

Who did *they* say they were?

The previous section of this chapter criticized the spatial equivocation that produces five metaphorical terms commonly used in contemporary ecclesiology: "discursive space," the gathered "*ekklesia*," "exodus-liberation," "colonization," and "standpoint." To that philosophical objection another must be added. Those metaphors also clash with the imagery in which Jesus' first followers named their own practices.

The imagery of leaven and salt, embraced by very early Christian communities after Calvary, describes deployment strategies for the kingdom of God that are not at all open, democratic, or liberating. Nor do these strategies constitute a discrete "standpoint." Rather, the paleochurch is a stealth operation. It presumes that imperial structures will remain intact so that they can be infiltrated. This is a resistance that exploits the empire; it does not defeat, neutralize, kill, or escape from its host. The paleochurch looks for the kingdom of God in the midst of occupied Palestine and Syria, not on some far shore where oppression has been left behind. Paul goes to Rome as a prisoner. This is not to deny that Christian theologians subsequently have been able to accomplish a creative synthesis in which exodus themes, leavening, sowing, and salting mutually enhance one another. But it seems clear that the notion of stealthy growth originated in a distinctive practice that is obscured if we insist on grasping it in terms of an exodus spatiality.

First, the "discursive space" of paleochurch practice is closed and secretive. This is abundantly clear in texts from the earliest stratum of the Sayings Gospel Q, and is corroborated in rabbinic traditions. The object of inquiry here is not Jesus, but very early ways of remembering him. The historical recovery of evidence for the practices and the teachings of Jesus' first followers is more easily accomplished than the recovery of the deeds and words of the "historical Jesus" himself. For this task, we do not have to determine whether a given practice that is reflected in early texts comes originally from Jesus or was an innovation by his followers. Either way, the practice is something that they embrace "in Jesus' name." The words of Jesus, as distinctively remembered and performed by some sector of the early church, disclose a great deal about that community's ideology and about its practices of memory and performance.

The parables of the Mustard Seed and the Leaven are juxtaposed in Q and they address the missionary work of the Q community. (Studies of the parables traditions by Wendy Cotter, Perry Kea, and John Kloppenborg support my own inferences about the industrial use of salt in the following account.) In Luke 10:2–11 the disciples of Jesus are sent out into dangerous circumstances, like lambs among wolves. Although they use the roads like tourists and business travelers, they go incognito, creating the false impression that they are locals by carrying no baggage. In towns they are to indigenize themselves by attaching to the family that employs them, "growing roots in the community in an unobtrusive manner," as Cotter says. The stealth tactics are understood to be temporary and provisional:

> There is nothing veiled that won't be unveiled, or hidden that won't be made known. And so whatever you've said in the dark will be heard in the light, and what you've whispered behind closed doors will be announced from the rooftops. (Luke 12:2–3)

To these people it seems only natural that God's kingdom must germinate and foment secretly at first, and that its eventual success is assured.

> It is like a mustard seed that a man took and tossed into his garden. It grew and became a tree, and the birds of the sky roosted in its branches. . . . It is like leaven that a woman took and concealed in fifty pounds of flour until it was all leavened. (Luke 13:19, 21)

In fact, mustard is not a tree but a big aggressive weed. Cotter points out that mighty trees like the oak and the cedar commonly represented political systems organized for domination; the pesky mustard shrub that the birds prefer is a parody. As for the leaven, it is "concealed" in the flour before it raises the whole wad of dough. Cotter concludes that the Q missionaries "had to hide their efforts from formal public scrutiny."

After sheltered beginnings hidden in the dark and in secret, the practices of the Q missionaries were supposed to burst forth into visibility: like a mustard plant, like a risen loaf, like a lamp on a lampstand (Luke 11:33), like a shout from a housetop. Other early Jesus constituencies apparently chafed at the stealth tactics of the Q people and wanted to "go public" more rapidly:

> Since when is the lamp brought in to be put under the bushel basket or under the bed? It's put on the lampstand, isn't it? After all, there is nothing hidden except to be brought to light, nor anything kept secret that won't be exposed. (Mark 4:21)

> A city sitting on top of a mountain can't be concealed. (Matt 5:14)

> A city built on a high hill and fortified cannot fall, nor can it be hidden. (Thom 32)

> No one lights a lamp and covers it with a pot or puts it under a bed; rather, one puts it on a lampstand, so that those who come in can see the light. (Luke 8:16)

> No one lights a lamp and then puts it in a cellar or under a bushel basket, but rather on a lampstand so that those who come in can see the light. (Luke 11:33)

Note the hiding places mentioned in the last two texts: under a bed, in a cellar, under a bushel, within a city. These would be places where *a person* could hide if the police ("those who come in," *eisporeuomenoi*) were searching house to house for troublemakers. In effect, these sayings propose a policy shift from secrecy to confrontative engagement with the authorities. But note as well that there is still no hint of escape, exodus, liberation.

Matthew's Jesus underscores the point of the metaphor: That lamp is you.

> You are the light of the world (*phōs tou kosmou*). . . . [Y]our light is to shine in the presence of others, so they can see your good deeds and acclaim your Father in the heavens. (Matt 5:14, 16; compare John 8:12 and 9:5, where the light of the world is *Jesus*.)

Matthew puts the same point on the salt metaphor: You are the salt of the earth (*halas tēs gēs*, Matt 5:13). The salt sayings that follow are notoriously obscure.

> But if salt loses its zing, how will it be made salty? It then has no further use than to be thrown out and stomped on. (Matt 5:13)

> Salt is good. But if salt loses its zing, how will it be renewed? It's no good for either earth or manure. It just gets thrown away. (Luke 14:34–35)

> Everyone [in Gehenna] is salted with fire. Salt is good—if salt becomes bland, with what will you renew it? Maintain salt among yourselves and be at peace with one another. (Mark 9:49–50)

These sayings baffle interpreters. Chemically it is not possible for salt to become unsalty. Therefore, they reason, some sort of mixture or unrefined raw material must be intended. The authors of the Gospel texts also seem to have amalgamated several diverse salt sayings whose meanings may already have become obscure by the end of the first century.

Fortunately, these sayings can be brought into clearer focus by considering the Galilean lakeside context in which they first circulated. Salt was used industrially in fish packing. Kinneret producers exported a briny gourmet fish sauce that was used as a condiment. A little of it went a long way. The "tainted" salt may refer to the occasional batch that was spoiled in production. When a load of fish spoiled, the mess could be composted as fertilizer to enrich the soil. But in case the brine was brewed up wrong, it could not be dumped in a field because doing so would prevent any crops from growing there. In fact, to salt a field would be an act of sabotage and would disrupt agricultural production. Bad brine would have to be dumped on bad land, that is, on a city pavement where it would do no more harm to the environment, but would actually improve the walking surface by sterilizing the urban filth and killing weeds.

"Earth" in Matt 5:13 does not mean the planet; it means the soil. Salt disables soil from producing crops. On the other hand, salt preserves food. It prevents fish from rotting, so that they can be shipped from the Kinneret to distant markets. The fish-packing plants in Magdala, on the shores of the freshwater "Sea of Galilee," would have to import salt overland in bulk from southern Judea or Idumea, on the other side of the Dead Sea. There may well have been spillage and agricultural damage along the roads, both from the raw salt and from the finished product. "Traveling salt," then, is a hazardous material. If it leaks, it can ruin crops and corrode the metal fittings on carts, casks, and weapons. Perhaps salt was shipped in unmarked containers to avoid arousing hostility from landowners along the way. This would make it something of a stealth commodity. Its potency would have been essential to the economy of the region, yet it would have to be brought in discretely. This industrial perspective aligns the metaphor of salt with the metaphors of the mustard seed, the leaven, and the oil lamp. Accordingly, paleochurch practices are such that they "turn on the lights" in a dark world that does not appreciate being lit up, and they "ship salt" across agricultural land. "You reveal the cosmos, you salt the soil," says Matthew, in effect (Matt 5: 13–4). We may read this as self-portraiture by the paleochurch.

If salt may be regarded as a controversial commodity, the controversy set one socio-economic class against another. In the first century it was increasingly common to find large tracts of agricultural lands held by absentee landlords. Many farmers were working for somebody else. Not so the fishing fleet. Family-owned boats seem to have been the norm, although many people also fished for hire. But you could always cast a net from the shore and sell your morning's catch to the fish-packing plant, or directly to tourists and local householders (as presumed in Mark 6:36–8 and parallels). Nobody owned the Lake. The "pro-salt" faction in the controversy, then, would be made up of small-scale boat owners, freelance fishers, and workers in allied industries like shipbuilding, fuel-gathering, and pot manufacture. If the Q missionaries are "salt of the soil," then they are in solidarity with all those workers as the workers resist powerful agribusiness interests. They have to be strategically sneaky in order to bring the harsh light of reality, and the purifying corrosion of salt, to bear upon the invisible interlocked web of imperial collusion by the wealthy, estate-owning class. The metaphor seems to indicate as much.

How did these sneaky practices look from the other side? Rabbinic tradition offers further evidence that the paleochurch made its initial approaches one-on-one through stealthy infiltration. According to the Mishnah, indigenous Judean authorities caught someone, maybe Peter, sneaking around in Lod and whispering heterodox teachings to one person at a time. Lod, or Lydda, was a fertile region where there were Hasmonean agricultural estates. Joshua Schwartz has examined the mishnaic and talmudic traditions about an individual identified as Ben Stada who is placed in Lydda under circumstances similar to those in which Acts 9: 32–35 places Peter there. The crime of beguiling people into false religious beliefs and practices was punishable by stoning.

Two witnesses ordinarily were required to establish guilt in a capital case. But the crime of the enticer (Hebrew *mesit*) was so serious and dangerous that some of the legal requirements of due process could be relaxed in order to enable the authorities to entrap the offender. The *mesit* was like salt in the soil. Schwartz (1995: 402) writes:

> The *mesit*, according to the Rabbis, threatened the very fabric of Jewish survival. The *mesit* preached action. . . . The *mesit* preached his message only in secret and often disguised it as a social encounter, preaching at a meal. The *mesit* spoke in a "low voice" and preferred to preach to individuals since "an individual does not ask outside advice and will err after him (= the *mesit*) while groups of many will seek advice and not err." . . . A *mesit* was neither a sage, Rabbi or prophet, but rather a "common man" . . . someone who would not automatically be recognized.

Schwartz argues persuasively that Peter operated in just this manner, according to details of his activities recorded in the Acts of the Apostles. When Peter healed, he did it privately, without fanfare. If people heard about the healing and came to him to inquire, Peter chose his words carefully to avoid charges of blasphemy. He played cat-and-mouse with the Sanhedrin and, unlike Paul or Stephen, preserved "the delicate balance of public and private activity" so as to keep one jump ahead of the law. (This contrasts with the practices of Jesus as reflected in Mark 14:44–49 and parallels, where Jesus protests to the arresting officers that he has taught openly and lawfully at the Temple.)

It is difficult to see how the sort of opportunistic infiltration practiced by a *mesit* like Peter could have been carried out under the guidance of a democratically self-governed assembly of Christians, the alleged "discipleship of equals." We have no evidence for any social mechanism to build consensus or to set policy. The paleochurch does not "gather" for social visibility; it scatters for invisibility and maximum disruption of other targeted institutions.

Even in the best of times, democracy is hard to manage. Democracy requires coordination of the judgments of individual members whose interests and insights are divergent. Decisions must be made in light of a perceived common good that may not coincide with the individual preference of anyone. The first century was not the best of times. Democracy no longer existed as a form of social organization at the level of the empire or its client states. Nor were there any democratically governed cities, industries, families, religions, or businesses. As the Stoic philosopher Epictetus amply attests, the realm of public affairs had become chaotic and precarious. The best that one could do was to govern one's own unruly desires and achieve an internal serenity. "Maintain salt among yourselves and be at peace with one another" (Mark 9:50). Epictetus could certainly agree with that.

One searches in vain for traces of democratic polity amid the vignettes of paleochurch decision-making that have been recorded in Acts. Consider these examples. The replacement for Judas is not elected, but chosen by lot (Acts 1:26). The material needs of the community are provided by benefactors who are wealthy merchants and householders, not by egalitarian tax or tithe (Acts 2:45; compare Rom 16:1–5). Christians who run afoul of community mores are summarily dispatched without benefit of due process (Acts 5:1–11). On his own initiative Peter makes important policy changes regarding gentiles, and explains it later to his associates (Acts 10:1–11:18). The Jerusalem church holds an assembly that issues orders to the church in Antioch (Acts 15:28–29). None of this is democratic or egalitarian.

But do these details perhaps pertain only to a relatively late period, after the paleochurch had abandoned some primitive form of governance in which property was communally owned and democratically administered, and in which teaching activities were coordinated by consensus? There is no evidence of primitive egalitarianism. Doctrinal uniformity and communal property are institutions attested in ancient sources, but the social mechanisms for producing them were not egalitarian. Paleochurch practices match the prevailing customs of their time, as studies by Brian Capper, John Kloppenborg, and others have shown. For example, Essene documents indicate that common ownership of property was an indigenous cultural practice in Palestine, but it entailed a two-tier social structure. Members who had permanently given over their property were an elite inner circle within a probationary group whose commitment was temporary. Administration of property or of teaching by consensus is not attested as a concept that would be intelligible in that society, much less as a cultural value. Our own Western values ought not to be projected onto the paleochurch. We must conclude that the urban churches generally operated ad hoc, by whatever means seemed expedient. They organized their activities according to available indigenous and colonial cultural patterns. We cannot conclude that they were any more democratic or egalitarian than any other institution taking shape in the Greco-Roman cities of the eastern empire.

The final section of this chapter will consider the question whether there is any enduring significance to the institutional contours emerging in the early urban churches; that is, whether the character of that institutionalization constitutes an imperative to be followed today. But first, the paleochurch's stealth tactics will be compared to the tactics defining the mainstream resistive constituency in first-century Palestine, which were discussed at length in an earlier chapter.

Alternative responses in early Judaism

Judaism as we know it today acquired several of its most profoundly self-defining practices through confrontation with the Romanization of Judea and Galilee, as we have seen. The historical term "Judaism" refers to the modification of Israelite religion socially and textually produced by the generations living from the late second-Temple period through the time of the editing of the Mishnah (roughly the middle of the first century BCE to 200 CE). After the Romans tore down Jerusalem's Temple in 70, the sacrificial practices set forth in the Torah no longer could be followed. However, the legal and instructional practices of the indigenous population continued and adapted. After 70, these practices were significantly shaped by the intention to preserve technical information about conducting the cult, and to preserve the lineage of cultic personnel (priests and levites), until the Temple could be rebuilt. But that hope gradually faded. The institutions of the rabbinic study house and the synagogue became more salient in their own right, and the scope of their authority expanded. Early on, they seem to have competed for leadership in the Land of Israel. By talmudic times (third and fourth centuries CE), however, they were architecturally joined. A single edifice symbolized the local Jewish community, its teaching and judicatory and charitable and social functions, its ritual observances, and its professional leadership.

This urban centralization suited the Romans. Their style of colonial administration depended on effective liaison with a few good men, the heads of compliant indigenous ruling families. Long before Rome became an empire, Jews had been a multinational presence. Dispersed among the cities of the Mediterranean and Mesopotamia, Jews (*Ioudaioi*, "Judeans") formed cohesive local communities, also called synagogues, whose functions were housed in distinctive structures. It is plausible to suppose that the first synagogues to be built in the Land of Israel itself, well before the destruction of the Temple, were built for the convenience of Diaspora Jews on holiday or traveling for business. Although formal prayer meetings may have occurred in them, that was not their primary use. After the Temple was razed, however, the religious practices and the architecture of Jews in Israel gradually conformed to those of Diaspora Jews.

But there are at least two significant exceptions to this general rule: the Mishnah, and the *miqveh* or ritual bathing tank, both of which originated in the Land of Israel under Roman colonial pressures and were subsequently exported to the Diaspora. Let us review what has already been said about them. The Mishnah is the compiled teachings of the early rabbis: rulings in legal cases, stories illustrating correct religious observances, legends, botanical lore, biblical exegesis, and more. Before being reduced to writing and contained within a definitive text around 200 CE, those teachings earlier had been produced and "contained" within an architectural innovation, the rabbinic study house. They did not circulate at large. The study house, as we have seen, was built to restrict access, keeping the teachings pure, enhancing their prestige, and associating them with an authoritative teacher. And as stated earlier, the *miqveh* is an architectural form designed to house the practice of ritual bathing, which although mandated anciently in Torah was accomplished outdoors or in ordinary bath facilities until precisely this era. We have also mentioned that a third tank-like architectural innovation may be identified in a distinctive new design for the synagogue hall. Seating was provided on steps rising along all four walls, so that participants sat in shadow looking inward and downward into a central area lit from above by a clerestory. There was no line of sight to the outdoors, and the flow of people in and out was regulated through doorways.

These "tanks" are resistive architectural gestures. They assert control and direction over their respective symbolic fluids. The study hall regulates teaching and memory, while the *halakhah* (religious law) developing within it re-conquers and regulates the times and spaces of everyday living in a colonized land: inch by inch, sabbath by sabbath. The clerestory synagogue hall regulates light for public reading and for observing the community assembled face to face; it also admits, encloses, and then releases the members of the community themselves. The *miqveh* regulates water by catching it from the heavens, without the intervention of Roman aqueducts; this special water therefore has the potency to remove various kinds of impediments to cultic purity. The tank-like structure is analogous in form and function to those of two older indigenous architectures that had embodied the national identity of the people, before being severely compromised by Roman occupation: the village house, and the Temple.

The Romans destroyed lots of houses and ultimately tore down the Temple itself, but that is not the point. The house, with its finely carved threshold, selectively admitted and enclosed the people associated with a patriline. It regulated their identity and their daily activities.

Colonial pressures distorted those indigenous work patterns, drawing labor away from the village and into the city, bringing massive social and cultural disruption. Thus the indigenous labor and kinship practices were distorted by Roman presence, often unwittingly. Rome violated Israelite thresholds. Moreover, Rome violated the proper flow patterns of commodities across the land itself. The Land of Israel remained "holy" as long as its God-given fertility was tithed and sacrificed. Grain and meat had to circulate in prescribed ways across the landscape and up to Jerusalem to the Temple. The colonial power tapped into those circulating commodities and diverted a great portion of them to imperial cities and other world markets. This produced real economic hardship; additionally, it produced cultural distress because it symbolically interfered with the indigenous material affirmation of Israel's covenant relationship with the deity.

In the same way, as we have seen, the seemingly benign Roman aqueducts wrested control of water away from the divine hand, secularizing and profaning one of the most profound and poetically powerful symbols of divine providence. When the aqueduct ran, who cared if God sent or withheld the rains? The *miqveh* tank and its associated practices constitute an alternative water system to that of the aqueducts. "Living" water—that is, water from rain or running streams that had not been lifted by human technology—was made available for purifying vessels and people. Passage through the *miqveh* tank after menstruation signaled the renewed eligibility of a Jewish wife to engage in lawful procreation; the *miqveh* had many other congruent uses as well. This new architectural form figured into the complex process of certifying Jewish descent, which became equivalent to Jewish identity. Since a patriline cannot be maintained as a closed system, it must open selectively to admit brides in each generation. The certification of brides, and therefore of continuity for the different castes of Israelites, became a matter of greater cultural concern in the Roman period than ever before, owing in part to the desire to preserve the priestly caste for the day when the Temple might be rebuilt. But it also signals a new strategy for ensuring national identity at a time when the integrity of the Land and its people was gravely compromised.

These "tanks" resist Roman power symbolically, in the indigenous idiom of Israelite religion, and in ways that the Romans would neither care about nor understand. The *miqveh*, the study house, the clerestory synagogue hall, and their associated practices symbolically take over the colonially breached functions of the village domestic threshold and the Temple. In the midst of imperial occupation, everyday life is now "housed" and "sanctified" by an emerging halakhic code whose practices erect another kingdom right under Roman noses in Palestine. Was the resistance effective? While not directly hampering the colonial power, these practices did indeed provide for the integrity and survival of a people identifying themselves as Jews. They persist as traditional elements of Judaism today.

Jesus and his followers used the same idiom to offer symbolic resistance, but at a slightly earlier period and in contrasting ways. Jesus lived in Galilee during Herodian times, while the Temple economy was still intact, in an era of increasing Judean hegemony, but before the establishment of Judean-influenced teaching centers at Sepphoris and Tiberias. Galilee, of course, had come under Hasmonean influence during the century before Jesus' birth. The Hasmonean dynasty was that of the Maccabees, whose rule was remembered as the last period of self-government in the Land of Israel (164 to 63 BCE). The beginning of the end for the Hasmonean house was their betrothal of Mariamme to Herod the Great, the up-and-coming client king of the Romans, in 42 BCE. As we have seen, Herod subsequently murdered not only Mariamme, but three young kinsmen of hers as well. They were the last Hasmoneans and had been popular with the people of Judea.

Neither Herod nor his son Herod Antipas, who took over in Galilee in 4 BCE when Herod died, had the respect of the people of Judea or Galilee. The people's desire for a return to Hasmonean rule, and to the independence that it represented, was expressed in an astonishing way. Herod had wiped out the Hasmonean patriline, and in killing Mariamme he had also removed the possibility of any direct Hasmonean descendants at all. People responded to the murder of Mariamme by starting to name their daughters after her. The land began to be populated with new Miriams. If "the virgin's name was Mary" (Luke 1:27) shortly after 29 BCE, when Herod murdered the last Hasmonean princess, that had to mean that the child's family wanted symbolically to counteract the effect of Herod's crime and to align themselves with the hope of independence. Virgin wombs all across Israel were designated ready to bring forth babies to re-establish what the Hasmoneans had meant to the people. In effect, to name a girl child "Mary" is to assert that Herod's takeover and sellout to the Romans cannot succeed, because the women of the land intend to bring more "Hasmoneans" into the world than Herod can murder—even without male Hasmoneans to father them into a proper patriline. The name Mary is unambiguously political, brave, and resistive. Jesus was born into such a family.

Nevertheless, the Herodians still held power after Jesus grew to adulthood. Jesus' use of the landscape and material culture of Galilee responds in some ways to Antipas's manipulation of them. Antipas, like his father Herod the Great, was known for architectural achievements. The Italianization of Galilee with the palace and city of Tiberias was mentioned above. Jesus countered with an architectural innovation of sorts: he taught in the open air, on the slopes overlooking Lake Kinneret. The Lake was Herod's little Mediterranean Sea, busy with wharves and commercial shipping. It was visible behind Jesus as he stood teaching people seated on the hillside. Jesus fed people with "free fish" from the Lake. But those particular practices could not be institutionalized and replicated on a large scale by his followers after Calvary, the paleochurch.

The generation after Jesus made the crucial decisions that made it possible for all subsequent generations to "see" Jesus as Lord and Savior after it became impossible literally to see and hear him against the backdrop of Herod's disneyworld, the Mediterraneanized Kinneret. Jesus' own refusal of urban interior space made sense only in terms of what it was refusing: the Roman disruption of traditional Galilean village networks through establishment of urban centers. Jesus' distribution of "free fish and bread" made sense only as a refusal of the imperial economic disruptions of local-market commodities circulation, including imperial co-optation of the leading priests, hereditary recipients of food tithes. Jesus' trope of "fatherhood" and his rejection of family values made sense in the idiom of lineage strategy as waged by the Herodians and their collaborators, the ruling Jerusalem priestly families. Jesus' detour out of the Jordan corridor after accepting John's baptism was a disengagement from Herodian multinational business traffic in particular and from Roman water management in general, which again was the spatial and cultural context in which it made sense. These material aspects of empire—urban architecture, commodities acquisition, manipulation of kinship-based traditional leadership institutions, and control of the water—would later evoke the different but comparable symbolic resistive responses of early Judaism discussed above. That is, Judaism would develop its own distinctive resistive features: novel closures of the architectural space of the synagogue and *miqveh*; elaboration of legal rulings to preserve or reestablish the sacral character of foodstuffs, instructions, and lineages; distinctive dining and washing practices.

These spatial forms and practices, "Christian" and "Jewish" alike, are resistive but not resistive enough to destroy the empire outright. What they do is to contradict the inevitability of the logic of empire. They attack its perceived reasonableness, its aura of efficiency and inevitability. They deprive it of its hegemonic ability to appear to offer

the superior rationale for organizing human activities. Most importantly, they frame and define the alternative to empire in terms of what
the empire is not.

Therefore, ironically, the paleochurch relies upon having a sound
and functioning empire, in order to maintain the resistive character of
the Jesus movement and to retain the focus of Jesus' teaching after
Calvary and beyond Galilee. The kingdom of God is not free-standing.
It has to be sought in the midst of something else. After Calvary, the
physical sites of the kingdom of God are precisely the Greco-Roman
urban spaces of Palestine and Syria. The means of propagation of the
gospel within cityspace become constitutive of the message itself. "*You
are* non-cooperation with agribusiness; *you are* non-compliance with
the cloaking mechanisms of worldly power" (paraphrasing Matt 5:13,
14). *You are* the realpolitics of free food in the hungry city.

▪ ▪ ▪

If churches today wish to conform themselves to the practices and
messages of their first ancestors in faith, then they need an accurate
account of the doings and teachings of the paleochurch. I have argued
that the mode of self-understanding and mission embraced by the
paleochurch was that of resistance from within imperial structures,
rather than liberation from them. It remains now to consider briefly
whether and to what extent present-day church practices can or should
be modeled after those of the mid-first century.

Christians often simply assume that the actions and intentions of Jesus
himself were replicated perfectly, or nearly so, in the pre-canonical
paleochurch and subsequently in the documentary record of the
Epistles and Gospels and in ecclesiastical institutions. Although historically that did not happen, the assumption still expresses an intention
to do as Jesus did. This intention was and remains a theologically powerful motive. On the other hand, churches today that seek guidance
from the past in a more historically nuanced manner will invest authority in those versions of Jesus' life and message that were captured at
some stage subsequent to Calvary; for example, in the texts of the
canonical Gospels, or in early ecclesiastical institutions. The texts or
the institutions become authoritative reference points and criteria
against which to measure and correct the activities of today's church. A
third ecclesiastical tactic today sidesteps historical questions altogether
by reducing "the Christian tradition" to whatever was believed and
handed on by the generation immediately before our own. The opinions of our parents then simply stand for "the tradition," no matter

what may be learned historically about Jesus and the paleochurch in their own social and geographical contexts.

It seems preferable to take with utmost seriousness the findings of historical scholarship, especially the finding that the paleochurch accommodated the words and practices of Jesus to the urban spaces of the empire. The paleochurch understood itself to be achieving solidarity and continuity with Jesus while adapting its activities to the evolving challenges of imperial colonization after Calvary. It achieved persistence amid historical change. What continued after Calvary was Jesus' refusal of the totalitarian claims of the empire that world markets and steeply stratified social classes were the best way or the only way to organize life on earth. The adaptive innovation put in place by the church from the start was the practice that I have termed stealth tactics. The way of salt and leaven is not absolutely authoritative; it is relatively authoritative insofar as churches today encounter circumstances like those in occupied Palestine.

As it happens, we do indeed live in comparable circumstances. The challenge for those who would follow Jesus today is therefore to devise means of material resistance to the hegemony of empire, which for Americans means the economic architecture of world capitalism supported by consumer ideology and substance abuse. There is no "liberation" from these. But resistance, in solidarity with the paleochurch, can take the form of small-scale refusals to comply with the alleged inevitability of the pomps and glamours of middle-class life. Among these could be named: automobiles and the commuting lifestyle; so-called "life insurance" and retirement funds; careerism; the "soccer mom" syndrome and the overscheduling of adolescent activities; fast food; fashionable clothing manufactured offshore under oppressive labor conditions; the subtle self-replicating practices of racism and classism; the relegation of the very young and the very old to caregiving institutions. Many other taken-for-granted practices could be identified as the means by which human life is colonized in our own everyday concrete experience.

What the paleochurch understood by Jesus' phrase "the kingdom of God" was an elusive reality that had to be sought in the midst of imperial distortions of human life. That reality cannot be fully defined on paper, either in the Gospels or here in this book. The kingdom of God is sought resistively, and therefore is redefined accordingly as historical circumstances change. After Calvary, the people of the paleochurch found it by working stealthily, on a small scale, and in the symbolic idiom of their own world. The next chapter takes up the terms that were available to Jesus before Calvary for imagining, describing, seeking, and finding the kingdom of God.

9 | A Kingdom of Contact

AS FAR AS JESUS IS CONCERNED, "where" and "when" are absolutely the wrong questions to ask about God's kingdom. This reality is one that flouts the spatializations and temporalizations experienced by people in the colonized Galilee of Jesus. Three ancient texts offer similar recollections of a pronouncement by Jesus concerning the *basileia*, God's kingdom:

> You won't be able to observe the coming of God's *basileia*. People are not going to be able to say, "Look, here it is!" or "Over there!" On the contrary, God's *basileia* is right there in your presence. (Luke 17:20–21)

> It will not come by watching for it. It will not be said, "Look here!" or "Look there!" Rather, the Father's *basileia* is spread out upon the earth, and people don't see it. (Gospel of Thomas 113:2–4; Coptic *tmntero* translates Greek *basileia*)

> If your leaders say to you, "Look, the *basileia* is in the sky," then the birds of the sky will precede you. If they say to you, "It is in the sea," then the fish will precede you. Rather, the *basileia* is inside you and outside you. (Gospel of Thomas 3:1-3 = POxy 654)

Logically, for Jesus to deny that God's *basileia* is spatialized, he must be framing that denial in terms of some particular cultural notion of what empire does to space. He must be articulating his denial with his feet planted on some particular terrain, some particular imperially occupied piece of real estate. Let us suppose that he makes these comments while walking past the fields south of Magdala along the lakeside road to Tiberias, with some of his friends around him. They would be looking into imperial space as they approached the capital city of Antipas. If they looked toward the sky, they would see Antipas' new palace on the cliff side, surrounded by administrative buildings, including perhaps the *basilika* or courthouse. If they looked toward the sea, their glance would take in the docks and boats, the transportation system drawing international business interests toward the provincial capital, the freight ships conveying fish products away to distant markets. In all of this, they would be seeing the *basileia* of Rome, and of the client ruler Antipas, and of Antipas' own clients, the local collaborating businesses. They would see this *basileia* embodied and deployed in the splendor of the capital and the bustle of the Lake.

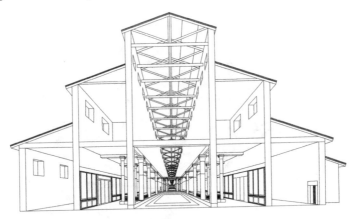

FIGURE 21: *The basilica building at Sepphoris, erected while Jesus was growing up in nearby Nazareth. Drawing by James F. Strange.*

If that is what *basileia* means, Jesus wryly remarks, then the fish and the birds have beaten you to it. The fish swarm into those nets, and the birds swoop through those colonnaded halls. That *basilika* or massive administrative edifice of Antipas is just a fancy perch for birds to nest and poop upon. Those little fishes volunteering to do their part for Kinneret commerce will not be around to share in the profits. The imperial rule of Antipas may look like a good thing at first. It may attract swarms of local collaborators, like eaves draw pigeons and nets catch fish. But there is another *basileia*, which secures the physical realities and business relationships upon which Herodian power depends.

Where did Jesus get such an idea? Hebrew prayer and the Hebrew Bible commonly address God as "King of the Universe." Conversely, all that is, the entire real world, is one universe inasmuch as it belongs to the one divine King. This universe and every part of it is governed from within by the natural tendencies of created things to go the way God intends them to go. Human beings cooperate with the divine rule when they intervene to adjust the universe at times of decision, or whenever things or people have gotten off the track. The thesis that I have advanced in this book is that an indigenous logic of "circulation and grounding" expressed this sense of the divine governance of reality, along with the human capacity to assist in channeling and correcting the flow of real relationships.

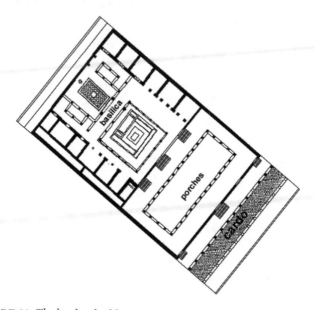

FIGURE 22: *The basilica building at Sepphoris. Plan of the ruin, after a drawing by James F. Strange. This building occupied a block approximately 40 by 60 meters on the Cardo or main street of the city. It was probably founded during the rebuilding of Sepphoris by Herod Antipas in the early first century* CE, *and subsequently was remodeled several times. This basilica would have been visible from Nazareth, some three miles away.*

Roman occupation, embodied and applied in urban architecture, was a tremendous affront to this cultural perception. Aqueducts, theaters, monumental roads, and above all, the *basilika* or central administrative building to which all roads led—these structures imposed a different governance upon the land. The *basileia* or empire of Rome disrupted virtually every material expression of divine sovereignty. Jesus' choice of the term *basileia tou theou*, "empire of God," is an ironic challenge to the empire of Caesar, which was so concretely deployed all around him in Galilee: in the land, on the sea, in the cliffs towering above the sea, where even the birds seemed to be transferring their allegiance to it.

As a spatial resistance, then, the *basileia* that Jesus was looking for would do the same sorts of things that were done in the Herodian *basilika*, but would do them in favor of the people of the land rather than for the benefit of the colonizers and their clients. Specifically, the kingdom of God would dispense justice. It would manage the distribution of food and other commodities. It would return tithes and tolls to the local economy. It would bring people together in new affinities and interests, apart from traditional kinship lines.

We must admit, then, that the *basileia* sought by Jesus was also contrary to the traditional laws of Israel, in the Judean aristocratic and collaborative version in which they were expressed in his own time and place. God's kingdom, in Jesus' view, would not govern through the reckoning of purity in kinship or in the tithing and handling of foodstuffs. The discourse of God's kingdom would not be enclosed in the built environment. Outdoor light, free food, and wild water would be the substances of this kingdom. Not in themselves, however. The openness, the untithedness, the wildness were meaningful *as a critique of* traditional religio-social practices, that is, as a reminder that it is God who governs while humans merely assist. Unlike his contemporaries the radical Cynic sages, Jesus does not advocate a return to some pre-civilized pure natural state, prior to Torah. He reminds people that there is nothing in existence prior to Torah, for God rules in all natural processes and human relationships, whether or not human beings have built their material structures to help or hinder.

This insight makes sense on the social frontier between what I have termed the indigenous logic of "circulation and grounding," and the material deployment of Roman colonial structures in Galilee. Jesus' notion of the *basileia* articulates the experience of someone living in a contact situation, at the troubled and complex interface of two or even three worlds. In the Galilee of Jesus, the Herodian-Roman *basileia* had arrived on the heels of the Hasmonean-Judean re-settlement and re-development of the land. The message of Jesus, then, is expressed as a blending of the indigenous idiom with the idiom of empire.

Companions on the edge

Jesus lived on the edge of empire, and he was not alone. In chapter seven we considered evidence that places Jesus within the orbit of

Antipas' imperial establishment at Tiberias, at least as a young man before his encounter with the anti-Herodian teachings of John the Baptist. The Gospel of Luke reports that Jesus attracted the attention of Joanna, the wife of Chuza, who was Antipas' chief of staff.

Joanna, as the wife of a high-ranking officer of the Herodian court, was an important and powerful personage. It is likely that her responsibilities included providing hospitality for guests at the palace in Tiberias. Plausibly, in that capacity she dealt with suppliers of food and entertainment from the local region. I have suggested that the Mary who was known as "Mary of Magdala" may have represented a purveyor of fresh fish, salt fish, and fish sauce in that town, which was a few miles north of Tiberias.

The fact that women were engaged in that kind of business in Herodian times is attested by an archaeological finding at Masada, the Judean desert fortress built by Antipas' father, Herod the Great. The massive storerooms at Masada yielded many storage jars, some of which were labeled with the names of their suppliers, according to Cotton and Geiger. The jars from local suppliers included four from "Salome," which is a woman's name. There was also one ostracon, that is, an inscribed sherd that may originally have been a tag attached to an amphora with twine, on which the name "Mary of Kypselos" was written, and another ostracon was thought to bear the name of a Nabatean woman. These women appear to have been suppliers of grain, oil, wine, or other comestibles for consumption by the court when Herod was in residence at Masada.

If women suppliers did business with the great Herodian houses, at least in the area of provisions for feasts and for everyday consumption by the palace staff and clients, then the purchasing agents for those houses also may very well have been women. The business firms of that era could be kinship groups, extended families. It would make sense to send a sister or an aunt to talk to the lady of the palace, if one knew that that lady was making decisions about what to serve at the banquets and what to feed the help. Greek texts indicate that women operated catering services to supply fine comestibles for fancy tables. For bulk foods, business women in Galilee could represent agricultural producers directly, or they could be wholesalers. As we have seen, this is a plausible context for the connection between Joanna, as a purchaser of foods for the tables of Antipas at Tiberias, and Mary, as a representative of the fish-packing interests in Magdala.

Food business was big business in Galilee. Considerations of place must be the starting point for reconstructions of the social world of Jesus, as Seán Freyne has persuasively argued in response to scholars who consider only the texts of sayings attributed to Jesus. In the Galilee of Jesus, food was bringing people together in new ways, as well as driving them apart. How you ate was a clear marker of who you were. Galilean villagers ordinarily ate a mush of cereal and beans, prepared in a common pot and dipped out with bread. Dairy products, poultry, figs, olives, and olive oil enhanced this cuisine. Wine was used sparingly to purify the water. The slaughter of an animal at festival time put meat on the menu, an unusual treat. When villagers began to go to the cities to work, they needed more portable food, or they needed to purchase meals from vendors in the city marketplace. This would have been quite a novel experience, for villages had no restaurants. Traditionally, before the Hasmoneans built their fortified towns, agricultural villas, and industrial installations, and before the Herods built their cities, travelers between villages could count on receiving hospitality and a meal at the home of someone whom they knew, someone with whom they might have distant kinship. This traditional practice is affirmed by Jesus' instructions to his followers that they must accept home hospitality.

Transplanted Judean families who had taken over agricultural estates in Galilee enjoyed a more plentiful and varied cuisine than the indigenous villagers did. Unlike the peasants, the Judeans had the furniture and the indoor spaces to hold banquets at which the diners reclined on one elbow. Reclining is an acquired skill. To recline and dine, you must be able to keep the drapes of your garments out of the fish sauce and out from under the elbows of your couch mates. You must know how to manage your feet and knees. You must have a staff of servers who will hand you the plates and remove them afterwards. You must drink your wine neither too fast nor too slowly. You must know how to make the polite conversation that is expected at dinner parties, a suitable kind of conversation for each of the courses served. Galilean villagers would not know how to conduct themselves in such a situation, without special instruction and practice. Workers and travelers from the surrounding villages might indeed be fed at the villas, but not in the *triklinai*.

On the other hand, someone who was accustomed to recline for banquets in the home of an old Hasmonean administrative family—for example, at a villa in or near Sepphoris—would indeed have the skills needed to accept invitations to dine with others in similar surroundings. This was one benefit of the "Hellenization" of Judean aristocrats. They were equipped to fit in well if they were invited to accept the hospitality of Herodian officials or of the Herodian court itself. They knew how to eat right. Thus, they could mix pleasure with business, and get along in the *basileia* of Antipas.

This brings us to a historical dilemma. It would seem that if Jesus knew how to recline to dine in a *triklinē*, then he was not a simple peasant villager. Or, if he was a peasant villager, then he did not "recline at table" and all those Gospel stories placing him on Greek couches must be inventions of the later Greek-speaking Christian community. This is a high-stakes dilemma. It determines whether we can plausibly claim that "open commensality" and table fellowship were the original embodiment of Jesus' own vision for the *basileia* of God.

It seems, then, that we cannot identify Jesus as a peasant. It is more likely that he gained Hellenistic dining skills at the home of his maternal grandparents who, judging by the fact that they were among those who named a daughter "Mary" to protest Herod's murder of his royal Hasmonean wife, were Judean nationalists residing in Galilee. In Jesus' generation, the political power of northern Judean families had waned, but their economic interests were still a considerable factor in Galilee as Antipas continued to encourage the growth of world markets for the region's agricultural produce. We have seen that Mary of Magdala and Joanna probably came from backgrounds similar to that which I am proposing for Jesus' mother.

In any event, we find Jesus traveling along the same routes where women's trading interests would have taken them. An illuminating example is that of the woman in Mark 7 whom Jesus meets near Tyre, a major port for shipping grain to Rome.

> Suddenly a woman whose daughter had an unclean spirit heard about him, and came and fell down at his feet. The woman was a Greek, by race a Phoenician from Syria. And she started asking him to drive the demon out of her daughter. He responded to her like this: "Let the children be fed first, since it isn't good to take bread out of children's mouths and throw it to the dogs." But as a rejoinder she says to him, "Sir, even the dogs under the table get to eat scraps dropped by children!" Then he said to her, "For that retort, be on your way, the demon has come out of your daughter." She returned home and found the child lying on the bed and the demon gone. (Mark 7:25–30)

This woman is called "a Greek" and "a Phoenician from Syria." Phoenicia was the country that lay along the Mediterranean coast west and north of Galilee, the country where the port of Tyre was located. Syria was the inland province east of Galilee that supplied huge grain shipments to Rome, sending them overland across Galilee to the port. A woman who is designated both Phoenician and Syrian likely was born in one place and then betrothed to the son of a house located in the other. A family that establishes such connections in both coastal Phoenicia and agricultural Syrian looks very much like a family that has organized itself to do business in the international grain trade.

If this woman addressing Jesus is also a "Greek" woman, she is a speaker of the language of international trade. As a Greek-speaking woman, then, she is socially defined in terms of her role as a facilitator of this grain trade, and not in terms of the circulation of "the work of her hands" (in the rabbinic phrase) back to the house of her husband's kin. That means that she is in the business of sending bread in the wrong direction: not to her husband's house to feed her children, but to the port of Tyre and off to Rome. Jesus obliquely suggests that she takes bread out of children's mouths and throws it to dogs. "The work of her hands" is circulating counter to what would seem right to traditional Israelite cultural sensibility.

Given that cultural perception, she is not a particularly appealing individual in the eyes of Jesus. His first response in the story may allude to her multinational "Greek" business practice as a violation of indigenous kin-based circulation patterns and a threat to the pedigrees that they construct and protect. Jesus' traditional assessment of this businesswoman does not surprise her at all. She seems to be familiar with the indigenous customs, and knows how she looks to a Galilean. But as a shrewd and experienced deal-maker, she is ready with the clever reply that convinces Jesus to grant healing for her daughter. The story of this encounter makes sense in a situation of cultural contact between indigenous expectations and imperial market practices. It also suggests that Jesus was traveling in circles where he would come across women doing business as international grain merchants.

Jesus also spent time in Capharnaum, on the "frontier" between the indigenous fishing economy and Roman tax collection. Capharnaum was near the point where two shipping routes crossed. The east-west route ran between Tyre or Caesarea, on the coast, and points east such as Damascus and Babylon. A north-south route went either over the Lake by ship or along the eastern shore by pack animal, through the Decapolis region, then along the Jordan valley toward Jericho. Tarriffs were collected on goods passing along those routes. Therefore, Roman troops and civil servants were stationed at Capharnaum.

It is sometimes said that Jesus welcomed "social outcasts" such as toll collectors and women with gynecological disorders. This term "outcast" tempts us arbitrarily to choose one of the many factions of Galilean society to be *the* dominant and defining group, and then accept that group's definitions of who the outcasts and out-castes are.

Some of the people who are out-caste according to Judean religious law would be reckoned as economically or politically elite on other scales. The woman who touches Jesus' cloak in Mark 5:25–34 apparently was a rather wealthy lady, for she had been attended by many expensive physicians, the story says. Matthew and Zacchaeus were members of the collaborating class, but no more so than the dealers who sold food to Antipas or accepted Antipas' help in arranging international shipping contracts, likely providing employment on the Lake for local people who had lost their land. The colonial situation already produced contacts and close cooperation among factions that, traditionally speaking, would have been "out-caste" to one another.

Jesus, then, is affirming a new intimacy among people that is already coming into being through social adaptations to the reality of the Roman occupation. He is following the lead of women like the clever bicultural woman of Tyre, or like Joanna, or like Mary of Magdala. He is accepting and applauding the way that they have already found, the way of moving forward to survival in the colonized situation. Specifically, what Jesus affirms is not the imperial disruption that is troubling the "circulation and grounding" patterns as traditionally expressed, but rather the survival strategies that people have worked out in the midst of empire. These are what enable Jesus to assert that the *basileia* of God persists in spite of imperial damage to the traditional patterns, for God's governance of the universe never did depend upon them. But he also insists that the *basileia* of the Herods and of Rome does not control the universe, all appearances to the contrary notwithstanding.

Insight dawning slowly

It appears, then, that there were two distinct stages in Jesus' recognition of the *basileia* of God, which can be tentatively sketched as follows. The first step was his involvement with Herodian business interests on the western shore of the Sea of Galilee. The way to this may have been opened to him through family connections among women from Judean lineages who had married into court circles, or through his skills as a craftsman in the shipyards or a healer at the lakeside hot springs. As a young man he accepted the sponsorship of senior Herodian women, including women of Judean lineage who had forged ties of kinship, business, or both with top aides of Antipas. Jesus then saw how *basileia* worked at the level of palace administration and the promotion of regional and world trade. He met elite travelers who were passing through Tiberias. He himself began to travel where the trade routes led, to Tyre and throughout the Decapolis. He also ventured south along the Jordan Valley in Judea, where John was waiting.

Jesus' encounter with John the Baptist would begin the second stage of his realization of the relationship between the *basileia* of Antipas and the *basileia* of God. John saw clearly the complicity between the Roman administration and the aristocracy of Jerusalem, who were running lucrative businesses that benefitted from the Temple sacrifices and the pilgrimage trade. If Jesus happened to be on the road to Jerusalem when he first saw John, he was going toward the Temple from Tiberias along a route "Italianized" by Antipas. John told him to "turn back" and cease to go with the flow of imperial business. Jesus' response to John was not a simple return to traditional perceptions of the correct flow patterns of goods, labor, and ideas in Israel. It was instead a recognition that ultimately it is God who makes things go the way they go. God sends the sun and rain to grow the grain that people ship from Galilee to Tyre to Rome. God quickens life in the womb for the birth of livestock to sell and buy for Temple sacrifice. God starts the springs that feed both the Roman aqueducts and the River Jordan. And God does not do it for profit.

The logic of "transmission and grounding" can serve as a baseline and grammar for interpreting some of the pronouncements and parables associated with Jesus and John the Baptist. For example in the Jesus and John traditions, the foods whose circulation conveys holiness are "wild" foods, those which fall outside the prescriptions for tithing: honey, locusts, fish, mother's milk (Thom 22). Bread, although tithed during kneading, is anomalous in being tithed by women. Wild food, not the regulated and tithed food of the Israelite "grounding" system, is what communicates the holiness of the "kingdom of God" in the Jesus tales. Moreover, the miraculous feeding stories are sited outdoors rather than in either the Roman urban built environment or village houses. Light from the heavens falls on the whole scene without any architectural assistance at all. Jesus interprets Torah without illumination arranged by human hands. Water, too, is wild and supersedes the need for water architecture. Even wine bursts out of wineskins.

The fantasy Jesus meal is everything that the "grounded, grounding, and housed" Israelite family meal is not: outdoors, untithed, unhindered by material scarcity, unconformed to kosher cooking customs, and unassociated with a patriline. No father presides. No kinship is constructed. No caste is nutritionally privileged. The management of "transmission and grounding" stops right here. But so does management according to a calculus of business advantage in the imperial markets. "The *basileia* of God is among you," no strings attached.

The inclusiveness and commensality attributed to Jesus' dining practices by Crossan, Corley, and many others should be re-examined in these indigenous terms. Clearly, they make sense in the idiom afforded by the basic logic of circulating commodities. But it is wrong to conclude from this that Jesus (or his friends) intended to change or subvert the indigenous logic. Rather, the dining practices associated with Jesus are but one expression *made possible by that very logic*, in the culturally and economically distressed situation of imperial contact. The subsequent historical development of those practices is, of course, a separate question.

What about women? Is there warrant for a claim that Jesus wanted to liberate women from oppressive social structures in general, or from the practices constituting the indigenous gender system in particular? The answer must be sought by considering what the material consequences would be if he could somehow bring the "circulation and grounding" of caste and other cultural "fluids" to a screeching halt— for female and male Jewish identities were constructed within those activities. In Jesus' Galilee, imperial economic interventions were already tampering with the practices that culturally constructed femininity and masculinity. In particular, they were diverting women's labor from the patrilineal households to which the women "belonged." They were undermining the perceived need for "fathers" and paternal lineages to stabilize women's economic productivity. Thus, the gender and kinship system that had nurtured Jesus was already damaged and partly dysfunctional. Provisionally we may say that all the women whom Jesus knew were working women. He did not mean to put a stop to work. He wanted to rechannel women's labor, like everyone else's, into "the one thing necessary," "the better portion," the *basileia* of God.

Jesus' own caste was questionable. The Gospels try to establish pure Israelite descent for him, but this effort must be read with suspicion. His flawed kinship likely made him ineligible to marry and unable to establish a household in a "grounded and grounding" Israelite house. As reckoned by Judean religious law, which probably was the law honored by his maternal kin, Jesus was a defective "man" and a defective "Jew" because caste had been lost through the circumstances of Mary's pregnancy. In any event, the Christian traditions indicate that Jesus did not become a householder and father. That means he did not achieve full manhood, as manhood was culturally constructed.

So it is incorrect to claim that the maleness of Jesus is entirely constructed in the rhetoric of twentieth-century historians and theologians, as some feminist interpreters have proposed. The maleness of Jesus was constructed and recognized in his own time and place, by the prevailing cultural logic, for it was configured in a pattern that, while partly strange to us, is also partly analogous to the constructions of maleness familiar to us in our own society. In terms of indigenous Judean and Galilean patterns, Jesus' maleness was constructed as anomalous, like the "defective" malenesses of slaves, freedmen, boys, proselytes, and gentiles. This deviance cannot be understood by us except in comparison with what it deviated from. In reconstructing the logic of first-century gender and kinship definitions, we cannot refuse to grant the partial analogy between them and twentieth-century patterns, or to admit that Jesus' contemporaries recognized him as a male human being. If we do refuse this analogy, then we cannot have even a partial grasp of what Jesus' maleness and kinship may have meant to him and to his family, friends, and enemies. In that case, we would miss important insights into what a "defective" male might have thought about the capacity of the logic of "transmission and grounding" to keep Israel "holy."

The African analogues

Fortunately, we have more than two gender and kinship systems to compare. The partial analogy between the ancient Palestinian conceptions of maleness, and maleness as we Westerners see it today, can be placed in the context of the distinctive kinship and gender reckonings of many other peoples, as described in recent anthropological literature. Comparative study is possible without imposing an essentialist definition of gender or kinship as categories of analysis for societies in which those terms would be alien and unintelligible. What is compared are analogues that are already similar in some ways, although different in other ways. People are quite able to tell anthropologists about the expectations for men and women in their societies. These reports always disclose points of similarity and points of difference with the expectations of other peoples (including the peoples from whom the anthropologists have come).

Moreover, comparative study can suggest hypotheses to guide further investigation. We do not know all the details of kinship and gender in Roman-era Galilee. At first we may not know what to look for in the evidence that we do have. More detailed descriptions of kinship practices in other particular societies may allow us to recognize similar practices in Galilee, or may provide heuristic clues where data are missing. The last two decades have seen the publication of a number of anthropological field studies investigating the gender and kinship practices of particular peoples or regions. These studies offer us cases for comparison. Of the many cases available, we should choose some that are similar to that of Roman-era Galilee in relevant ways. For example, societies where inheritance and descent are reckoned through the father's lineage, where brides transfer residence from the father's home to that of the husband, and where political forces have stressed or disrupted those indigenous practices would offer very apt comparisons for the gender and kinship practices that Jesus knew in occupied Galilee.

A cluster of such societies has been described by Karen Brodkin Sacks in her landmark publication of 1979, *Sisters and Wives*. Sacks studied traditional societies in Africa, at a time when their indigenous kinship practices remained intact or at least were retained in living memory while transitions to Western forms of political and economic "development" were under way. The choice to consider data from Africa is by no means a choice to examine peoples who are somehow "primitive," animalistic, or lingering in some "natural" state prior to human cultural refinement, as might be wrongly supposed by someone laboring under a Eurocentric bias.

Rather, African regional studies offer several distinct advantages for comparison with the Galilee of Jesus. First, in Africa we can get to know societies where traditional practices may be both adapting to, and creatively resisting, newly introduced pressures of state formation, imperial culture, and world markets. These resistive adaptations are matters of living experience and memory in many parts of Africa; while the era of contact between empire and indigenous social practices has already closed in most parts of the Americas and throughout Europe. Today's European and American kinship practices, which are shared by the majority of scholars who seek to investigate the historical Jesus, are in fact profoundly shaped by the pressures of empire and state formation that our ancestors had to cope with in the eighteenth or sixteenth or tenth or third century. Gender and kinship, as *we* know these realities, are inseparable from the mechanisms of control by the state and global business interests. The duties and prerogatives of kinship in our own context are still being renegotiated on fronts such as the provision of care for seniors, children, and adults unable to work in the waged economy. Nevertheless, it is difficult for us to see through assumptions that have become the common wisdom only recently, such as the assumption that rights and responsibilities inhere in individuals. We can identify such assumptions as accommodations to economic forces, and we can question the trade-offs that they represent, when we have the advantage of observing how other people are working out different compromises in similar situations. Anthropology of African societies gives us this advantage.

Comparative data from Africa are helpful for understanding the Galilee of Jesus in several other respects. Contact between the civilizations of the Nile Valley and the peoples of Palestine is older than recorded history itself. This fact strengthens the plausibility that social practices in the two lands may have common ancient antecedents, or may have mutually influenced one another. Thus, African gender and kinship practices might be expected to bear a closer resemblance to indigenous Galilean practices than do the practices of people from farther west, such as Greeks and Romans. In recent decades, much light has been shed on gender practices in ancient Palestine by extrapolating from studies in "classical" antiquity, by which is meant the literature and art of the Greeks and Romans. That interpretive work has been premised in part upon the thesis that the Galilee of Jesus was a "Mediterranean" society, a thesis that was challenged and rejected in chapter four.

Whatever "Mediterranean" might have meant in Roman-era Galilee, it certainly included a large component of African cultural practices. The Romans decorated their public buildings in Galilee with mosaics depicting the Nile, its delta, its vegetation, and the wonderful wild beasts both mythic and real that were thought to inhabit its banks. The writers of the New Testament quoted from an African translation of the Hebrew Bible, the Septuagint. We need not insist upon causal or cultural links between architectural or literary motifs and village customs in the two lands, and we need not affirm continuities of social practice between Roman-era Egypt and sub-Saharan peoples of the nineteenth and twentieth century. We merely observe that Roman-era Galilee was no less "African" than "Mediterranean." Or more precisely: comparative cases drawn from traditional African societies in recent times can enhance our grasp of gender and kinship practices in the Galilee of Jesus, and can compensate for the bias introduced in Jesus Studies by exclusive reliance upon Greek and Roman parallels and the "Mediterranean" anthropology of the 1960s and 1970s.

Let us turn, then, to a brief and generalized account of Sacks's findings in her study of gender and kinship in several traditional African societies. (The following account is a composite, illustrating how gender roles and kinship construct each other. It does not exactly fit any of the particular societies that were so carefully described by Sacks.)

The category of "woman" as such was not a particularly meaningful one among the peoples whose practices Sacks reports. Persons whom we might see as women, and whom we might expect to possess items of property or to exercise rights and responsibilities, were in fact able to alternate between roles having different possessions, expectations, and duties. The two roles named in the title of Sacks's work, sister and wife, are filled by one woman depending upon where she is. One person has the prerogatives of a sister when she is in the household into which she was born, and the prerogatives of a wife when she is in the household into which she was married.

A man, who is someone who stays in one household all his life, sees both sisters and wives around him there. The *sisters*, like himself, have been there since birth. They have various entitlements to the goods and the food of the household, and they reap the benefit of the labor of the wives. The *wives*, who entered the household by marriage, must work to feed and support those who were born there, including the sisters, the men, and the children. Wives rise in seniority as they bear children into the household, for those children have a claim on the labor of the other wives. An individual who is a wife in one house may return to visit in the household where she was born. In her natal house, she remains a sister and is entitled to the fruits of the labor of those who have married into the house (whom we would call her sisters-in-law).

Sisters are valuable, because the household receives cattle as bridewealth when they are married. These cattle are needed by the sons of the house (whom we would call the bride's brothers) so that they can be exchanged in turn for brides who will come into the house to work. Wives are valuable because their labor enriches the house into which they have married and because their children become the sons and daughters of that house. A wife works to support herself in her husband's house, but she can always return to the house where she was born in order to receive food and the benefits of the labor of her brothers' wives. There are many variations on this general pattern in the societies that Sacks studied, and the strategies for arranging marriages are quite complex and ingenious. But this much will suffice to sketch the main details.

We notice immediately that, as in Israel, femininity is mobility in relation to masculinity, while masculinity is stability and is tied to the household. But the African wives are *more* mobile, for they can move back and forth between their natal and marital residences. As in Israel, the gender and kinship system functions to manage labor and to distribute the fruits of labor, particularly the food. There is no such thing as an individual who carries qualities, rights, and duties within himself or herself, apart from his or her social context. Even what we call gender is not a two-valued parameter that can be determined for a given individual apart from her location. There seem to be two ways of being a woman, which every woman oscillates between: as sister, and as wife. Moreover, sisters prior to marriage are different from married-off sisters, for the latter have brought their brothers the ability to marry by bringing bridewealth into the household, while the former are keeping their brothers from marrying and so keeping the household from acquiring new workers. Similarly, wives prior to childbearing are different from wives who have brought new sisters and brothers into the household, or from senior wives whose sons have brought in brides to work and whose daughters have brought in bridewealth so as to make that possible.

Complex variations on this basic pattern provided for the organization of labor and property in traditional societies. Western industrial organization disrupted the flow of goods and labor along traditional kinship lines, first during colonial times in Africa, and then with the formation of Western-style nation states. In capitalist market systems, the labor of wives was taken for granted as the invisible source sustaining the labor of working men. Working women lost their traditional control of markets and marketing networks. They lost access to the food and goods that they traditionally had tapped in to when residing at their natal homes, while their wages accrued to households into which they had married. Western assumptions about land ownership and farming practices also put wives at a nutritional disadvantage. Conversely, new possibilities for working and for retaining the fruits of one's work had an impact not only on the economy, but on gender and kinship as well, since these systems were culturally bound up with the management of labor and could not be conceptualized apart from it. World markets and the nation state brought the possibility of seeing oneself as an individual, but they also took away the social network that had insured a basic level of subsistence for everyone.

Jesus and mobile women

Using the African data heuristically, let us recall that kinship in Roman-era Galilee was also a means of managing labor and property. As we have seen, in Judean religious law the lines of imputed entitlement to the productivity of land and people followed the lines of perceived kinship, which were congruent with the trajectories of the real displacement of brides from the households of their fathers to those of their husbands. Any anomaly in a bride's trajectory could deprive her and her children of property and the fruits of labor that otherwise would have been theirs. But *every* bridal trajectory carried a girl away from her father's house and support. Unlike the African brides whom Sacks described, wives in Israel did not retain the prerogatives of sisters in their natal homes. They had no claim on the labor of their brothers' wives. Instead, they took dowries with them to the households of their husbands, households that henceforth would benefit from their labor. In the event that the husband failed to prosper, the Israelite caste system did not provide for the wife to return to the house of her father and brothers and resume the prerogatives of sisterhood. A prodigal daughter would be unthinkable. The story told in Luke 15:11–32 could not be rewritten starring a girl whose husband wasted her inheritance.

Kinship practices in Galilee probably functioned on the average to maximize the well-being of the people by discouraging the begetting of children in irregular circumstances, since defects in lineage carried heavy economic sanctions and could not be repaired. The averages shifted sharply with the advent of Roman occupation forces. Many young people in and around Sepphoris were sexually assaulted when the city was besieged and burned in 4 BCE. It is plausible that the mother of Jesus was one of the victims of this violence. Jane Schaberg has cited literary evidence to make a case that Jesus, who died the victim of imperial terrorism, was begotten in a similar manner. The archaeological evidence of the siege of Sepphoris confirms at least one event during which Roman soldiers combed through Mary's neighborhood and, following their standard procedure, raped whomever they could catch.

According to provisions later recorded in the Mishnah, every girl in a besieged city lost her high-caste marriageability, regardless of whether a soldier had laid a hand or even an eye upon her. If Mary conceived Jesus after being raped in Sepphoris or in nearby Nazareth, or even if she were merely hiding in Sepphoris when it fell to the siege of 4 BCE, the perceived directionality of her life as a prospective bride went irreparably astray on that day. In either case, Christian belief in Mary's free assent to a divine invitation (Luke 1:26–38) would not be overturned, but it would have to be redirected toward a much more courageous decision on her part. Not an archangel but an enemy soldier would then be the one to deliver the news to Mary that her future was to be quite different from that which she had planned. The assent that the Almighty asked of Mary was her decision to go on living, to survive rather than take her own life after realizing that she had lost eligibility to become a mother in a legitimate Israelite lineage. She chose not to prevent the birth of an out-caste child in her father's house. The word that became flesh in Mary was the brave word "yes," the word of trust that God would find a way to provide a future for her and for Israel, the involuntarily occupied land.

Mary's father proceeded with her wedding. Luke's and Matthew's Gospels assert that Joseph always had been the intended husband. This is doubtful, if Mary's lineage was Judean and her family had come to

Galilee in Hasmonean times, a thesis for which I have been making a case in this book. If my arguments have been sound, then Mary's family originally would have been looking for a better match than Joseph the craftsman. They would have had their sights set upon an alliance like that made by Joanna's father when he betrothed her to Chuza, a Herodian administrator with good political prospects, or like that made by Elizabeth's father when he found a husband for her within his own priestly caste (Luke 1:5). The disaster at Sepphoris would have ended any such aspiration. Joseph was the solution to the problem of Mary's pregnancy, from her family's point of view. Joseph was the family's second choice but God's first choice, we may surmise, and Joseph made his own courageous assent to this proposal (Matt 1:18–25).

We have indirect evidence that Mary's father did not close the doors of his house against her after she went to reside with Joseph, but continued to welcome Mary and the child into his home. In other words, Mary had the privileges of an African sister in her natal home—not by law and custom, but by the kindness of her family of origin. The evidence for this is of two kinds. First, when Jesus grew to maturity he apparently did not marry or seek to marry. This indicates that he accepted the definition of himself as ineligible to contract a proper marriage under Judean religious law. He declined to go ahead and marry without regard to Israelite caste, like the unobservant "people of the land." He chose to forgo founding a household of his own, because he was not eligible to do so. He did not bring into the world any more children outside of Israelite caste. This decision indicates that Jesus both knew and honored the interpretation of the Law that was taught by Judean religious authorities. He learned it somewhere. The Gospels attest that Jesus knew the Law on many other points, could argue about it effectively with learned scribes from Jerusalem, and had developed his own new interpretation of it. But this was later, in his maturity, about the age of 30. Jesus would have been half that age, a teenager like his mother when she conceived him, at the point in time when he realized that no betrothal would be arranged for him. This fact, and coming to grips with its legal rationale, is plausibly at the heart of Jesus' own revisioning of the Law and the principles for applying it in human lives. We may think of the young man pondering the contrast between a grandfather's house where he was lovingly welcomed, and a Law which was read so as to close the doors of Israelite kinship and shut out people like himself, who were a large and growing portion of the population of Galilee.

The second sort of evidence that supports this scenario is the fact that Jesus reportedly had acquired the skills for participation in elite

Hellenistic social situations. He was at ease at formal dinners. He knew how to recline at table. He was in demand as a dinner-party guest. He could speak well to wealthy hosts, and he could effectively address large crowds. He probably could speak and think in Greek as well as Aramaic. He sounded like a Cynic sage. Jesus could argue with learned emissaries from Jerusalem, and for their part, they took the trouble to engage him in conversation. Influential businesswomen noticed him. Herod Antipas, tetrarch of Galilee, wanted to meet him. The picture of Jesus that the Gospels paint is of someone who had acquired the manners and the self-confidence to go where Galilee's indigenous "people of the land," the peasants and artisans, did not go. The most plausible source for such skills is access to a home where they were taught by example. Not in the house of Joseph the worker, but rather in the house of a Hasmonean retainer who had named his daughter Mary, do we find a place where the young Jesus could have learned how to conduct himself properly in elite Greco-Jewish and Greco-Roman circles. The most subtle lesson that Jesus learned was that proper behavior could be crafted into profoundly potent resistance. For Joseph taught him what to do with tools.

A *basileia* of sisters

We see Jesus, his deeds, and his teachings in a new light when we consider the kinship and gender practices of his society. In Jesus' day those practices were not engaged in placid maintenance of a traditional society; they were disrupted by and creatively adapting to the incursions of empire. Jesus himself fits into no one simple category. He passes as a Judean gentleman at Hellenistic symposia meals, but he also passes as a Galilean waterman on the docks at the Magdala fishworks. The frontiers of his land project into his soul: indigenous Galilean, transplanted Judean, dancing with Herodians and Romans. He is *mestizo*, culturally mixed, out-caste, transgressive of borders. This is why he can see things in a new way.

When Jesus talks about the kingdom or *basileia* of God, he is taking the reality of *basileia* as he knows it and giving it a novel spin. The real *basileia* that Jesus knows is the tetrarchy of Herod Antipas, with its head at Tiberias and its tentacles draped across the Sea of Galilee and the fertile inland valleys. It is not a totally bad beast. Jesus met some good people in the service of Rome, people who were able to do good and do well by cooperating with Antipas' enterprises. He was particularly impressed, perhaps, with what women could accomplish when cut loose from traditional kinship-based labor practices. (In any event, we do not hear him advising Joanna, the Magdalene, the Syro-Phoenician bilingual, or any other woman of means to leave her business affairs behind and return to her husband's house. He thinks that Mary of Bethany has chosen well in refusing traditional labor.) The *basileia* of God, quite like the *basileia* imposed upon Galilee by Roman colonization, will facilitate the entrepreneurship of women.

This is not to say that human beings are the ones who establish God's empire. God's *basileia* is already here in our midst, no matter what we do for or against it. It is the matrix from which we are born and grow. For Jesus, God is not only king but father. God's *basileia* is a father's household. In fatherhood, we have another metaphor whose meaning depends upon the cultural meanings of the term in the society of Jesus. As we have seen, the father is perceived as the stabilizer of a lineage in Israel, and must protect it from vulnerabilities that might be introduced by the wrong kind of bride. The divine Father overcomes all defects in lineage, for no one is excluded from inheriting the riches of this household.

Conventionally, Christians have meditated upon divine fatherhood in terms of a father-son relationship. But the African anthropological data now enable us to explore the meaning of this metaphor in different terms, terms which might very well have occurred to Jesus in his cultural vocabulary, but which are difficult to grasp in our own Western context. We can now ask: What kind of daughters does the divine Father have in his household? Are the women of God's *basileia* sisters or wives, in the African sense of those terms? *Wives* remain "outsiders" to the houses into which they marry. They must labor for the benefit of others, and they have no entitlement to the goods of the house. *Sisters* are always "insiders" to the houses in which they were born, even after they have married and gone to take up residence in another house. Any woman can arise and return to the house of her father. She will always be received as someone entitled to the goods and the care of that household.

In my reconstruction of Jesus' boyhood experience, Mary was in fact treated like an African sister when she visited the home of her father. In my reconstruction, Mary's father was under no further obligation to his daughter after he had settled her with a dowry in the house of Joseph to bear her out-caste child and to work as a proper wife. Nevertheless, Mary's father did not shut the doors of his house to her, but welcomed her with joy and feasting whenever she returned to him. In my reconstruction, Mary's father treats her like the father treats the errant son in Luke 11. The boy Jesus is there watching, and he keeps all these things in his heart.

God the Father, as Jesus knows him, runs a household where all the women have the same birthright. All are "sisters," with full entitlement to the goods of the *basileia*. There are no "wives," in the sense of latecomers, second-class laborers, who sweat to sustain others while they are grudgingly and gradually allowed to earn places of their own through childbearing. I am using the terms "sister" and "wife" in the African sense described by Karen Sacks, and not with the meanings that these terms commonly have in Western discourse. In the traditional societies that Sacks studied, these terms have to do with the management of labor and the distribution of commodities, as well as with inheritance and social identity. The African terminology does not perfectly coincide with that of Jesus' society, but neither does our own. What the African terms do is to throw new light on the range of kinship meanings that were available to Jesus, and out of which he crafted his version of God as Father of a household, King of a *basileia*.

Most importantly, there are no bastards in the Father's house. There are no defects of lineage, no breaks in the lines of entitlements to God's provident care. Women cease to pose any threat to the proper maintenance of acceptable religious identity as Israelite caste. Or more precisely, women remain vulnerable to violent attack by the military and economic forces of empire. Women and men may indeed still be abused and murdered, like Herod killed Mariamme, her brother and her sons. This violence breaches the lineages of Israel, but it does not breach the lines of the Father's provident care for Israel. It does not slam the door of God's *basileia* in the victims' faces. The virgin does not lose the value of virginity when she is the victim of violence. In Christian tradition, victims of persecution who were routinely and legally raped by the Romans before being murdered have been acclaimed as *virgin* martyrs for twenty centuries. The doctrine of the virgin birth of Jesus is not a gynecological doctrine.

The cultural meaning of virginity, for the people among whom Mary and Jesus grew up, was to designate a girl who was about to cross thresholds, to transfer residence from her father's house to the house of her husband. The virgin daughter is still under her father's protection and still labors for the benefit of the household into which she was born and whose wealth she shares. The married daughter does not; she labors for someone who is not her father, someone from whom she does not stand to inherit anything. To say that God is Father is to say that women need never leave the Father's house, the *basileia* of God. No matter where they may travel or live or work, they are entitled to God's protection and they are to labor on behalf of God's *basileia*. One of the senses in which Mary the mother of Jesus remains virgin is that she recognizes this fact and takes advantage of it. Mary is the first of the "sisters" to claim her inheritance in the Father's house, notwithstanding any marital transfer or defect of caste. She belongs to God's royal household by birth, not marriage. She is a daughter; she does not have to earn her place there by pleasing anyone else.

Besides his mother, Jesus came across a number of other women in the *basileia* of Antipas who were pushing the envelope of indigenous labor and gender practices, as we have seen. Their example helped him to imagine a Father whose household was more like the Roman empire than the Israelite household, in that certain important circulation patterns had been exploded beyond repair. There was no turning back to a system of local and regional distribution of commodities, for example. There was no hope of repairing Israelite lineages for the majority of the population in Galilee, after so many generations of immigration, buy-outs of ancestral farms, displacement of young people to the cities as laborers, and routine use of rape as a military tactic to terrorize and control the people. Traditional integrated practices of gender, kinship, labor management, and food distribution were wrecked. Jesus' quest for the *basileia* of God is an attempt to sort out the pieces, patching together a new vision that can inspire hope and creative engagement with the situation as he saw it.

Jesus combined aspects of Israelite fatherhood with aspects of secular empire in his vision of the *basileia* of God the Father, as we have just seen. In this *basileia*, the flow patterns of kinship no longer need be reckoned with; they no longer matter. The cultural idiom of circulation and grounding is retained, but is represented now in novel practices. Jesus and his band travel among households to spread a new teaching among those who are not their kin, even going contrary to the wishes and the interests of their kin. They develop practices of feeding people with no strings attached. Jesus accepts immersion by John the Baptist, but apparently practices no further water rituals himself. He repairs the damage to human lives and bodies that has been wrought by sickness, injury, or demonic interference. He looks to the Father to correct the errant flow of human lives and the ravages of empire. The career of Jesus comes to an abrupt end when he attempts to interrupt the commercialized flow of sacrificial animals through the Jerusalem Temple.

Historians of early Christianity, of baptism and the eucharist, can find a starting point for the subsequent development of sacramental traditions in these gestures.

▪ ▪ ▪

In conclusion, it is clear that the indigenous caste system is the proper target of research for those who wish to reconstruct the Galilee of Jesus. Caste was an integrated set of practices for the symbolic and material management of commodities and of other entities culturally defined as fluid. Caste found its architectural expression and its chief means of implementation in the Israelite house. The practices of caste were pervasively, even if inadvertently, disrupted by Roman imperial contact. Yet these Judaism-constituting practices were resilient enough to devise symbolic resistances in their own idiom, resistances whose traces can be read from the landscape of Israel today.

Judaism's adaptation to imperial colonization was still in its early stages when Jesus of Nazareth came up with his own, rather different proposals for the future of God's people amidst the Roman Empire. Early rabbinic Judaism and early Christianity have different histories, but they are both responses to the disruption of cultural practices by Roman occupation, and they both make material proposals for viable co-existence with the empire. Our understanding of both of these histories can be enhanced by comparative research guided by the archaeology of gender and caste. Such work must supplement social reconstructions deduced from universal sociological and ideological models.

Research that draws its evidence from material remains as well as from texts can overcome the objections of feminist critics who have charged that historical Jesus research is necessarily positivist in its scientific practices and rhetoric. For as we undertake to give an account of the social construction of gender, ethnicity, and economic class—not only in twentieth-century scientific discourse, but also in the built environment as well as the texts of the first century—what we are about is precisely an empirical, historical task. The landscape provides another angle of vision and of access to the conflictive social practices constituting the Galilee of Jesus.

10 Bibliographical Commentary

ARGUMENTS AND INFORMATION FROM A VARIETY OF SOURCES have been used in this volume. Readers may wish to examine those sources directly, and may wish to know how they have been weighted in my construction of the case for objective study of the places and spaces that comprised the Galilee where Jesus lived. The following discussion arranges the sources into several categories:

1. reference works
2. on ways to make sense of the past:
    2.1 sociological models, systems, and comparative studies
    2.2 "the archaeology of mind"
    2.3 contact theory
    . 2.4 "situated knowledge" versus recursive practice
3. on ancient technologies
4. on gender
5. on caste and kinship
6. on "Jewishness"
7. on Herod and the Herodians
8. on architectural forms:
    8.1 the house
    8.2 the Temple in Jerusalem
    8.3 the synagogue
    8.4 the *miqveh* or ritual bathing tank
    8.5 the study house
    8.6 the basilica
9. on the landscape:
    9.1 land
    9.2 water
10. on Galilee
11. archaeological site reports
12. history and theology of early Christianity

1. REFERENCE WORKS

The Gospels of the New Testament canon and other ancient texts convey early Christian portraits of Jesus, as well as a wealth of incidental information about his society. A collaborative effort by the fellows of the Jesus Seminar has produced new translations of those texts. The translations are furnished with background notes concerning the seminar's judgments about the relative age of the various sayings and deeds attributed to Jesus. I have endorsed the Jesus Seminar's general method of historical study, although I have given priority to the landscape and to material remains other than texts in my reconstructions of the Galilee of Jesus. The following are basic research tools:

Robert J. Miller, editor. *The Complete Gospels: Annotated Scholars Version*. Revised and expanded edition. Sonoma, CA: Polebridge Press, 1994. This volume has text and limited notes for the 20 known ancient documents that fit into the literary genre of "gospel."

Robert W. Funk, Roy W. Hoover, and the Jesus Seminar. *The Five Gospels: The Search for the Authentic Words of Jesus*. New York: Macmillan Publishing Company and Polebridge Press, 1993. More extensive commentary is offered for the Gospels of Matthew, Mark, Luke, John, and Thomas.

Robert W. Funk and the Jesus Seminar. *The Acts of Jesus: The Search for the Authentic Deeds of Jesus*. San Francisco: HarperSanFrancisco and Polebridge Press, 1998. Commentary on the deeds attributed to Jesus in the canonical Gospels and in several of the non-canonical gospels.

John S. Kloppenborg, Marvin W. Meyer, Stephen J. Patterson, and Michael G. Steinhauser. *Q Thomas Reader*. Sonoma, CA: Polebridge Press, 1990. This is a convenient presentation of the two principal "sayings gospels": the reconstructed Q gospel and the Gospel of Thomas.

John Dominic Crossan, designer and editor. *Sayings Parallels: A Workbook for the Jesus Tradition*. Philadelphia: Fortress, 1986. This indispensable tool for gospel study predates the Jesus Seminar but was used in their work.

For integrating textual evidence with the findings of archaeologists, the best starting point will often be the relevant article in:

John J. Rousseau and Rami Arav. *Jesus and His World: An Archaeological and Cultural Dictionary*. Minneapolis: Fortress Press, 1995.

Summaries of archaeological findings at individual sites are presented in:

Ephraim Stern, editor. *The New Encyclopedia of Archaeological Excavations in the Holy Land*. New York: Simon & Schuster, 1993.

Two excellent multi-volume commentaries provide background information, summaries of the scholarly discussion, judicious interpretation, and suggestions for further research:

John P. Meier. *A Marginal Jew: Rethinking the Historical Jesus*. Volume 1: The Roots of the Problem and the Person. Volume 2: Mentor, Message, and Miracles. New York: Doubleday, 1991 and 1994.

Raymond E. Brown, S.S. *The Death of the Messiah: From Gethsemane to the Grave*. Two volumes. New York: Doubleday, 1994.

2. ON WAYS TO MAKE SENSE OF THE PAST

The spatial approach to understanding Galilee, as proposed and practiced in this volume, has been presented as an alternative to several "modeling" strategies that are widely used in Jesus studies today, particularly in the so-called social science approach to interpreting the New Testament. Those ways of modeling the past were enumerated in chapter three as: an economic conflict model, a gender-ideological conflict model, and an "honor-shame" model. Chapter four went on to criticize the premises and claims of each of those strategies. Here are some of the sources mentioned in that discussion.

2.1. SOCIOLOGICAL MODELS, SYSTEMS, AND COMPARATIVE STUDIES

Although it is sometimes mistaken for an "anthropological" and "cross-cultural" interpretive program, the "Lenski-Kautsky model" draws heavily on the academic disciplines of sociology and empirical political science, as practiced in mid-century America. The original publications were:

Gerhard Lenski. *Power and Privilege: A Theory of Social Stratification*. New York: McGraw-Hill, 1966.

Gerhard Lenski. "Rethinking Macrosociological Theory." *American Sociological Review* 53 (1988) 163-171.

John Kautsky. *The Politics of Aristocratic Empires.* Chapel Hill: University of North Carolina Press, 1982.

Karl Kautsky. *Foundations of Christianity* [1908]. Translated by Henry F. Mins. New York: S.A. Russell, 1953.

Karl Kautsky. *Are the Jews a Race* [1914]. Translated from the second German edition. New York: International Publications, 1926.

Karl Kautsky. *The Materialist Conception of History* [1927]. Abridged and annotated by John H. Kautsky. Translated by Raymond Meyer. New Haven: Yale University Press, 1985.

Lenski collated empirical findings from a great number of actual societies in order to construct a generalized account of certain regularities and correlations that he found to hold constant across comparable cases. In this he was influenced by the "systems theory" of his day. A "social system" is an analogical construction. The analogy is drawn between the metabolic processes by which an individual organism interacts with its environment and maintains itself in a state of physiological equilibrium, and the social "processes" by which a society maintains itself amid historical change. Both are regarded as if they were automatic and mechanical.

Reliance upon this analogy imports certain presuppositions into the study of society: that society is unified and organic, that it is driven by quasi-organic forces of adaptation and evolution, and that decisions and purposes are irrelevant to the system. As sociological systems theory became more nuanced and complex, it overcame some of the theoretical drawbacks of that analogy. But it never abandoned the basic premise that society runs on causal forces that can be measured and that can serve as the basis of prediction. Thus, social systems theory continued to base itself upon a general premise that holds true for physical reactions: like causes always yield like effects. That, in turn, was taken as a warrant for supplying missing pieces from data sets. Since any missing data could be regarded as "results" produced by some antecedent combination of forces, all the researcher would have to do was to find some similar combination of forces in another society, and observe how things turned out there. The "results" in the society that had been thoroughly observed would indicate what "results" must have taken place in the society where observation had been deficient.

General models like that of Lenski were compiled in order to facilitate just this maneuver. This is what I criticized in chapter four as the export of data from models. What models of social systems yield, properly speaking, are hypotheses: scientific guesses that become the basis for further research, leading to confirmation or disconfirmation. It is simply a misuse of sociological method when historians take the hypothesis itself to be data, with no further ado.

Three further considerations might be mentioned. First, if the Galilee of Jesus can be regarded as a social system at all, it was not a system maintaining a state of organic equilibrium. It was a severely stressed system struggling to persist in the face of massive and deliberate imperial incursions. It was a frontier where social, political, economic, and cultural "systems" were colliding. Second, several factors that were significant to the indigenous Galilean and Judean culture were never included in the generic model of Lenski. Kinship, gender, and religious ideology are among the un-modeled factors. Third, there exists no real society that instantiates any of Lenski's ideal-typical social forms. Nothing real ever worked this way. John Kautsky, quoting another social scientist with approval, characterizes his own intention thus:

> My goal . . . is to discover "causal regularities across the various historical cases," to develop generalizations about politics in traditional aristocratic empires—though I am well aware that, in fact, all I can produce is tentative hypotheses. . . . I construct an ideal type of aristocratic politics and develop a general, if very partial and tentative, explanatory theory showing functional linkages among various elements in aristocratic empires. . . . (1982: xii–xiii).

As a source for testable hypotheses, then, the Lenski-Kautsky model remains a general rule and should not be regarded as a complex of universally binding causal relations. John Dominic Crossan has made creative and provocative use of this model in:

John Dominic Crossan. *The Historical Jesus: The Life of a Mediterranean Jewish Peasant.* San Francisco: HarperSanFrancisco, 1991.

John Dominic Crossan. *Jesus: A Revolutionary Biography.* San Francisco: HarperSanFrancisco, 1994.

John Dominic Crossan. *The Birth of Christianity: Discovering What Happened in the Years Immediately After the Execution of Jesus.* San Francisco: HarperSanFrancisco, 1998.

It is also used by Richard A. Horsley in the titles mentioned below (in section 10, Galilee).

John Kautsky followed in the footsteps of earlier marxian economic interpretations of the ancient world. Notable for its methodological restraint was the classic study:

G.E.M. de Ste. Croix. *The Class Struggle in the Ancient Greek World From the Archaic Age to the Arab Conquests.* Ithaca, NY: Cornell University Press, 1981.

De Ste. Croix subscribed to the general marxist perception of history as the inexorable conflict of social forces. Yet he was careful not to project nineteenth- and twentieth-century categories of social analysis back onto the relationships of the ancient world. He writes:

When imperialism leads directly to exploitation of a conquered people, or at any rate the primary producers among them, for the benefit of the foreign rulers, that is a situation *closely resembling* class struggle . . . as certainly happened for example, in Seleucid Palestine and even more in Roman Palestine. . . . (1981: 442, italics added; see also 1–2 and 42–49)

De Ste. Croix made no attempt to corroborate his findings by coming up with material evidence to support them. The ancient texts were his entire universe of data. In this, his work is methodologically and ideologically similar to that of Karl Kautsky (1908), although in a later work Kautsky (1914) called upon many kinds of empirical data to support arguments against both anti-Semitism and Zionism, and in favor of revolution. Yet de Ste. Croix rightly maintained the distinction between his evidence (the texts) and his model ("class struggle"). He asserted resemblance, not identity.

Marxian social theory is used by the anthropologist Karen Sacks as she correlates gender with control over the means of production. Sacks's categories of "sister" and "wife," which designate labor relations as well as kinship relations in the African societies that she studied, emerge from empirical data through comparative investigation of the practices of several peoples. That is why they were suitable for use in chapter nine as a heuristic key to unlock meanings in yet another set of cultures, those of Roman-era Galilee. Sacks's work is discussed further below (in section 4, gender).

2.2. "The archaeology of mind"

Cognitive archaeology stands in stark contrast with the use of sociological "modeling," which, as we have just seen, all but excludes meaning from the past so as to focus on the impersonal and inexorable operation of quasi-natural causal forces of one sort or another. Cognitive archaeology tries instead to discern the meanings that were being negotiated by people living in a particular context. In chapter four I criticized the wholesale transfer of a questionably derived idiom of "honor and shame" from the twentieth to the first century. While I affirm the orientation toward meaning and personal motivation embraced by those who make ancient Galilee out to be an "honor-shame" society, my objection is that this key distinction was not indigenous to the Galilee of Jesus, but arose from mid-twentieth century anthropological studies that have come in for devastating criticism in the years since they first were advanced.

In "cognitive archaeology," a phrase which I borrow from A. Martin Byers, the patterns uncovered at excavated sites are regarded as expressions of the meaningful activities of the people who inhabited them. Mark P. Leone and his colleagues have proposed an "archaeology of mind" for interpreting the colonial and early republican architecture and artifacts of Annapolis, Maryland. Kent G. Lightfoot and colleagues are working on similar premises as they attempt to discern the "underlying organizational principles" of the different groups who lived together in nineteenth-century Fort Ross on the northern coast of California. The recent reports of these two research teams provide an introduction to this new way of interpreting material remains. Their findings and their practices are suggestive for innovations in archaeological work in Israel.

Kent G. Lightfoot. "Culture Contact Studies: Redefining the Relationship Between Prehistoric and Historical Archaeology." *American Antiquity* 60 (1995) 199–217.

Kent G. Lightfoot, Antoinette Martinez, and Ann M. Schiff. "Daily Practice and Material Culture in Pluralistic Social Settings: An Archaeological Study of Culture Change and Persistence From Fort Ross, California." *American Antiquity* 63 (1998) 199–222.

A. Martin Byers. "Intentionality, Symbolic Pragmatics, and Material Culture: Revisiting Binford's View of the Old Copper Complex." *American Antiquity* 64 (1999) 265–87.

Mark P. Leone. "Some Opinions About Recovering Mind." *American Antiquity* 47 (1982) 742–760.

Mark P. Leone. "A Historical Archaeology of Capitalism: Considering Political Context." *American Anthropologist* 97 (1995) 251-68.

Mark P. Leone and Barbara J. Little. "Artifacts as Expressions of Society and Culture: Subversive Genealogy and the Value of History." *History from Things: Essays in Material Culture*, 160–181. Edited by Steven Lubar and W. David Kingery. Washington: Smithsonian Institution Press, 1993.

Mark P. Leone. "The Productive Nature of Material Culture and Archaeology." *Historical Archaeology* 26 (1992) 130–133.

Mark P. Leone, Parker B. Potter, Jr., and Paul A. Shackel. "Toward a Critical Archaeology." *Current Anthropology* 28 (1987) 283–292.

Parker B. Potter. "Critical Archaeology: In the Ground and on the Street." *Historical Archaeology* 26 (1992) 117–29.

P. Shackel and B. Little. "Post-Processual Approaches to Meanings and Uses of Material Culture in *Historical Archaeology*." *Historical Archaeology* 26 (1992) 5–11.

The term *recursive* is used by Leone, B. Little, P. Potter, and their colleagues to characterize the way in which artifacts affect the people who have made them and who use them. Potter writes that "the recursive quality of material culture is the capacity of objects to teach their users ways of thinking and behaving." Leone says that "using things substantiates and reproduces all the same social actions that went into the artifact in the first place. Just as language reflects and in use creates, so things that are made reflect but also substantiate and verify, and thus reproduce the processes that led to making them." The notion of recursivity in archaeology is akin to proposals made recently in several other fields. In literary criticism, for example, see Elaine Scarry's phenomenological account of how creativity redounds from the artifact to act upon its creator. In architecture, see Amos Rapoport's work on the meanings of urban architectural design and the uses of urban spaces.

Elaine Scarry. *The Body in Pain: The Making and Unmaking of the World* (New York: Oxford University Press, 1985).

Amos Rapoport. *The Meaning of the Built Environment: A Nonverbal Communication Approach*. Beverly Hills: Sage Publications, 1980. Second edition 1990.

Changes in architecture can be both result and agent of changes in social practices. This insight is developed in:

Matthew Johnson. *An Architecture of Capitalism*. Cambridge, MA: Blackwell, 1996.

P. Lewis. "Common Landscapes as Historic Documents," in *History From Things: Essays in Material Culture*, ed. S. Lubar and W. Kingery, 115–39 (Washington: Smithsonian Institution Press, 1993).

Johnson demonstrates ways of interpreting architecture, landscape, and other material culture as both expressions and instruments of political and economic transition in England from about 1400–1800 CE. Particularly suggestive are the notions of an archaeology of closure and enclosure, and archaeologies of authority. Buildings are effective to the extent that they invoke the particular "grammar" of space and movement that is shared by contemporary people. Lewis reads landscape as a historical document disclosing purposive action. By "cultural landscape," Lewis designates "everything that humans do to the natural earth for whatever purpose but most commonly for material profit, aesthetic pleasure, spiritual fulfillment, personal comfort, or communal safety" (p. 116).

The contrast between social system and intentional meaning is the key distinction between so-called "processual" approaches in archaeology and "postprocessual" approaches such as cognitive archaeology. For an overview of these terms see:

Stephen L. Dyson. "From New to New Age Archaeology: Archaeological Theory and Classical Archaeology—A 1990's Perspective." *American Journal of Archaeology* 97 (1993) 195–206.

Gender and kinship, which were vitally important indigenous cultural meanings in ancient Galilee, are more adequately understood in cognitive archaeology than they were in the sociological models favored by processual archaeology. Elizabeth Brumfiel gave expression to this insight in a now-classic paper, and Alison Wylie has developed the methodological implications in a number of articles.

Elizabeth M. Brumfiel. "Breaking and Entering the Ecosystem: Gender, Class, and Faction Steal the Show." *American Anthropologist* 94 (1992) 551–567.

Alison Wylie. "Putting Shakertown Back Together: Critical Theory in Archaeology." *Journal of Anthropological Archaeology* 4 (1985) 133–147.

Alison Wylie. "The Interpretive Dilemma." *Critical Traditions in Contemporary Archaeology*, 18–28. Edited by Valerie Pinsky and Alison Wylie. Cambridge: Cambridge University Press, 1989. Albuquerque: University of New Mexico Press, 1995.

Alison Wylie. "Invented Lands / Discovered Pasts: The Westward Expansion of Myth and History." *Historical Archaeology* 27 (1993) 1–19.

Alison Wylie. "A Proliferation of New Archaeologies: 'Beyond Objectivism and Relativism'." *Archaeological Theory: Who Sets the Agenda?*, 20–26. Cambridge: Cambridge University Press, 1993.

Alison Wylie. "Evidential Constraints: Pragmatic Objectivism in Archaeology." *Readings in the Philosophy of Social Science*, 747–765. Edited by Michael Martin and Lee McIntyre. Cambridge, MA: MIT Press, 1994.

Alison Wylie. "Angles of Vision: The Engendering of Archaeology Past and Present." Paper presented to conference on "The Women and Gender Question in Science," Minneapolis, 1995.

Alison Wylie. "The Constitution of Archaeological Evidence: Gender, Politics, and Science." *The Disunity of Science: Boundaries, Contexts, and Power*. Edited by Peter Galison and David J. Stump. Stanford, CA: Stanford University Press, 1996.

Wylie's astute analyses of the scientific methods, aspirations, and practices of archaeology have guided my own critical thinking in this book. I have discussed her philosophy of science in:

Marianne Sawicki. *Body, Text, and Science: The Literacy of Investigative Practices and the Phenomenology of Edith Stein.* Dordrecht: Kluwer Academic Publishers, 1997. See especially chapter six.

In the titles mentioned above as examples of "cognitive archaeology," the meaningful categories were elicited from the indigenous cultures themselves, by inference from patterns discerned in the archaeological record, and they were corroborated by several independent inference chains—the so-called "suite of evidence." This is precisely what is missing from contemporary "social science" models of ancient Galilee that have applied the category of "honor and shame" to an ancient society and thereby constructed it as "Mediterranean." If Galilee had been intrinsically Mediterranean in its social practices and sensibilities in Jesus' day, then the Herods would not have had to work so hard to "mediterraneanize" it—an irony pointed out above in chapter seven. The sensibilities of Italy and of the eastern empire were being architecturally and economically promulgated in Israel in the first centuries BCE and CE. Today's "social science approach" to New Testament studies is unwittingly taking the side of Herod and of the Greek-speaking empire, against the indigenous Galilean and Judean cultural expressions that the mediterraneanizing Romans were trying to stamp out.

Although there is indeed a real body of water, bounded by lands that are hilly to mountainous, that is called "The Mediterranean," there is no reason to suppose that this real territory corresponds to a homogenous cultural group, the Mediterranean area. The cultural Mediterranean is a research construct produced by anthropologists. It took shape in publications such as the following:

Julian A. Pitt-Rivers, ed. *Mediterranean Countrymen: Essays in the Social Anthropology of the Mediterranean.* Paris: Mouton & Co., 1963.

J. G. Peristiany, ed. *Honor and Shame: The Values of Mediterranean Society.* London: Weidenfeld and Nicolson, 1965.

Jane Schneider. "Of Vigilance and Virgins." *Ethnology* 9 (1971) 1–24.

J. Davis. *People of the Mediterranean: An Essay in Comparative Social Anthropology*. London: Routledge & Kegan Paul, 1977.

David D. Gilmore. "Anthropology of the Mediterranean Area." *Annual Review of Anthropology* 11 (1982) 175–205.

David D. Gilmore, ed. *Honor and Shame and the Unity of the Mediterranean*. Washington: American Anthropological Association, 1987.

More recently, a number of anthropologists have offered critiques of this construction.

Michael Herzfeld. "Honor and Shame: Problems in the Comparative Analysis of Moral Systems." *Man* 15 (1980) 339–351.

Michael Herzfeld. "The Horns of the Mediterraneanist Dilemma." *American Ethnologist* 11 (1984) 439–454.

Michael Herzfeld. "'As in Your Own House': Hospitality, Ethnography, and the Stereotype of Mediterranean Society." In *Honor and Shame and the Unity of the Mediterranean*, 75–89. Edited by David. D. Gilmore. Washington: American Anthropological Association, 1987.

Lila Abu-Lughod. "Zones of Theory in the Anthropology of the Arab World." *Annual Review of Anthropology* 18 (1989) 267–306.

Mediterranean-area anthropology of the 1960s reflected the practices of traditional societies in the twentieth century. It was borrowed and used as a foundation for a novel approach to the New Testament by Bruce Malina, John Pilch, Jerome Neyrey, K.C. Hanson, and their colleagues. Important works from this school include:

Bruce J. Malina. *The New Testament World: Insights from Cultural Anthropology*. Atlanta: John Knox Press, 1981.

Bruce J. Malina. *Christian Origins and Cultural Anthropology: Practical Models for Biblical Interpretation*. Atlanta: John Knox Press, 1986, revised edition 1993.

Bruce J. Malina. *The Social World of Jesus and the Gospels*. New York: Routledge, 1996. This is a collection of articles previously published in *Biblical Theology Bulletin* and in other journals and edited volumes. Hypotheses about child-rearing practices in first-century Palestine provide a starting point for speculation about relationships among men and women in that era.

Jerome H. Neyrey, ed. *The Social World of Luke-Acts*. Peabody, MA: Hendrickson Publishers, 1991.

Jerome H. Neyrey. *What Is Social-Science Criticism?* Minneapolis: Fortress, 1993.

K.C. Hanson and Douglas E. Oakman. *Palestine in the Time of Jesus: Social Structures and Social Conflicts*. Minneapolis: Fortress Press, 1998. This work is enhanced by a website where additional instructional materials are available, although users should be aware of the methodological problems.

John J. Pilch and Bruce J. Malina, editors. *Handbook of Biblical Social Values*. Peabody, MA: Hendrickson Publishers, 1998. The danger of this work is that its format—a specialized dictionary—camouflages the weak methodological basis on which a great deal of the information relies.

Halvor Moxnes. "BTB Readers Guide: Honor and Shame." *Biblical Theology Bulletin* 23 (1993) 167–176.

Halvor Moxnes, editor. *Constructing Early Christian Families: Family as Social Reality and Metaphor*. New York: Routledge, 1997.

Critiques of Mediterranean-area anthropology and of the projection of the honor-shame template onto first-century Palestine were presented in two earlier works of mine. In a more recent and extensive study, F. Gerald Downing concurs, and goes on to point out further difficulties.

Marianne Sawicki. "Making the Best of Jesus." Paper presented to the Society of Biblical Literature, November 1992, and posted on the IOUDAIOS list server ever since. This paper will be printed in a forthcoming volume of the Feminist Companion series, edited by A.-J. Levine, from Sheffield Academic Press.

Marianne Sawicki. *Seeing the Lord: Resurrection and Early Christian Practices*. Minneapolis: Fortress Press, 1994. See pages 246–249.

F. Gerald Downing. "'Honor' Among Exegetes." *Catholic Biblical Quarterly* 61 (1999) 53–73.

When parables or *chreiai* in the Gospels seem to exhibit a concern with "Mediterranean values" of honor and shame, this should be taken to indicate that they come from strata of the early Jesus movement that accepted Herodian and Roman cultural practices, which were not indigenous to Galilee.

2.3 CONTACT THEORY

In the 1990s there has been an explosion of interest in post-colonial studies, in academic fields ranging from literature to architecture to the social, behavioral, and environmental sciences. Western academic frameworks of analysis are increasingly recognized to be ideologically complicit with the structures and practices of empire. Scholars and writers in newly independent nations are assessing their experiences of having learned the truths of the colonial culture during their early years, and then having attempted to return to some sort of indigenous cultural life. They report that it has proved impossible for them to do so. Colonized people take on a version of the oppressor culture. It becomes for them a medium of creativity and innovation, but not without a good deal of soul-searching and guilt.

The experiences of people in post-colonial situations today have shed new light upon the past. We can now see Galilee as a land where Judean and then Roman occupation produced cultural compromises that are in some respects comparable to today's colonial and post-colonial cultural experiences. They are not identical, of course; but the twentieth-century experience can guide historians in formulating new questions and expectations about the past. In the Americas, a new interest in "contact" situations has emerged among archaeologists.

"Contact" is the shorthand term for the complex and negotiated borders between two or more cultures when representatives of those cultures live together. The borders are differently drawn, depending upon what sector of daily life may be in question. Perhaps when a woman cooks and weaves, she uses materials and practices that are familiar from her family of origin; but when she participates in group activities such as agriculture or trade, she adopts the customs of the family into which she has married, who may be colonists. Young and old, rich and poor, male and female may alternate between cultures at various times and in various circumstances. The studies of Kent Lightfoot at Fort Ross, mentioned above, report on a site of contact among Russian colonials, Eskimo workers, native Californians, and their mixed offspring. European imperialism produced many contact sites in the Americas, but other ancient contacts are known as well. For example, the Inka colonized many other native peoples in ancient South America. The literature of contact is vast and still growing, but the following titles can serve as an introduction:

J. Levy and C. Claassen. "Engendering the Contact Period." In *Exploring Gender Through Archaeology: Selected papers from the Boone Conference*, 111–126. Edited by C. Claassen. Madison, WI: Prehistory Press, 1992.

S. Suleri. *The Rhetoric of English India*. Chicago: University of Chicago Press, 1992.

J. Buttigieg and P. Bové. "An Interview With Edward W. Said." *Boundary* 2 20 (1993) 12.

M. Pratt. *Imperial Eyes: Travel Writing and Transculturation*. London: Routledge, 1992.

2.4. "SITUATED KNOWLEDGE" VERSUS RECURSIVE PRACTICE

The claim is often heard that all knowledge is "situated." An account of the rise of this metaphor in twentieth-century philosophy has been proposed by Neil Smith and Cindi Katz, who find that its popular acceptance is largely owing to an essay by Adrienne Rich.

Neil Smith and Cindi Katz. "Grounding Metaphor: Toward a Spatialized Politics." *Place and the Politics of Identity*, 67–83. Edited by Michael Keith and Steve Pile. London: Routledge, 1993.

Adrienne Rich. "Notes Toward a Politics of Location." *Blood Bread and Poetry: Selected Prose, 1979–1985*. New York: W.W. Norton, 1986.

In fact, Leibniz had already linked physical location to identity at the turn of the eighteenth century, and this was a point on which Isaac Newton famously disagreed with him. In the nineteenth century, Hegel and Marx regarded knowledge as socially situated. Durkheim brought that notion into sociology. In the descriptive tradition stemming from those writers, the "social locators" of knowledge and identity include factors such as economic class, ethnic heritage, gender practices, and nutritional prerogatives.

It is important to recognize that these factors have nothing to do with real, material position. Although they are spatially expressed, as all human realities are, these factors operate in all localities. For example, a segregated "white neighborhood" in an American city is not a place where there are only white people and no people of color. Rather, it is a place where whites sleep and eat while people of color work at various jobs under surveillance. Racial "segregation" is actually intimate contact: a finely orchestrated cohabitation of one physical space by people whose so-called "social locations" differ. Thus while the common knowledge that is race is spatially deployed, it is not equivalent to a location. In critical social analysis, terms of spatial location become metaphors for one's assigned racial identity. But analysis founders when metaphorical and literal senses are confused.

One danger of such spatial equivocation is that it imposes a one-to-one mapping of social knowledges onto physical places. Although place determines what someone can physically see while occupying it, place does not entirely determine the knowledges or the practices that can transpire within it. Different subjects can physically occupy the same space (as in the example of races in a "segregated" neighborhood). This distinction becomes particularly important when one space is supporting many successive overlays of use patterns. In the outdoor history parks in Israel that I discussed, a single physical space situates three contrasting programs of socially located information access: an ancient elite pattern, an ancient service pattern, and a twentieth-century scientific pattern. The frontiers among these situations—two synchronic, one diachronic—cannot be adequately conceptualized unless the real and metaphorical senses of "social location" are kept strictly distinct. The urban built environment always lends itself to uses beyond and even contrary to those that it was originally intended to facilitate.

A second danger posed by spatial equivocation is that it obscures human creative action. Whatever people do may be regarded as a mere predictable result of the social and physical situations within which they live. This brings up an issue widely debated within social theory: whether to accord priority to "agency" or to "structure." Anthony Giddens argues that the two are not opposed but are embedded in one another.

Anthony Giddens. *Central Problems in Social Theory: Action, Structure, and Contradiction in Social Analysis*. Berkeley: University of California Press, 1979.

In other words, social structures are the persistent regularities of human actions that tend to endure unchanged, even though their influence may be modulated by emotions and other subjective psychological determinants of action. Structures gradually mutate, or, in our metaphor, positions subtly shift, as the subjects' actions "reflexively" both amplify and modify them. According to Giddens, then, subjects themselves are the principal targets of their own reflexive monitoring.

But other theorists invest reflexivity in structuration itself, altogether doing away with subjectivity as the bearer of structure. For example:

Scott Lash and John Urry. *Economies of Signs and Space*. London: Sage, 1994. See pages 31–109, especially 64.

Lash and Urry develop the notion of reflexivity as a principle of innovation in systems of production. It is an aesthetic, hermeneutic principle rather than a principle of causality. Nevertheless, subjectivity boils down to the reflexive component of structuration, a mere feedback mechanism. Or, in our metaphor, the subject coincides with its social location.

Clearly, this makes sense metaphorically but not literally. Subjects literally inhabit physical structures, but we are in no way identical with our houses and cities. We engage in significant reciprocal relations with these built places, but those relations are not "reflexive." Rather, they are "recursive," the term favored by Leone and his colleagues in cognitive archaeology (in titles listed above in section 2.2). Objects of material culture have the capacity to reproduce the social relations obtaining among those who first made them. Yet, recursion can be resisted and redirected. Innovations happen. Places and things can be turned to uses unforeseen by their makers. They are not causes in relation to human actions, and cannot completely determine the paths through them that people pursue. Physical things, by virtue of their very physicality, remain capable of multiple uses. Places are big tools.

There is a third danger in confusing "social location" with physical space, and particularly the bodily space enclosed by one's own skin: the social factors that "situate" knowledge and praxis may be reduced to mere biographic or demographic facts. This privatizes and individualizes the epistemological "standpoint," as David Harvey argues.

David Harvey. "Class Relations, Social Justice and the Politics of Difference." *Place and the Politics of Identity*, 41–66. Edited by Michael Keith and Steve Pile. London: Routledge, 1993.

Harvey (pages 57–58) criticizes this individualization as a "vulgar" conception of situated knowledge, according to which "I see, interpret, represent, and understand the world the way I do because of the particularities of my life history." After this reduction, it becomes impossible in principle ever to understand someone else. Each person is the infallible authority concerning his or her own experience, but can never communicate it. Harvey would retain the metaphor of "situation" in its non-vulgar, dialectical sense: that knowing occurs as participation in an ecological, economic chain of production and consumption amid limited resources.

The social location of discourse is invoked in a contrasting sense by Habermas and his followers.

Jürgen Habermas. *Strukturwandel der Öffentlichkeit: Untersuchungen zu einer Kategorie der burgerlichen Gesellschaft.* Neuweid: Luchterhand, 1962. Translated by Thomas Burger as *The Structural Transformation of the Public Sphere: An Inquiry into a Category of Bourgeois Society.* Cambridge, MA: MIT Press, 1989.

Jürgen Habermas. *Theorie des kommunikativen Handelns.* Two volumes. Frankfurt am Main: Suhrkamp, 1981. Translated by Thomas McCarthy as *The Theory of Communicative Action.* Boston: Beacon Press, 1984–1987.

Seyla Benhabib. *Situating the Self: Gender, Community and Postmodernism in Contemporary Ethics.* New York: Routledge, 1992.

Benhabib, following Habermas, calls for the establishment of a public sphere, a pseudo-space constituted by procedures ensuring democratic participation by all people in reaching consensus for concerted action. Anyone who would be affected by norms and decisions would have to have a say in their formulation. But Benhabib's proposal entirely overlooks the real spatial constraints on any democracy.

This brings us to a fourth danger of equivocating between metaphorical and material placement: the jargon of discourse-as-space and space-as-discourse. This jargon de-localizes the subject altogether and disperses it among many "places" or "discursive regimes." The physical body, indivisible as it is, somehow gets misplaced—that means lost—so that the individual subject now is virtually unavailable even to itself. Knowledge becomes more idiosyncratic and inaccessible than ever. Personal identity becomes mere inscription.

The "inscription" metaphor introduces further spatial equivocation. Events occurring "in the depths" of the human psyche are correlated with "surface" features of the human body. This dismisses the body's potential for action and motion. Bodily spatiality is reduced from three dimensions to two, like a flat page awaiting the application of signs. The body, or more precisely, its skin, is imagined to be the raw material out of which the human subject is made. This twist on spatial equivocation is rooted in psychoanalytic theory. Elizabeth Grosz examines the sources of inscription theory in Nietzsche and Freud.

Elizabeth Grosz. "Bodies and Knowledges: Feminism and the Crisis of Reason." *Feminist Epistemologies*, 187–215. Edited by Linda Alcoff and Elizabeth Potter. New York: Routledge, 1993. See especially pages 195–199.

Elizabeth Grosz. "Bodies—Cities." *Sexuality & Space*, 241–253. Princeton Papers on Architecture, volume 1. New York: Edited by Beatriz Colomina. Princeton Architectural Press, 1992.

The inscribed body is also a favorite metaphor of Michel Foucault and is current among French feminists. Gender, sexuality, class, race, and other identity-assigning structures are then regarded as mere significations written onto the receptive surface of the body. Accordingly, the places that the body inhabits are reduced to representations or simulacra of the inscribed body itself. The city is just the body writ large. And the body is a city writ small. Grosz (1992) discusses the theorization of the city as a representational analog isomorphic with the body. She traces this metaphor back to Hobbes's *Leviathan*, and criticizes its implicit claim that the city is something natural and organic that "just grew." Grosz also criticizes an alternative model: the city as artifact rationally designed and built to serve human purposes. In any case, the "spatialization" of discourse has troubling implications. It pretends that there is a realm of access to reality "apart from" the common toil of listening, interpreting, discovery, feedback, and cooperation. The flight to discursive pseudo-space is a flight from political responsibility.

Finally, a fifth danger is that the sense of concreteness owing to the material reality of physical places may bleed over rhetorically onto "social locations." Statements which display their rootedness in some social situation tend to claim superior truth-value over against statements intending general applicability. The avowedly "situated" knowledge purports to partake of the nontheorized and unmediated concreteness of the body's sensations of its physical surroundings. But that is a ruse. The body is the physical location of the subject; whether the body is tantamount to social location is quite another question and requires further inquiry. That inquiry is cut short, however, if we too hastily assume that the factors constituting "social location" are straightforwardly available as bodily realities.

The bogus epistemology of situation and inscription is not without its allure. But its equivocations foreclose the possibility of engagement with projects and possibilities that cannot even be framed in the current vocabulary of "feminist standpoint," "situated knowledge," "social inscription," and "discursive space." As a small step toward confronting the troubles and dangers set forth above, I have tried to keep in mind a simple principle: Real space always allows more pathways, more sequences of access, than have already occurred. This principle can function as a definition: real space *is what* always allows one more path, one more sequence of access. Reality is the abundance of possibility over actuality. It embraces both what has been realized and what will be realized.

There is always "another way," physically and therefore epistemologically. For the past, this principle says that the epistemic portals currently in operation in today's sciences necessarily hide some of the pathways with which people have inhabited the surface of the planet. For the future, it says that our habitual action routines are fewer than the physical possibilities offered by the land we live on and the bodies that do the living.

The real space that we have got to share—this *here* world, the only one—is crossed by many paths, and our resources are drained off in many directions. But the channels built for these comings and goings are vulnerable to subversive use, precisely because they are material. In archaeology we cannot adequately understand the social frontiers and boundaries of ancient society until we recognize the problematic character of another boundary: the interface between those ancient landscapes and the landscape of access cut into them by present, ideologically informed archaeological investigation. In the case of the dining rooms discussed above, ancient agenda collide with contemporary agenda such as the reproduction of female aesthetic objects and the Israeli political strategy of colonizing the past as a precedent for future settlement in the Golan and the West Bank. All of these projects, and their attendant truths, have the same "locations." They occupy the same space, both literally and discursively. Their differences therefore are not differences of "situation."

Their differences lie, rather, in the differential patterns of movement associated with each. The built environment of ancient Galilee channeled the flow of commodities, services, labor, and information. It continues to do so today. Thus, "location," whether in its literal or its metaphorical sense, remains a partial and unhelpful cipher for "identity." The fuller meaning of "location" is access. Who you are *is* what moves you can make. That capability is correlated with architecture: literally, with the built environment of roads, houses, and cities; and also figuratively, with the data architecture that excavates Grandpa's house at Qatzrin and invites tourists to feast their eyes on feminine beauty at Sepphoris. The action patterns that we learn by walking through such templates in museums determine where we can reach with the virtual hands and feet of the mind and what we can do with the physical hands and feet of our bodies. But this determination is partial. Some discretion remains, owing to the superabundance of possibility that is inherent in real places and real bodies.

In summary, the thesis of the "social location" of knowledge can be taken to assert that demographical and biographical factors entirely determine what is true for any individual knower. Or, it can mean that knowledge is tied to the particular human body of the person who knows, or to particular parts of that body or experiences that the body has undergone. The former version of the claim is made by theorists whose intellectual heritage is broadly marxist or materialist. The latter version of the claim comes from psychoanalytic theorists and their successors. Both versions of the claim are false, and lead to an insupportable relativism.

The claims can be defeated in two ways: logically, and empirically. Logically, the claims themselves take the form of claims to a knowledge that is itself unsituated and independent of any particular circumstances. These claims themselves, strictly speaking, are claiming exemption from the very rule that they articulate. Moreover, these claims would enforce a privatization of knowledge in which all communication would become impossible. Each person would become the ultimate and infallible authority concerning that which he or she had experienced, because no one would be able to say that he or she had understood another, much less whether the other had gotten something wrong or right. But this is absurd; for in that case, human social life would cease, and proponents of the theory would not be able to communicate any warning or diagnosis of its failure to the rest of us.

Empirically, the claims are disproved in the practice of science, by the fact that investigators in different places and different bodies routinely do confirm one another's results. Conversely, people who occupy the same spaces can have very different experiences of those spaces, and very different consciousness. This was the case, for example, for the elite diners and the serving women who occupied the same space in the dining rooms in ancient Galilee and the Golan, discussed in chapter five. Moreover, the metaphorical use of "place" and "viewpoint" as a synonym for "opinion" makes it difficult to make a critical study of real spaces and vistas. Thus, these claims have been more persuasive in literary theory than in the empirical sciences.

It is necessary, however, to make clear the distinction between these claims, and the premise of the "recursive" power of material culture that supports the cognitive archaeological theory of Leone, Lightfoot, and their colleagues. Proponents of "situated knowledge" hold for a material, quasi-causal determination of knowledge by circumstances. Accordingly, persons' opinions and the truths that they profess are thought to be a function of the way they earn their living, or of the style of childrearing followed by their mothers. This hard causal relation excludes the possibility of acquiring a novel opinion, or changing one's mind, or dissenting from received doctrine, or learning the ways of another. It robs individuals of their initiative, ingenuity, and discretion.

Recursive theories of material culture also affirm the real power of places and things to determine human thoughts; but that is only one half of the picture. The thesis of the recursive power of artifacts, in contrast with theories of absolutely "situated knowledge," asserts that human discretionary practices also shape and reshape the equipment and architecture of the everyday world during routine use and innovation. A situation may give rise to knowledge, provisionally; but then a thought or choice or transgressive use can alter the material structure of the situation, too. Causality arcs from things to knowledge, but it also arcs back in the other direction (as Elaine Scarry has succinctly put it). Every tool, every place in the built environment, offers opportunities for both standard and innovative uses. Every material thing is intrinsically capable of being bent to a novel use. Particularly in contact situations, ethnologists and archaeologists see plenty of evidence of innovation in material culture. Those material transgressions would be impossible if the strict causality upon which "situated knowledge" is premised were correct.

For these reasons, I have avoided psychoanalytic theorists and have made only sparing use of materialist epistemology, although the following have been helpful:

Nancy Hartsock. "The Feminist Standpoint: Developing the Ground for a Specifically Feminist Historical Materialism."

Discovering Reality: Feminist Perspectives on Epistemology, Metaphysics, and Philosophy of Science, 238–310. Edited by Sandra Harding and Merrill B. Hintikka. Dordrecht: Reidel, 1983.

Ched Myers. *Binding the Strong Man: A Political Reading of Mark's Story of Jesus*. Maryknoll, NY: Orbis Books, 1988.

Rosemary Hennessy. *Materialist Feminism and the Politics of Discourse*. New York: Routledge, 1993.

See pages 68–73 of Hennessy, where feminist standpoint theories are criticized for grounding knowledge in reports about individual women's life experiences and for reducing the objective condition of people's lives to a position. Hennessy would detach the spatial metaphor from "objective material conditions" and transpose it to speech practices. Rather than individual lives or experiences, according to this proposal, "situation" now would mean "discursive position" and the subject would be "theorized as an ensemble of discursive positions."

Among standpoint theories, the work of the feminist theologian Elisabeth Schüssler Fiorenza merits special consideration. Her proposal of "critical feminist biblical interpretation for liberation" endorses the "hermeneutic of suspicion" first described by Paul Ricoeur as characteristic of the theories of Karl Marx and Sigmund Freud, from which today's theories of situated knowledge derive. For the hermeneutical background, see:

Paul Ricoeur. *De L'interpretation: Essai sur Freud*. Paris: Éditions du Seuil, 1965. See especially page 40.

John H. Hall. *Cultures of Inquiry: From Epistemology to Discourse in Sociohistorical Research*, 6–29. Cambridge: Cambridge University Press, 1999.

In Schüssler Fiorenza's hermeneutical program, gender determines knowledge but gender itself is naturalized and taken to be a stable vantage point amid the flux of historical and cultural events. On one hand, she rightly points out that women scholars have brought unique insights to New Testament studies that seemed to be unavailable to men. This fact suggests women can know things that men cannot, either because of their distinctive physiological makeup, or because of their experiences of oppression in our sexist society. On the other hand, Schüssler Fiorenza's program is premised upon the universality of a single standpoint or epistemological location for all "oppressed" people, women and men alike, ancient and contemporary alike. This is in keeping with a generally marxian and materialist account of history as an inexorable struggle fueled by the consciousness of contradictions in relations between social classes.

The fortification and healing of consciousness have both political and therapeutic value in Schüssler Fiorenza's proposal for a reconstruction of Christian Origins after the model of *memory* rather than scientific history. Memory is intended as an alternative to liberal positivistic historical-Jesus studies. It remains unclear how memory also differs from the other extreme that Schüssler Fiorenza wishes to avoid: relativistic literary studies of the New Testament. Reconstruction as memory cannot yield "facts," that is, data about the first century. But it can yield something else: hypotheses to guide further empirical investigation. The mnemonic reconstructions advanced by Schüssler Fiorenza, though rhetorically potent, fall short of the epistemological status that she and others often claim for them. Yet one aspect of their rhetorical potency is their ability to inspire further research initiatives and to assist in the framing of hypotheses to be confirmed or disproved with empirical evidence. Schüssler Fiorenza's re-description of Christian origins is not factual, but it can become part of a research program to produce and secure facts. This rhetorical thrust toward validation is thwarted, however, if the formulations achieved through practices of feminist-liberatory reconstructive memory are promulgated and accepted as dogma.

Although Schüssler Fiorenza has made admirable contributions as a historian herself, she has increasingly criticized the premises of historical study. In recent writings, she generally dismisses investigations into the life and world of the historical Jesus as "malestream" and necessarily complicit with socially oppressive practices in the academy today. Her most important works include:

Elisabeth Schüssler Fiorenza. *In Memory of Her: A Feminist Theological Reconstruction of Christian Origins*. New York: Crossroad, 1984.

Elisabeth Schüssler Fiorenza. *Bread Not Stone: The Challenge of Feminist Biblical Interpretation*. Boston: Beacon Press, 1985.

Elisabeth Schüssler Fiorenza. "Text as Reality—Reality as Text: The Problem of a Feminist Historical and Social Reconstruction Based on Texts." *Studia Theologica* 43 (1989) 19–34.

Elisabeth Schüssler Fiorenza. "The Politics of Otherness: Biblical Interpretation as a Critical Praxis for Liberation." *The Future of Liberation Theology: Essays in Honor of Gustavo Gutiérrez*, 311–325. Edited by Marc H. Ellis and Otto Maduro. Maryknoll: Orbis Books, 1989.

Elisabeth Schüssler Fiorenza. "A Discipleship of Equals: Ekklesial Democracy and Patriarchy in Biblical Perspective." *A Democratic Catholic Church: The Reconstruction of Roman Catholicism*, 17–33. Edited by Eugene C. Bianchi and Rosemary Radford Ruether. New York: Crossroad, 1992.

Elisabeth Schüssler Fiorenza. *But She Said: Feminist Practices of Biblical Interpretation*. Boston: Beacon Press, 1992.

Elisabeth Schüssler Fiorenza. "The Rhetoricity of Historical Knowledge: Pauline Discourse and Its Contextualizations." *Religious Propaganda and Missionary Competition in the New Testament World: Essays Honoring Dieter Georgi*, 443–469. Edited by Lukas Bormann, Kelly del Tredici, and Angela Standhartinger. Leiden: Brill, 1994 [a].

Elisabeth Schüssler Fiorenza. "The Bible, the Global Context, and the Discipleship of Equals." *Reconstructing Christian Theology*, 79–98. Edited by Rebecca S. Chopp and Mark Lewis Taylor. Minneapolis: Fortress Press, 1994 [b].

Elisabeth Schüssler Fiorenza. *Jesus Miriam's Child, Sophia's Prophet: Critical Issues in Feminist Christology*. New York: Continuum, 1995.

Elisabeth Schüssler Fiorenza. "Jesus and the Politics of Interpretation." *Harvard Theological Review* 90 (1997) 343–358.

The emendations to this work that I have proposed are based upon three premises. First, facts can be shared. Knowledge is not "perspectival" in the sense that a fact could be accessible in some "social locations" but not in others. The perspectival character of knowledge consists only in this: that reality can be illuminated from various angles by various investigative methods, and that those methods or "views" can themselves be made visible for critical analysis. Therefore I can accept the assertions of feminist reconstructive memory only as hypotheses that require, inspire, and rhetorically motivate further scientific research.

Second, the empirical evidence that we have from antiquity includes the landscape, architecture, and other items of material culture; it is not confined to texts, as Schüssler Fiorenza supposes. Even the texts themselves may be regarded as a class of artifact that was used in conjunction with other items of the built and cultivated environment. Material culture offers itself for analysis through methods that take account of the recursive character of its production and use in real space. Third, I resist the import of contemporary social descriptions into the first century. Indigenous practices for constructing gender and class can be understood, to a great extent, in terms of the prevailing cultural logic of the caste system as known to us from both texts and the archaeological record. It cannot simply be assumed that the liberal modern political rhetoric of "democracy," "liberation" and "equality" applies to events of the first century, as their participants lived them in the midst of empire.

3. ON ANCIENT TECHNOLOGIES

Having chosen material spaces and things as my starting point, rather than texts, I relied on archaeological studies of ceramics, roads, architecture, and other aspects of technology and material culture. The primary source for reports on current excavations in Israel is the illustrated journal *'Atiqot*, which carries English summaries of articles in Hebrew. A special issue in 1998 was devoted to "industrial and agricultural installations." Along with the site reports and other titles mentioned below (in sections 8 , 9, and 10), I depended upon:

Daniel Sperber. *The City in Roman Palestine*. New York: Oxford University Press, 1998. Sperber's two earlier volumes are listed below in section 9.1, land.

Ze'ev Safrai. *The Economy of Roman Palestine*. New York: Routledge, 1994.

David Adan-Bayewitz. *Common Pottery in Roman Galilee: A Study of Local Trade*. Bar-Ilan Studies in Near Eastern Language and Culture. Ramat-Gan: Bar-Ilan University Press, 1993.

David Adan-Bayewitz and Isador Perlman. "The Local Trade of Sepphoris in the Roman Period." *Israel Exploration Journal* 40 (1990) 153–172.

Joshua Schwartz. "Treading the Grapes of Wrath: The Wine Press in Ancient Jewish and Christian Tradition." Two parts. *Theologische Zeitschrift* 49 (1993) 215–228 and 311–324.

Douglas R. Edwards and Thomas McCollough. "Transformation of Space: The Road Systems of Sepphoris and the Galilee in the First and Second Centuries." *Archaeology and the World of Galilee: Texts and Contexts in the Roman and Byzantine Periods.* Edited by Douglas R. Edwards and Thomas McCollough. University of South Florida Studies in Judaica. Atlanta: Scholars Press, 1997.

D. Dorsey, *The Roads and Highways of Ancient Israel.* Baltimore: Johns Hopkins University Press, 1991.

M. Avi-Yonah. *The Jews Under Roman and Byzantine Rule: A Political History of Palestine From the Bar Kokhbah War to the Arab Conquest.* Jerusalem: Magnes Press, Hebrew University, 1984.

Jacob Neusner. *The Economics of the Mishnah.* Chicago: University of Chicago Press, 1990.

Miriam Beth Peskowitz. *"The Work of Her Hands": Gendering Everyday Life in Roman-Period Judaism in Palestine (70–250 CE), Using Textile Production as a Case Study.* Ann Arbor: UMI, 1993. (Ph.D. dissertation, Duke University)

Perry V. Kea. "Salting the Salt: Q 14:34–35 and Mark 9:49–50." *Foundations & Facets Forum* 6 (1990) 239–44.

For comparison, archaeological studies from the Americas also were suggestive:

Elizabeth M. Brumfiel. "Weaving and Cooking: Women's Production in Aztec Mexico." *Engendering Archaeology: Women and Prehistory*, 224–251. Edited by Joan M. Gero and Margaret W. Conkey. Cambridge, MA: Basil Blackwell, 1991.

Christine A. Hastorf. "Gender, Space, and Food in Prehistory." *Engendering Archaeology: Women and Prehistory*, 132–154.

Carmen A. Weber. "The Genius of the Orangery: Women and Eighteenth-Century Chesapeake Gardens." *The Archaeology of Gender*, 263–269. Proceedings of the Twenty-Second Annual Conference of the Archaeological Association of the University of Calgary. Calgary: Archaeological Association, 1991.

For theoretical approaches to the place of technology in human life, see titles listed above in section 2.2 as examples of "cognitive archaeology," as well as the following:

Donna J. Haraway. "A Cyborg Manifesto: Science, Technology, and Socialist-Feminism in the Late Twentieth Century." *Simians, Cyborgs, and Women: The Reinvention of Nature*, 148–181 and 243–248. New York: Routledge, 1991.

Martin Heidegger. *Poetry, Language, Thought*. Translated by Albert Hofstadter. New York: Harper Colophon, 1971.

4. ON GENDER

My earlier work on gender in social theory was published in a book and an article in 1994. These two titles offer a methodological introduction and review of the literature of the 1980s and early 1990s, which need not be repeated here.

Marianne Sawicki. *Seeing the Lord: Resurrection and Early Christian Practices*. Minneapolis: Fortress Press, 1994. See in particular my account of gender as a means of production of meaning, that is, a genre, pages 229–241, 292–295, and passim. (The title that I intended for this work was: *Making Jesus: Resurrection and the Practices of Gender, Race, and Class*. This title and the opening paragraph of the Preface were suppressed by the publisher.)

Marianne Sawicki. "Archaeology as Space Technology: Digging for Gender and Class in Holy Land." *Method & Theory in the Study of Religion* 6 (1994) 319–348.

Archaeology is a science, a disciplined way of knowing, that manipulates space in the very effort to understand how space has been managed previously. Yet, I argued, it is possible to achieve an objective grasp of the practices that constructed gender and other social classifications. The stance of "chastened realism" that I advocated was roundly attacked by Miriam Peskowitz, who rejects the feminist empiricist principles that my case was founded upon.

Miriam Peskowitz. "Empty Fields and the Romance of the Holy Land: A Response to Marianne Sawicki's 'Archaeology' of Judaism, Gender, and Class." *Method & Theory in the Study of Religion* 9 (1997) 259–282.

Marianne Sawicki. "Having Been Outed As a Crypto-Christian Anti-Semite, Can One Say 'Shalom'?" *Method & Theory in the Study of Religion* 9 (1997) 283–293.

Peskowitz meanwhile published a constructive and readable study of gender dynamics in rabbinic texts:

Miriam B. Peskowitz. *Spinning Fantasies: Rabbis, Gender, and History*. Critical Studies in Jewish Literature, Culture, and Society 9. Berkeley: University of California Press, 1997.

As she did in her dissertation (1993, listed above in section 3, ancient technologies), Peskowitz continues to treat material practices and items of material culture as if they were texts and words, as if their potency and meaning were entirely rhetorical or literary and could tolerate no other kind of interpretation. This reflects her reliance upon an interpretive tradition stemming from French psychoanalysis, particularly Jacques Lacan and Luce Irigaray, and Michel Foucault. This branch of psychoanalytic theory emphasizes desire rather than material relationships. It models its arguments after the psychotherapist's diagnosis of neurosis through analysis of dreams, slips of the tongue, reflex associations, and other covert communications from the unconscious. Thus, it is well suited for use in the literary interpretation of texts. By definition, however, it excludes from consideration any real, material, effective relation between text and material context.

Irigaray's concept of an "imaginary" stands for the fragile and constructed coherence of any given dream world, and in her estimation, there simply are no other kinds of worlds *that can be known*. "World" reduces completely to description, with no residue of independent reality. This reductive move can be helpful in certain aspects of historical study. The world projected in rabbinic writings can be analyzed as a dreamed world, a fiction, a literary construct. Peskowitz brilliantly unravels the ways in which the fictional world of the rabbis was knit together. But the method itself hampers and defeats her attempts to connect this literary analysis with concrete worldly realities today.

In the first place, Irigarayan analysis cannot be consistently carried out. It always falls into preformative contradiction. The interpreter needs a few solid terms that are naively accepted, or stipulated to be unconstructed markers of realities that do not arise from texts. In Peskowitz's account, such terms include "domestic," "Jew," and "woman." She equivocates on the logical status of these terms. Sometimes they are "under construction" but often they stand for entities independent of text. I have argued that we need to look at material things in order to see how work is rendered "domestic" behind the doors of the house. We need to look at built mechanisms for rhetorical defense of caste status and lineages of "Jews." We need to interrogate indigenous gender practices to indentify varieties of people who could be perceived as "women."

Peskowitz agrees with me (1994b: 337, 340) that the Talmuds produce rabbinic Judaism as a way of regulating the comings and goings of everyday life, and that this textual agenda was inaugurated under the social stresses of Roman occupation. But she overlooks the other adaptation to Roman cultural disruption, the one that was inaugurated by Jews in Galilee about 170 years before Judah ha-Nasi framed the Mishnah, the one that eventually produced Christianity. I have treated early Christian and early Jewish adaptations to Roman disruptions as different but comparable resistive strategies, framed in a common indigenous idiom, and addressed to the concrete, material ways in which the empire eroded both the real sustenance and the symbolic universe (or "imaginary") of the people of Palestine. Peskowitz takes the textual construction of the wife in Proverbs 31:10–11, 13–31 (leaving out v 12, where the wife "brings good to her husband") for a kind of baseline, disclosing relationships "before" the rabbis subjected wives to control by husbands, under Roman influence. Ironically, if I am correct in my findings that Judean women in Galilee were both the models for and the promoters of the *basileia* of God announced in Jesus' name, and if Peskowitz is also correct in her finding that rabbinic texts produce privilege for males as they promulgate what comes to be accepted as mainstream Judaism, then we must confront some rather uncomfortable conclusions. Either women made no contribution to shaping Judaism as we know it (a premise that I take to be contrary to fact), or the methods of analysis chosen by Peskowitz are not suitable for discovering, describing, and celebrating that contribution.

Labor is more than a cipher in an imaginary. We need a synthetic investigative practice that can connect literary analyses, like Peskowitz's, with analyses of realia. Christine Ward Gailey has asserted two universal principles about gender as understood in the social sciences: "It is not identical with sex differences, and . . . it provides a basis for a division of labor in all societies." See:

Christine Ward Gailey. "Evolutionary Perspectives on Gender Hierarchy," in *Analyzing Gender: A Handbook of Social Science Research*, ed. B. Hess and M. Ferree (Beverly Hills: Sage Publications, 1987), 37.

Several general works on the archaeology of gender have appeared recently.

Elisabeth A. Bacus et al., eds. *A Gendered Past: A Critical Bibliography of Gender in Archaeology.* Technical Report 25. Ann Arbor: University of Michigan Museum of Anthropology Publications, 1993.

Kelley Hays-Gilpin and David S. Whitley, eds. *Reader in Gender Archaeology.* New York: Routledge, 1998.

This convenient reprint makes available 21 excerpts and articles that often are cited as defining and shaping this sub-field of archaeology, 1987–1997. Article #16, by Cohen and Bennett, discusses skeletal evidence and the reading of bone and teeth. Alison Wylie, whose work was mentioned above as an example of "cognitive archaeology," continues to offer excellent theoretical discussions of gender in archaeology. Wylie argues in favor of feminist science, refusing to reject the possibility of objective knowledge through scientific investigation of the realities of gender. See also:

Sarah Milledge Nelson. *Gender in Archaeology: Analyzing Power and Prestige.* Walnut Creek, CA: Alta Mira Press, 1997.

Jenny Moore and Eleanor Scott, eds. *Invisible People and Processes: Writing Gender and Childhood into European Archaeology.* New York: Leicester University Press, 1997.

Several of the articles in the Moore and Scott collection argue that viable human populations in the past must have been about half female and half juvenile. Women and children labored and engaged in craft production.

An important study of the prerogatives of women in ancient society is:

Kathleen E. Corley. *Private Women, Public Meals: Social Conflict in the Synoptic Tradition.* Peabody, MA: Hendrickson, 1993.

Anthropological investigations of how gender was negotiated in living traditional societies in Africa offer parallels that are suggestive of hypotheses about gender in ancient Galilee. I have relied especially upon:

Karen Brodkin Sacks. *Sisters and Wives: The Past and Future of Sexual Equality.* Contributions to Women's Studies 10. Westport, CT: Greenwood Press, 1979.

Karen Brodkin Sacks. "Toward a Unified Theory of Class, Race, and Gender." *American Ethnologist* 16 (1989) 534–550.

Monica L. Udvardy. "The Lifecourse of Property and Personhood: Provisional Women and Enduring Men Among the Giriama of Kenya." *Research in Economic Anthropology* 16 (1995) 325–348.

Monica L. Udvardy. "Theorizing Past and Present Women's Organizations in Kenya." *World Development* 26/9 (1998) 1749–1761.

Monica L. Udvardy and Maria Cattell. "Gender, Aging, and Power in Sub-Saharan Africa: Challenges and Puzzles." *Journal of Cross-Cultural Gerontology* 7/4 (1992) 275–288.

5. On caste and kinship

Although I began my research with a narrow focus upon gender, I gradually realized that gender cannot be understood apart from the particular kinship structures and practices of the society in question. A helpful review of the anthropology of kinship, with astute methodological assessment, is:

Ladislav Holy. *Anthropological Perspectives on Kinship*. London: Pluto Press, 1996.

Kinship in first-century Israel is difficult to study directly. Most of the textual sources are rabbinic texts from a slightly later period. The works that I found most helpful were:

Paul Virgil McCracken Flesher. *Oxen, Women, or Citizens? Slaves in the System of the Mishnah*. Atlanta: Scholars Press, 1988.

Stuart S. Miller. *Studies in the History and Traditions of Sepphoris*. Leiden: Brill, 1984.

Shaye J.D. Cohen. "The Matrilineal Principle in Historical Perspective. *Judaism* 34 (1985) 5–13.

Shaye J.D. Cohen. "The Origins of the Matrilineal Principle in Rabbinic Law." *AJS Review* 10 (1985) 19–53.

M. Peskowitz, "'Family/ies' in Antiquity: Evidence from Tannaitic Literature and Roman Galilean Architecture," in *The Jewish Family in Antiquity*. Brown Judaic Studies 289, ed. S. Cohen (Atlanta: Scholars Press, 1993).

Joshua Schwartz. "On Priests and Jericho in the Second Temple Period." *Jewish Quarterly Review* 79 (1988) 23–48.

Joshua Schwartz. "Once More on the Nicanor Gate." *Hebrew Union College Annual* 62 (1991) 245–283.

Jane Schaberg. *The Illegitimacy of Jesus: A Feminist Theological Interpretation of the Infancy Narratives*. San Francisco: Harper & Row, 1987.

Margaret H. Williams. "Palestinian Jewish Personal Names in Acts." In *The Book of Acts in Its Palestinian Setting*, 79–113. Edited by Richard Bauckham. Grand Rapids, MI: Eerdmans, 1995. Williams presents evidence in support of the conclusion that the name Mary signaled a family's nationalistic, pro-Hasmonean sympathies.

Sylvia Junko Yanagisako and Jane Fishburne Collier. "Toward a Unified Analysis of Gender and Kinship." *Gender and Kinship: Essays Toward a Unified Analysis*, 14–50. Edited by Jane Fishburne Collier and Sylvia Junko Yanagisako. Stanford, CA: Stanford University Press, 1987.

The threats to caste and to indigenous cultural patterns of circulation, grounding, and closure that I perceive in Galilee in the first century CE, owing to penetrations of the land by imperial markets, have been found to be escalating in the second and third centuries by Cynthia M. Baker, in a provocative study of contrasts between home and market as represented in the rhetoric of the rabbis:

Cynthia M. Baker. "Bodies, Boundaries, and Domestic Politics in a Late Ancient Marketplace." *The Journal of Medieval and Early Modern Studies* 26 (1996) 39–66.

Kinship has not received much attention among scholars of the New Testament; but see:

John Dominic Crossan. "Mark and the Relatives of Jesus." *Novum Testamentum* 15 (1973) 81–113.

Mary Rose D'Angelo. "Abba and 'Father': Imperial Theology and the Jesus Traditions." *Journal of Biblical Literature* 111 (1992) 611–630.

Mary Rose D'Angelo. "Theology in Mark and Q: Abba and 'Father' in Context." *Harvard Theological Review* 85 (1992) 149–174.

Adriana Destro and Mauro Pesce. "Kinship, Discipleship, and Movement: An Anthropological Study of John's Gospel." *Biblical Interpretation* 3 (1995) 266–284.

6. On "Jewishness"

Three distinct questions, at least, should be sorted out in regard to ascertaining Jewish identity among people of the past. First, how can a meaningful Jewish identity today and tomorrow be secured through claiming certain people, places, and practices of the past as the antecedents and sources of one's own Jewishness? This question I respectfully leave for Jews to address; a Christian has no business trying to tell Jews how to be who they are. But the other two questions are properly historical, and they are open to objective investigation. In the past, what practices were recognized as identifying people as "Jews" to themselves, to other Jews, and to gentile neighbors? And how do archaeologists today discern whatever traces those practices may have left in material artifacts, including both the landscape and ancient texts?

These latter two questions must be addressed independently of the first question. Unfortunately, they are conflated in some discussions of archaeology in Israel. For example, preliminary reports and discussions of the city of Sepphoris assert that it was certainly a Jewish city; see:

Eric Meyers. "The Challenge of Hellenism for Early Judaism and Christianity." *Biblical Archaeologist* 55/2 (1992) 84–91.

The assumption that the categories "Jew" and "gentile" are names that pick out discrete, mutually exclusive, and plainly observable qualities, is often found in the older standard scholarly studies of Roman Galilee. However, it needs to be re-examined in light of recent empirical research. The multicultural complexity of Palestine in the era of Roman occupation is evident in recent studies of Galilee (listed below in section 10) and in classic studies such as:

Joachim Jeremias. *Jerusalem in the Time of Jesus: An Investigation into Economic and Social Conditions During the New Testament Period*, trans. F. and C. Cave. Philadelphia: Fortress Press, 1969.

For evidence and arguments that "gentiles" lived in various degrees of association with the Jewish community, see:

Shaye J.D. Cohen. "Crossing the Boundary and Becoming a Jew," *Harvard Theological Review* 82 (1989) 13–33.

Cohen suggests that someone not of Jewish birth who nevertheless followed sabbath practices and participated in Jewish holiday observances in a Roman city might be considered a Jew *ipso facto* by his neighbors and perhaps by himself. If the criteria for defining a person to be Jewish were so fluid even in the ancient world, then there is no simple way to determine whether and how a city, a house, or an artifact could be recognized as "Jewish" by archaeologists today. Hence my proposal that we look instead for evidence of an intention and a project to construct Jewish identity in ever new ways in the face of ever new threats from the material imposition of empire on the land. The methodological difficulties in identifying artifacts, structures, and inscriptions as "Jewish" are examined in:

L. Rutgers. "Archaeological Evidence for the Interaction of Jews and Non-Jews in Late Antiquity," *American Journal of Archaeology* 96 (1992) 101–18.

Ross Kraemer. "On the Meaning of the Term "Jew" in Greco-Roman Inscriptions," *Harvard Theological Review* 82 (1989) 35–53.

Byron R. McCane. "Jews, Christians, and Burial in Roman Palestine (Israel)" (Ph.D. diss., Duke University, 1992).

Kraemer discusses the difficulty of interpreting the term "Jew" in ancient inscriptions, but begs the question of how an investigator decides which inscriptions ought to be included in one's sample of "Jewish inscriptions." McCane found that there is no reliable way to distinguish between Jewish and Christian burials in the Roman period.

7. On Herod and the Herodians

The Herodian dynasty illustrates the resilience and the pliability of kinship in Palestine of the first centuries BCE and CE. The Herods were builders, and they built for the purpose of rhetorically establishing their legitimacy, and thus their real power, to rule in the land of Israel. They built cities out of stone, and they built their royal identity out of strategic intermarriage with Hasmonean aristocrats as well as with the daughters of eastern ruling families. Information about Herodian constructions—the palaces and the dynasty itself—comes principally from the historical works of Josephus and from excavations of Herodian sites in Israel. For recent interpretations of archaeological findings, see:

Klaus Fittschen and Gideon Foerster, eds. *Judaea and the Greco-Roman World in the Time of Herod in the Light of Archaeological Evidence*. Göttingen: Vandenhoeck & Ruprecht, 1996. The following two papers are especially relevant:

Hannah M. Cotton and Joseph Geiger. "The Economic Importance of Herod's Masada: The Evidence of the Jar Inscriptions." *Judaea and the Greco-Roman World in the Time of Herod*, 163–170.

Reinhard Förtsch. "The Residences of King Herod and Their Relations to Roman Villa Architecture." *Judaea and the Greco-Roman World in the Time of Herod*, 73–119.

Cotton and Geiger present evidence that women were purveyors of commodities to the Herodian court, apparently as independent businesswomen. Förtsch calls attention to Herod's habit of exploiting "extreme" landscapes and incorporating them into his grand architectural plans. Roman and Eastern architectural styles were combined at Herodian sites. The more public rooms and reception rooms followed Roman conventions. The more private rooms provided for the comfort of inhabitants through Eastern practices such as using very thick walls and water installations to cool the air in "summer rooms." This is an instance of an adaptive "contact" architecture.

Herodian kinship has been discussed in detail by Hanson and Oakman 1998, mentioned above, where I criticized its reliance upon the spurious identification of first-century Palestine as a "Mediterranean" society with an "honor-shame" ethos. This work is flawed by a few errors of historical fact as well, and was based upon Hanson's earlier research on the Herods:

K.C. Hanson. "The Herodians and Mediterranean Kinship, Part I: Genealogy and Descent." *Biblical Theology Bulletin* 19 (1989) 75–84.

K.C. Hanson. "The Herodians and Mediterranean Kinship, Part II: Marriage and Divorce." *Biblical Theology Bulletin* 19 (1989) 142–51.

K.C. Hanson. "The Herodians and Mediterranean Kinship, Part III: Dowry and Inheritance." *Biblical Theology Bulletin* 20 (1990) 10–21.

These articles, too, must be read with caution. They do not always distinguish accurately between individuals whose names were similar or identical, and they sometimes invoke anthropological terms in nonstandard ways. However, Hanson is quite correct to call attention to the significance of the Herods and their creative kinship strategies for understanding the social world of Jesus. Few New Testament scholars have taken seriously the likelihood of a connection between Herod Antipas and Jesus; but see:

Ben Witherington, III. "On the Road with Mary Magdalene, Joanna, Susanna, and Other Disciples—Luke 8: 1–3." *Zeitschrift für neutestamentliche Wissenschaft* 70 (1979) 243–248.

For a recent general study of Herod the Great, see:

Peter Richardson. *Herod: King of the Jews and Friend of the Romans.* Columbia: University of South Carolina Press, 1996.

Articles written nearly a century ago for *The Jewish Encyclopedia* (New York: Funk & Wagnalls, 1903–1906) were based on very careful readings of ancient rabbinic and historical texts. They are still useful today, both as introductions and as indexes to the classical texts:

"Herod I." By Isaac Broydé.

"Herodian Dynasty." By Frederick T. Haneman. With a lineage chart.

"Antipas (Herod Antipas)." By William Milwitzky.

"Mariamne." By Samuel Krauss.

"Maccabees." By Max Seligsohn.

"Hasmoneans." By Heinrich Bloch.

8. ON ARCHITECTURAL FORMS

There is no up-to-date general study that provides a typology of the kinds of structures that are excavated in Roman-era Palestine. Until very recently, archaeologists paid most attention to the sites of ancient cities, and to monumental urban architecture. They compared these ruins to those found elsewhere in the empire, and in doing so they minimized any features that were distinctive. This practice did little to advance the question of whether there might be indigenous architectural and landscape forms emerging in the Land of Israel, as an adaptive response to Roman occupation. My use of the available sources, therefore, has been highly eclectic.

8.1. THE HOUSE

The places and practices that comprise domestic space have attracted increasing scholarly attention in many disciplines within social theory. A helpful guide to the literature is provided by:

> Richard E. Blanton. *Houses and Households: A Comparative Study*. New York: Plenum Press, 1994. See especially the preface and the first two chapters.

Blanton has compiled a comparative data base in which he describes interactions between household behavior and its built environment in a number of areas of the world, but primarily in Asian societies. In his analysis, houses achieve two kinds of communication. "Canonical communication" expresses and reinforces the order of the universe, as perceived among a particular people, while "indexical communication" signals the rank of a particular house within that order. The canonical or cosmological function of the house, as Blanton describes it, might at first seem to be a useful conceptual tool with which to explicate the idiom of "circulation and grounding" that I have identified in the architecture, landscape, and religious practices of early Roman-era Palestine. But on closer consideration, it becomes clear that the very concept of "canonical communication" itself performs what I call the "grounding" or stabilizing function; there is no way to *think* "flow" or "circulation" or "redirection" within Blanton's category of "canonical communication." He presumes that a house is a static thing that secures the world against any fluctuation. In the Israelite house, as I have suggested, doors and roofs must open and close at the appropriate times in order to catch certain kinds of fluids, shelter and stabilize them, then allow them to go forth on their proper trajectories.

In Blanton's account, there is only one basic scale of measurement: the degree to which the house arrests flow and takes things out of circulation altogether. For example, doors are meaningful to the extent that they are costly to build. The effort and materials that "go into" the building of doorways will never come out again. So the number of doors and the ratio of doors to walls are treated only as measures of the complexity of the house and the costs that its builders were willing to sustain. Blanton describes a house's cosmological communication function as that of producing statements or propositions, of establishing boundaries, of making categorical oppositions and reducing all kinds of difference to binary pairs of is / is not. For example, the sole indigenous meaning allowed for every and any door is just this: the line between is / is not. Lost here is any nuance of facilitating connection, modulation, transition, partial retention, partial release, and so forth. Sets of binary oppositions are then laid end to end to form scales. The indexical communication function, which establishes status, presumes the existence of scales and the meaningfulness of scaling for the people whose houses are being studied.

The very terms of Blanton's analysis signal arrested motion or stasis. Moreover, they betray the origin of this conception in Western logic, rhetoric, and literacy. We in the West use the techniques of scientific classification in order to arrest reality and nail it down, in order to make ourselves feel safe and secure. It may be that we do this because we are the descendants of peoples whose indigenous built environments were breached repeatedly by imperial initiatives, and words are all we have left to build with. Unwittingly, we now try to read the houses of other peoples as if they were sentences. We look for the nails and miss the hinges.

In Blanton's model, the house is not only static, but altogether inert with respect to the intergenerational propagation of households. Agency and initiative are invested entirely in the occupants, in terms of rational strategies imputed to them. House design and complexity are theorized as either a result of those strategies or as a passive tool wielded in waging them. This feature of the model keeps the researcher from noticing whatever congruence there may be between the design of the house itself and the patterns in which its occupants think through their various social strategies and live out their life histories. For Blanton, mind must be something altogether different from house; house cannot embody and deploy mind. Blanton's research model is the most careful and rigorous proposal yet to appear for the study of households, but it must be applied within the empirical parameters that he has set forth, and also with due caution as to its hidden assumptions.

David A. Feinsy's study of the land in the Herodian period (listed below in section 9.1, the land) has a chapter on peasant households and villages that exhaustively discusses the available evidence. Feinsy refrains from inferring family structure from the architecture. Others do not:

Yizhar Hirschfeld. *The Palestinian Dwelling in the Roman-Byzantine Period*. Studium Biblicum Franciscanum Collectio Minor 34. Jerusalem: Franciscan Printing Press, 1995.

Ann Killebrew and Steven Fine. "Qatzrin: Reconstructing Village Life in Talmudic Times." *Biblical Archaeology Review* 17 (1991) 44–56.

Cynthia M. Baker. "'Ordering the House': On the Domestication of Jewish Sexuality." Paper presented to the Society of Biblical Literature, Chicago, 21 November 1994. Revised as "'Ordering the House': On the Domestication of Jewish Bodies." *Gender and the Body in Mediterranean Antiquity*. Edited by Maria Wyke. Malden, MA: Blackwell, 1998.

Santiago Guijarro. "The Family in First-Century Galilee." *Constructing Early Christian Families: Family as Social Reality and Metaphor*, 42–65. Edited by Halvor Moxnes. New York: Routledge, 1997.

Guijarro relies in part upon the report of modern-day peasant housing practices in:

T. Canaan. The Palestinian Arab House: Its Architecture and Folklore." *Journal of the Palestine Oriental Society* 13 (1933) 1–83.

For comparisons and comparative method, see also:

S. Kent, ed. *Domestic Architecture and the Use of Space: An Interdisciplinary Cross-Cultural Approach*. New York: Cambridge University Press, 1990. Two of the articles in this volume are of particular interest:

D. Sanders. "Behavioral Conventions and Archaeology: Methods for the Analysis of Ancient Architecture." *Domestic Architecture*, 43-72.

M. Jameson. "Domestic Space in the Greek City-State." *Domestic Architecture*, 92–113.

The use of cross-cultural comparative method in the study of housing must be balanced by intra-cultural comparisons with works in other media that can enhance our understanding of what houses "said to" and "did for" the people who dwelled in them. The quest for this balance requires us to read both the texts and the nonliterary material remains of ancient Galilee, without presuming that the relationship between those different sorts of evidence is merely one of reference.

Text can trope house. In an article listed above (in section 5, caste and kinship), Cynthia Baker examines the house and the marketplace as contrasting *literary* constructions, at a slightly later period than that which interests us. What she calls "the symbolic typography of the rabbis" does not give us direct evidence about the built environment of ancient Palestine. But it does show us something of what the built environment could mean to people who lived in it and thought with it. Baker writes (pp. 405–6):

> In the symbolic typography of the rabbis, *shuk* and *bayit*—market and home—are diametrical opposites. . . . This *bayit-shuk* opposition takes on particular significance when considered within the context of the massive economic shifts occurring in the region in the early rabbinic period. In the second and third centuries, the Galilee lay at the heart of an expanding and increasingly open Roman provincial economy, in which indigenous "markets" were being readapted to service the needs of the wider empire. Export production was increasing as lands were devoted more and more to agricultural products destined for nonindigenous consumption.
>
> . . . Greater numbers of the indigenous populations were likewise being drawn into work in export industries and into merchant trade. High on the list of such export industries, and central to the developing economy of the Galilee in the second and third centuries, was textile production.
>
> . . . Could it be that the rabbinic prohibition on women "spinning in the *shuk*" . . . is . . . an expression of conflicts between opposing economic realities?

Baker's analysis substantially concurs with that of Miriam Peskowitz on several points. However it opens here to the possibility of engagement with material reality, in ways that are foreclosed by the methodology that Peskowitz has chosen.

8.2. THE TEMPLE IN JERUSALEM

Little archaeological work has been possible on the site of the Temple in Jerusalem, given its character as a place sacred to Muslims, Jews, and Christians alike. Virtually all of the information we have about the layout of the Temple comes from ancient texts. This information was ably summarized in *The Jewish Encyclopedia* nearly one hundred years ago, and the floor plans presented there continue to be taken as the best reconstruction available.

J.D. Eisenstein. "Temple in Rabbinical Literature." *The Jewish Encyclopedia*. New York: Funk & Wagnalls, 1906. Two diagrams of the Temple layout are included.

Jonathan Z. Smith. *To Take Place: Toward Theory in Ritual*. Chicago: University of Chicago Press, 1987.

Bruce Chilton. *Pure Kingdom: Jesus' Vision of God*. Grand Rapids, MI: Eerdmans, 1996.

8.3. THE SYNAGOGUE

The multi-ethnic urban social milieu of the Hellenistic and early Roman periods is the context in which Jews, like other expatriates, began to adapt non-sacred spaces for community uses that included but were not limited to religious rituals. The need to accommodate a worshiping assembly was only one of numerous civic, religious, business, and social needs that prompted Jews to establish synagogues in fixed locations in urban neighborhoods throughout the empire. The earliest synagogues, like contemporary *mithraea* and so-called house churches, had no particular distinctive architectural form but took over spaces that had been parts of homes or shops, as Michael White has shown.

L. Michael White. *Building God's House in the Roman World: Architectural Adaptation Among Pagans, Jews, and Christians*. ASOR Library of Biblical and Near Eastern Archaeology. Baltimore, MD: Published for the American Schools of Oriental Research by Johns Hopkins University Press, 1990. Reprinted as volume 1 of The Social Origins of Christian Architecture. Harvard Theological Studies 42. Valley Forge, PA: Trinity Press International, 1996.

L. Michael White. *Texts and Monuments for the Christian Domus Ecclesiae in Its Environment*. Volume 2 of The Social Origins of Christian Architecture. Harvard Theological Studies 42. Valley Forge, PA: Trinity Press International, 1997.

Descriptions and images of ancient synagogues are available online at a website maintained by Donald D. Binder at Southern Methodist University.

www.smu.edu/~dbinder

This site also hosts learned discussions of disputed historical issues. The last decade has been an exceptionally fruitful one for synagogue research. The emergence of synagogue architectural designs as such, particularly in the Land of Israel, is discussed in:

Lee I. Levine. "The Nature and Origin of the Palestinian Synagogue Reconsidered." *Journal of Biblical Literature* 115 (1996) 425–448.

Dan Urman and Paul V.M. Flesher, eds. *Ancient Synagogues*: *Historical Analysis and Archaeological Discovery*. Leiden: Brill, 1995. See especially the following articles:

J. Gwyn Griffiths. "Egypt and the Rise of the Synagogue." *Ancient Synagogues*, 3–16.

Dan Urman and Paul V.M. Flesher. "Ancient Synagogues: A Reader's Guide." *Ancient Synagogues*, xvii–xxxvii.

Gideon Foerster. "The Ancient Synagogues of the Galilee." *The Galilee in Late Antiquity*, 289–319. Edited by Lee I. Levine. New York: The Jewish Theological Seminary of America, 1992.

James F. Strange. "The Art and Archaeology of Ancient Judaism." *Judaism in Late Antiquity*. Part I: The Literary and Archaeological Sources, 64–114. Handbuch der Orientalistik 16.1. Leiden: E.J. Brill, 1995.

R. Hachlili. *Ancient Jewish Art and Archaeology in the Land of Israel*. Leiden: E.J. Brill, 1988.

Lucille Roussin. "The Zodiac in Synagogue Decoration." *Archaeology and the World of Galilee: Texts and Contexts in the Roman and Byzantine Periods*, 83–96. Edited by Douglas R. Edwards and Thomas McCollough. Atlanta: Scholars Press, 1997.

Lester Ness. "Astrology." Archaeology in the Biblical World 2 (1992) 44–54.

8.4. THE MIQVEH OR RITUAL BATHING TANK

Ronny Reich. *Miqwa'ot* (Jewish Ritual Baths) in the *Second Temple Period and the Period of the Mishnah and Talmud*. (In Hebrew, with English summary.) Doctoral Dissertation, Hebrew University, Jerusalem, 1990.

Ronny Reich. "The Synagogue and the Miqweh in Eretz-Israel in the Second-Temple, Mishnaic, and Talmudic Periods." In *Ancient Synagogues: Historical Analysis and Archaeological Discovery*, 289–297. Edited by Dan Urman and Paul V.M. Flesher. Leiden: Brill, 1995.

Carol Barbara Selkin. *Exegesis and Identity: The Hermeneutics of* Miqwā'ôt *in the Greco-Roman Period*. Ann Arbor: UMI, 1993. (Ph.D dissertation, Duke University)

Benjamin G. Wright, III. "Jewish Ritual Baths—Interpreting the Digs and Texts: Some Issues in the Social History of Second Temple Judaism." *The Archaeology of Israel: Constructing the Past, Interpreting the Present*, 190–214. Edited by Neil A. Silberman and David B. Small. Sheffield: Sheffield Academic Press, 1997.

R. Wasserfall. "Menstruation and Identity: The Meaning of Niddah for Moroccan Women Immigrants to Israel." *People of the Body: Jews and Judaism from an Embodied Perspective*, 309–27. Edited by H. Eilberg-Schwartz. Albany: State University of New York Press, 1992 .

8.5. THE STUDY HOUSE

Dan Urman. "The House of Assembly and the House of Study: Are They One and the Same?" *Journal of Jewish Studies* 44 (1993) 236–257. Reprinted in *Ancient Synagogues: Historical Analysis and Archaeological Discovery*, 232–255. Edited by Dan Urman and Paul V.M. Flesher. Leiden: Brill, 1995.

Shaye J.D. Cohen. "The Place of the Rabbi in Jewish Society of the Second Century." *Galilee in Late Antiquity*, ed. L. Levine, 157-73; see also

Lee I. Levine, "The Sages and the Synagogue in Late Antiquity: The Evidence of the Galilee." *The Galilee in Late Antiquity*, 201–22. Edited by Lee I. Levine. New York: The Jewish Theological Seminary of America, 1992.

8.6. THE BASILICA

Any handbook of the architecture of classical Antiquity will describe the form and function of the basilica in the Roman city. My argument in chapter nine builds upon two facts that are so obvious that they might be missed. First, any city with a basilica was a Roman city, not a Greek or Hellenistic city, and therefore in Galilee not a Hasmonean city. The presence of the basilica both signals and enacts the intrusion of Roman imperial business and government. Second, despite its thoroughly Roman and imperialistic character, this edifice went by a name that was a Greek loan-word. The language of administration in the eastern empire was Greek. The empire was called *basileia* and its local administrative center was the *basilika*. These terms were not translated into Aramaic; the basilica was not indigenized, and could not be indigenized. The building where the empire did its business was called the basilica by the indigenous people in Galilee, for it brought the *basileia* home to them. Outside of the Land of Israel, the architectural form of the basilica could be adapted to house a local Jewish community, as its "community center," where community affairs could be managed. Inside of the Land of Israel, in the first century, this form was too alien and invasive for any such architectural adaptation. Jesus' rhetorical adaptation of the concept of *basileia* was shocking and troubling indeed.

Daniel Sperber remarks (on page 73 of his 1998 book, listed in section 3, technologies):

> The one building that stands out as peculiarly Roman is the basilica, a large covered hall that performed the functions of the ubiquitous stoas of Hellenistic architecture, and is obviously loosely related to them, but had a form that appears to lack any clear parallel in the Greek world. The basilica is often identified with the courts of justice. However, this identification is by no means clear. Indeed, it served either as a court of law and seat of the magistracy or as a place of meeting for merchants and men of business. These two uses were so mixed that it is not always easy to state which was the principal.

9. ON THE LANDSCAPE

The phrase "Land of Israel" carries profoundly theological and emotional overtones. Caution is therefore in order whenever the term is used. Gathering empirical information can be difficult. I relied on the following sources for facts about the land and its waters.

9.1. LAND

David A. Feinsy. *The Social History of Palestine in the Herodian Period: The Land Is Mine.* Studies in the Bible and Early Christianity 20. Lewiston: Edwin Mellen Press, 1991.

Daniel Sperber. *Roman Palestine 200–400: The Land: Crisis and Change in Agrarian Society as Reflected in Rabbinic Sources.* Ramat-Gan, Israel: Bar Ilan University, 1978.

Daniel Sperber. *Roman Palestine 200–400: Money and Prices,* second edition. Ramat-Gan: Bar-Ilan University, 1991.

9.2. WATER

A recent volume in Hebrew presents discussions of the major ancient water projects built in the land of Israel. The many maps, drawings, and photographs make this work relatively accessible even for those who cannot read modern Hebrew. See:

D. Amit, Y. Hirschfeld, and J. Patrich, eds. *The Aqueducts of Ancient Palestine: Collected Essays.* [In Hebrew.] Jerusalem: Yad Izhak Ben Zvi, 1989.

For Greco-Roman waterworks and the everyday practices that they made possible, see:

F. Yegül. *Baths and Bathing in Classical Antiquity.* New York: The Architectural History Foundation, 1992.

G. Fagan. *Three Studies in Roman Public Bathing: Origins, Growth, and Social Aspects.* Ph.D. dissertation, McMaster University, 1992.

D. Crouch. *Water Management in Ancient Greek Cities.* New York: Oxford University Press, 1993.

Aqueducts in various locations throughout the empire are examined in volumes published by the Frontius Gesellschaft:

Die Wasserversorgung antiker Städte: Pegamon, Recht/Verwaltung, Brunnen/Nymphäen, Bauelemente. Geschichte der Wasserversorgung vol. 2. Mainz: Philipp von Zabern, 1987.

Die Wasserversorgung antiker Städte: Mensch und Wasser, Mitteleuropa, Thermen, Bau/Materialien, Hygiene. Geschichte der Wasserversorgung vol. 3. Mainz: Philipp von Zabern, 1988.

See also the titles listed above under *miqveh* and below under site reports. It is difficult to distinguish pools designed for secular uses from ritual bathing tanks. See:

David Small. "Late Hellenistic Baths in Palestine," *Bulletin of the American Schools of Oriental Research* 266 (1987) 59–74.

The baths that Small discusses are not representative of Israel as a whole, for all of them were built for the members of the Herodian dynasty. Thus, they cannot support inferences about typical Jewish bathing practices.

For the fishing industry on the Sea of Galilee, see:

K.C. Hanson. "The Galilean Fishing Economy and the Jesus Tradition." *Biblical Theology Bulletin* 27 (1997) 99–111.

10. ON GALILEE

The source for my premise that Roman-era Galilee was a society of uneasy contact among at least three cultural groups is:

Richard Horsley. "The Historical Jesus and Archaeology of the Galilee: Questions From Historical Jesus Research to Archaeologists." *Society of Biblical Literature 1994 Seminar Papers*, 91–135. Edited by Eugene H. Lovering. Atlanta: Scholars Press, 1994.

Richard Horsley. *Galilee: History, Politics, People.* Valley Forge, PA: Trinity Press International, 1995. See especially pp. 34–61.

Richard Horsley. *Archaeology, History, and Society in Galilee: The Social Context of Jesus and the Rabbis.* Valley Forge, PA: Trinity Press International, 1996.

However, I have relied most heavily on the work of Seán Freyne.

Seán Freyne. *Galilee From Alexander the Great to Hadrian 323 BCE to 135 CE: A Study of Second Temple Judaism.* Wilmington: Michael Glazier, 1980.

Seán Freyne. *Galilee, Jesus, and the Gospels: Literary Approaches and Historical Investigations*. Philadelphia: Fortress Press, 1988.

Seán Freyne. "Urban-Rural Relations in First-Century Galilee: Some Suggestions from the Literary Sources." *The Galilee in Late Antiquity*, 75–94. Edited by Lee I. Levine. New York: The Jewish Theological Society of America, 1992.

Seán Freyne. "The Geography, Politics, and Economics of Galilee and the Quest for the Historical Jesus." *Studying the Historical Jesus: Evaluations of the State of Current Research*, 75–121. New York: Brill, 1994.

Seán Freyne. "Herodian Economics in Galilee: Searching for a Suitable Model." *Modeling Early Christianity: Social-Scientific Studies of the New Testament in Its Context*, 23–46. Edited by Philip F. Esler. New York: Routledge, 1995.

Seán Freyne. "Galilean Questions to Crossan's Mediterranean Jesus." *Whose Historical Jesus?*, 63–97. Studies in Christianity and Judaism 7. Edited by William E. Arnal and Michel Desjardins. Wilfrid Laurie University Press, 1997.

The cumulative effect of Roman colonization upon the well-being of the people of the Galilee remains to be securely established. The term "colonization" is used here in its modern political and economic sense, not in its ancient honorific sense, of course. Economic relationships within Galilee have been addressed by Douglas Edwards in his recent research, coordinating textual evidence with archaeological findings at Sepphoris and at Cana. See:

Douglas R. Edwards. "First-Century Urban/Rural Relations in Lower Galilee: Exploring the Archaeological and Literary Evidence." *Society of Biblical Literature 1988 Seminar Papers*, 169–182. Edited by David J. Lull. Atlanta: Scholars Press, 1988.

Douglas R. Edwards. "The Socio-Economic and Cultural Ethos of the Lower Galilee in the First Century: Implications for the Nascent Jesus Movement." *The Galilee in Late Antiquity*, 53–73. Edited by Lee I. Levine. New York: The Jewish Theological Seminary of America, 1992.

Edwards argues that imperial contact brought benefits to Galilee commensurate with the wealth that was extracted, at least during the first century CE. But the physical evidence, including floral and faunal materials, that could clarify this picture has yet to be excavated.

Neither indigenous constructions of caste nor archaeological evidence for the character of the dining facilities commonly available in Galilean villages of the first century have yet been considered seriously in historical-Jesus research; for example, in the work of the Jesus Seminar or in the otherwise very careful investigations of table fellowship traditions by Dennis E. Smith.

Robert W. Funk and the Jesus Seminar. *The Acts of Jesus: The Search for the Authentic Deeds of Jesus*. San Francisco: HarperSanFrancisco, 1998.

Dennis E. Smith. "What Really Happened at Ancient Banquets? Evaluating the Evidence for Ancient Meal Practices." Paper presented to the Society of Biblical Literature, 1993.

Dennis E. Smith. "Table Fellowship and the Historical Jesus." *Religious Propaganda and Missionary Competition in the New Testament World: Essays Honoring Dieter Georgi*, 135–162. Edited by Lukas Bormann, Kelly Del Tredici, and Anglea Standhartinger. Leiden: Brill, 1994.

The issue, aptly formulated by Smith, is this: "whether the picture of Jesus utilizing table fellowship with a symbolic meaning as part of his teaching program can be plausibly reconstructed as a real event in first-century Palestine."

11. ARCHAEOLOGICAL SITE REPORTS

Ehud Netzer. *Greater Herodium*. Qedem 13. Jerusalem: Institute of Archaeology, The Hebrew University, 1981.

Moshe Dothan. *Hammat Tiberias: Early Synagogues and the Hellenistic and Roman Remains*. Jerusalem: Israel Exploration Society, 1983.

Moti Aviam. "A Second-First Century BCE Fortress and Siege Complex in Eastern Upper Galilee." *Archaeology and the Galilee:*

Texts and Contexts in the Graeco-Roman and Byzantine Periods, 97–105. Edited by Douglas R. Edwards and Thomas McCollough. Atlanta: Scholars Press, 1997.

James F. Strange. "Six Campaigns at Sepphoris: The University of South Florida Excavations, 1983–1989." *The Galilee in Late Antiquity*, 339–55. Edited by Lee I. Levine. New York: The Jewish Theological Seminary of America, 1992.

Eric M. Meyers, Ehud Netzer, and Carol L. Meyers. *Sepphoris*. Winona Lake, IN: Eisenbrauns, 1992.

Joshua J. Schwartz. *Lod (Lydda), Israel: From Its Origins Through the Byzantine Period, 5600 BCE–640 CE*. BAR International Series 571. Oxford: Tempus Reparatum, British Archaeological Reports, 1991.

Virgilio C. Corbo. *Cafarno*. Gli Edifici della Citta Publicazioni dello Studium Biblicum Franciscanum 19. Jerusalem: Franciscan Printing Press, 1975.

Eric M. Meyers, James F. Strange, and Carol L. Meyers. *Excavations at Ancient Meiron, Upper Galilee, Israel 1971–72, 1974–75, 1977*. Cambridge: The American Schools of Oriental Research, 1981.

David Adan-Bayewitz, Mordechai Aviam, and Douglas R. Edwards. "Yodefat, 1992." *Israel Exploration Journal* 45 (1995) 191–197.

12. HISTORY AND THEOLOGY OF EARLY CHRISTIANITY

Along with titles listed above under specific categories, the following titles entered into my historical reconstructions.

John S. Kloppenborg. "Literary Convention, Self-Evidence and the Social History of the Q People." *Early Christianity, Q and Jesus*. Semeia 55. Edited by John S. Kloppenborg and Leif E. Vaage. Atlanta: Scholars Press, 1992.

John S. Kloppenborg. "The Sayings Gospel Q and the Quest of the Historical Jesus." *Harvard Theological Review* 89 (1996) 307–44.

John S. Kloppenborg. "Egalitarianism in the Myth and Rhetoric of Pauline Churches." *Reimagining Christian Origins: A Colloquium Honoring Burton L. Mack*, 247–263. Edited by Elizabeth A.

Castelli and Hal Taussig. Valley Forge, PA: Trinity Press International, 1996.

Brian Capper. "The Palestinian Cultural Context of Earliest Christian Community of Goods." *The Book of Acts in Its Palestinian Setting*, 323–356. The Book of Acts in Its First Century Setting 4. Edited by Richard Bauckham. Grand Rapids, MI: Eerdmans, 1995.

Joshua J. Schwartz. "Peter and Ben Stada in Lydda." *The Book of Acts in Its Palestinian Setting*, 391–414. The Book of Acts in Its First Century Setting 4. Edited by Richard Bauckham. Grand Rapids, MI: Eerdmans, 1995. An earlier version appears in Schwartz's book on Lod, listed above.

Wendy J. Cotter. "The Parables of the Mustard Seed and the Leaven: Their Function in the Earliest Stratum of Q." *Toronto Journal of Theology* 8 (1992) 38–51.

Finally, the following titles are to be read with great caution, for they tend to import twentieth-century ideological constructions into the first century:

Rebecca S. Chopp and Mark Lewis Taylor, eds. *Reconstructing Christian Theology*. Minneapolis: Fortress, 1994.

Francis Schüssler Fiorenza. "Christian Redemption between Colonialism and Pluralism." *Reconstructing Christian Theology*, 269–302. Edited by Rebecca S. Chopp and Mark Lewis Taylor. Minneapolis: Fortress Press, 1994.

Shelley Davis Finson. *Women and Religion: A Bibliographic Guide to Christian Feminist Liberation Theology*. Toronto: University of Toronto Press, 1991.

Norman K. Gottwald. "The Exodus as Event and Process: A Test Case in the Biblical Grounding of Liberation Theology." *The Future of Liberation Theology: Essays in Honor of Gustavo Gutiérrez*, 250–260. Edited by Marc H. Ellis and Otto Maduro. Maryknoll: Orbis Books, 1989.

Norman K. Gottwald and Richard A. Horsley. "Introduction: The Bible and Liberation: Deeper Roots and Wider Horizons." *The Bible and Liberation: Political and Social Hermeneutics*, xiii–xxi.

Revised edition. Edited by Norman K. Gottwald and Richard A. Horsley. Maryknoll, NY: Orbis Books, 1993.

Ronald G. Musto. *Liberation Theologies: A Research Guide*. New York: Garland Publishing Company, 1991.

Luise Schottroff. *Lydia's Impatient Sisters: A Feminist Social History of Early Christianity*. Translated by Barbara and Martin Rumscheidt. Louisville: Westminster John Knox Press, 1995.

▪ ▪ ▪

This bibliographical survey gives an account of the sources that I used, and why I used them. Despite its length, it falls far short of adequate coverage for any of the theoretical and historical topics that it touches upon. Readers are challenged to use this work as a stepping stone in their own research and analysis, in hopes of achieving better understanding of the Galilee of Jesus.

Index

Abu-Lughod, Lila, 210
Adan-Bayewitz, David, 94–5,
 224, 248
Africanist anthropology, 9, 10,
 91, 187–91, 193, 195–6, 229–30
Alcoff, Linda, 217
Amit, D., 244
anthropology, 5, 9, 36, 38, 64, 67,
 75–6, 78–9, 161, 187–9, 205,
 209–10, 225, 230
Antipas. *See* Herod Antipas.
aqueducts, 15, 23–5, 37, 58,
 99–101–3, 116–8, 120, 122–3,
 126, 128, 170–1, 178, 185,
 244–5
Arav, Rami, 30, 53, 146, 201
archaeological excavation, 5, 7,
 10, 39, 86, 92, 94, 201,218
archaeological excavation, display of, 101–9, 214
archaeology of mind, 13–4, 37,
 41, 44, 48, 56–7, 62, 75, 81,
 205–212
architectural forms. *See individual forms. See also* material
 culture.
Aristotle, 78
Arnal, William, E., 246
artifacts, power of. *See* recursivity.
Avi-Yonah, M., 225
Aviam, Mordechai, 248
Aviam, Moti, 248

Bacus, Elisabeth A., 229
Baker, Cynthia M., 36, 98, 231,
 238–9

banquets. *See* dining rooms.
basileia. See kingdom. *See also*
 Roman administration in Israel.
basilica, 83, 114, 117, 126,
 177–9, 243–4
baths. *See* tanks.
Bauckham, Richard, 231, 249
Benhabib, Seyla, 216
bet midrash. See study house.
Bethsaida, 19, 92, 112, 146
Bianchi, Eugene, C., 223
Binder, Donald D., 25, 241
Blanton, Richard E., 236
Bloch, Heinrich, 235
body, human, 24–5, 37, 47, 59,
 62–3, 71, 87, 101–3, 106–7,
 109–10, 132, 197, 216–9
book, 15, 31–2, 70–1, 84–7, 99,
 161, 170
borders. *See* contact theory.
Borman, Lukas, 223, 247
Bové, P., 213
bride. *See* wife.
Brimlow, Robert, viii
Brown, Raymond E., 201
Broydé, Isaac, 235
Brumfiel, Elizabeth M., 208, 225
Budde, Michael I., viii
built environment, 13–5, 29, 33,
 37, 44, 56, 59–62, 70–71, 79,
 82, 85, 87–8, 98, 100, 102,
 120, 128, 132, 185, 198, 214,
 219, 237, 239 *See also* architectural forms.
businesswomen, 90, 105–7, 113,
 127, 134–5, 144, 147–8, 163,